Entrepreneurship in Hospitality and Tourism

A Global Perspective

Maureen Brookes and Levent Altinay

Entrepreneurship in Hospitality and Tourism

A Global Perspective

Maureen Brookes and Levent Altinay

(G) Goodfellow Publishers Ltd

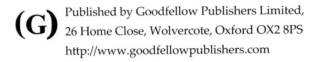

Published by Goodfellow Publishers Limited,
26 Home Close, Wolvercote, Oxford OX2 8PS

http://www.goodfellowpublishers.com

British Library Cataloguing in Publication Data: a catalogue record for this title is available from the British Library.

Library of Congress Catalog Card Number: on file.

ISBN: 978-1-910158-28-9

Design and typesetting by P.K. McBride, www.macbride.org.uk

Cover design by Cylinder

Printed by Marston Book Services, www.marston.co.uk

Contents

Introduction

This textbook has been designed to develop your understanding of entrepreneurship within hospitality and tourism. Schumpeter (1934: 354) is often credited with the first definition of entrepreneurs as those 'individuals whose function is to carry out new combinations of means of production'. While entrepreneurship can therefore be considered the process by which individuals carry out this function, there is no universally accepted definition of entrepreneurship (Spencer *et al.*, 2008). Academics have examined entrepreneurs and entrepreneurship, from a wide range of theoretical perspectives and within a variety of different contexts. Entrepreneurship has been explored through decision sciences, economics, management, sociology and psychology. Entrepreneurs and entrepreneurship have been studied through the endeavours of individuals working for themselves, and individuals working within corporations. They have been explored as part of social and professional networks, including franchising. Additionally, the value of entrepreneurship has also been considered from both economic and social perspectives. Despite this diversity, there is general consensus that entrepreneurs and entrepreneurship make an economic contribution at both a national and global level.

There is also a general agreement that there are two concepts fundamental to entrepreneurship. The first concept is opportunities, which are argued either to be created or discovered by entrepreneurs and which arise out of market dynamics or inefficiencies (Edelman and Yli-Renko, 2010). These opportunities are the situations in which new means of production can be carried out (Shane and Venkataraman, 2000). The Global Entrepreneurship Monitor (Singer *et al.*, 2014) identifies that entrepreneurs have the capability to detect opportunities, seize them and transform them into a venture, whether this be for economic or social gains. In fact, some view entrepreneurship as the nexus of the individual and the opportunity (Sarason *et al.*, 2006). The second concept fundamental to entrepreneurship is innovation, or more specifically, the new or novel combination of resources identified to address an opportunity (Schumpeter, 1934) that yields new products, services, methods of production or markets. Entrepreneurs are the creative force behind innovation, and entrepreneurial mindsets support innovation, change and growth (Chirico *et al.*, 2011).

Entrepreneurs and entrepreneurship are vitally important within the hospitality and tourism industries. Although frequently considered distinct industrial sectors, hospitality and tourism are closely intertwined sectors that meet customers' recreation, leisure and entertainment needs, and the needs of international and domestic business and leisure travellers. Subsectors include, hotels and other types of lodging, restaurants, pubs, bars, nightclubs, contract catering, gaming, events, visitor attractions and travel and transport (International Labour Office (ILO), 2010). Combined, hospitality and tourism contribute significantly to local, regional, national and global economies. According to the UNWTO (2014), international tourist arrivals grew to 1.135 billion in 2014, generating US$ 1.5 trillion in export earnings. International visitor spending on hospitality, including accommodation, food and drink, entertainment, shopping and other services reached an estimated US$ 1,245 billion (Euro 937 billion). Forecasts are for continued growth with 1.8 billion international tourist arrivals predicted by 2030. Arrivals in emerging economy destinations (Asia Pacific, Central and Eastern Europe, Middle East and Africa) are expected to increase at twice the rate of those in advanced economies. Like entrepreneurship therefore, hospitality and tourism are important to many national economies, creating jobs and contributing to national gross domestic product (GDP). For many countries, domestic tourism is also important to economic health and the provision of stable revenue streams, particularly in times of environmental uncertainty (OECD, 2014).

History identifies numerous hospitality and tourism entrepreneurs across the different industry subsectors who were influential in developing the industry as we know it today. One of the best known hotel entrepreneurs is Conrad Hilton, who bought his first hotel in Cisco, Texas in 1919. He subsequently expanded throughout the US and formed the Hilton Hotels Corporation in 1946. In 1948, the name was changed to the Hilton International Company which became the world's first international hotel chain. Today, Hilton International has 540 hotels in 78 countries and 6 continents, operating under 13 different brands (www. hilton.com, 2015). JW Marriott was another hospitality entrepreneur who started out with a root beer stand in Washington, DC in the USA in 1927. That business soon became a family restaurant known as The Hot Shoppe. It wasn't until 1957 that Marriott opened his first hotel, the Twin Bridges Motor Hotel in Arlington, Virginia. In 1967, he formed Marriott Inc. expanding through the development of hotels, different restaurant brands, airline in-flight food service, and contract catering. Today Marriott International has a portfolio of 19 lodging brands and 4200 properties, operating in 79 countries across the globe (www.marriott.com, 2015). One of the world's largest fast food brands, also began life through an entrepreneurial founder by the name of Fred DeLucca. As a 17 year old, DeLucca was trying to fund his university tuition when a family friend suggested opening a submarine sandwich shop and provided a loan to start the enterprise in 1965 in

Connecticut, USA. The partners grew the outlets slowly and began to franchise in 1974. Today, the Subway empire comprises over 43,000 outlets in over 110 countries (www.subway.com , 2015).

One of the world's most famous visitor attractions is Disneyland. This theme park would not have been opened without the efforts of the entrepreneurial Walt Disney, best known as an animator and film maker. This entrepreneur first envisaged the idea for a theme park in the late 1940s as a place where his employees could spend time with their children (http://thewaltdisneycompany.com/about-disney, 2015). With funding from the Bank of America, Disneyland, one of the world's first theme parks, opened on July 17, 1955 in California and attracted visitors from around the globe. Disney theme parks were later opened in Florida, Japan, France and Hong Kong and at the time of writing this book, a new theme park is scheduled to open in Shanghai, China. Within the travel and transport sector, Sir Freddie Laker, an English entrepreneur, was best known for founding Laker Airways in 1966, considered the original no-frills airline business model which many airlines such as Southwest Airlines and EasyJet replicate successfully today   (http://www.telegraph.co.uk/news/obituaries/1510173/Sir-Freddie-Laker.html , 2015). Richard Branson is also a well-known entrepreneur within the airline sector, starting Virgin Atlantic Airways in 1984, and subsequently a number of other regional airlines. His most recent tourism entrepreneurial venture however is Virgin Galactic, a space tourism company launched in 2004 (http://www.virgingalactic.com/, 2015).

In addition to these famous hospitality and tourism entrepreneurs, there are countless individuals who represent the backbone of the industry and operate many small to medium-size enterprises (SMEs). These individuals identified opportunities which could be fulfilled through the development of a hospitality or tourism business, but did not develop their enterprise into larger international organisations such as those described above. In the UK, SMEs represent 80% of the hospitality and tourism sector (Tourism Alliance, 2010) and there are more than 250 million hospitality and tourism SMEs in Europe (ILO, 2010). While there are wide variations across countries, the ILO (2010) also reports that 80% of people employed in the hospitality and tourism sectors are within SMEs. This employment was created by the numerous hospitality and tourism entrepreneurs who identified market opportunities within these industrial sectors and pursued them.

There is no global agreement on the definition of an SME. The European Union defines an SME as an organisation with less than 250 employees, with turnover of no more than Euros 50 million and a balance sheet of no more than Euros 43 million. In the US, however SMEs are businesses with fewer than 500 employees and the maximum revenue varies depending on industrial sectors. While the definition changes depending on geographical location, there is general agreement that SMEs are essential for economic prosperity and job creation. However, SMEs are also noted for their failure rate. European Commission research suggests that only 50% of firms are still trading 5 years after their start up (EC, 2015). As such, SMEs are argued to reflect what Schumpeter (1934) termed as 'creative destruction'. Schumpeter argued that business failure is an inherent part of economic growth in a free market economy. As some enterprises fail, other new enterprises are started and this situation leads to competition and innovation, which in turn drives change, productivity and economic growth.

It would seem therefore that both entrepreneurs and entrepreneurship drive innovation and economic growth. In addition, entrepreneurs are extremely important in the hospitality and tourism industries, through the development of SMEs which are the backbone of the industry, or through the subsequent creation of global, multi-sector industries. This textbook therefore has been designed to develop your understanding of the different types of entrepreneurship within hospitality and tourism. It is structured around three key themes. The first section introduces you to different theoretical perspectives of entrepreneurs and entrepreneurship. The second section identifies different types of entrepreneurship that exist within these sectors today, including social, corporate, ethnic minority, franchising and social franchising. The third and final section explores the growth of entrepreneurship and some of the challenges entrepreneurs face when trying to grow their business enterprises. Each theme is introduced by an editorial which explains the relevance of the theme and provides an overview of the chapters contained within that theme. The different chapters contain case study examples of hospitality and tourism entrepreneurs and entrepreneurial enterprises from different countries to illustrate the key arguments presented. Each chapter also contains a number of questions to aid your understanding of the chapter content and its application to hospitality and tourism. We hope you enjoy reading this text.

Maureen Brookes & Levent Altinay
Oxford School of Hospitality Management
Oxford Brookes University, UK

References

Anon (2006) Sir Freddie Laker, *The Telegraph,* downloaded from http://www.telegraph. co.uk/news/obituaries/1510173/Sir-Freddie-Laker.html on 18 June, 2015.

Chirico, F., Ireland, R. and Simon, D. (2011) Franchising and the family firm : Creating unique sources of advantage through familiness, *Entrepreneurship Theory and Practice,* **35**, 483-501.

Disney, W. (2015) downloaded from http://thewaltdisneycompany.com/ on 22 June, 2015.

Edelman, L. and Yli-Renko, H. (2010) The impact of environment and entrepreneurial perceptions on venture-creation efforts: Bridging the discovery and creation views of entrepreneurship, *Entrepreneurship Theory and Practice,* **34**(5): 833-856.

European Commission (2015) A second chance to entrepreneurs, downloaded from http://ec.europa.eu/enterprise/policies/sme/business-environment/failure-new-beginning/index_en.htm on 22 June, 2015.

Hilton Hotels and Resorts (2015) downloaded from http://www3.hilton.com/en/about/index.html on June 22, 2015.

International Labour Organization (2010) *Developments and challenges in the hospitality and tourism sector,* Geneva: International Labour Office.

Marriott (2015) downloaded from https://www.marriott.co.uk/marriott/about-marriott.mi on 21 June, 2015.

Organisation for Economic and Co-operation and Development (OECD) (2014) *OECD Tourism Trends and Policies 2014,* France: OECD Publishing.

Sarason, Y., Dean, T. and Dillard, J. (20060 Entrepreneurship as the nexus of individual and opportunity: A structuration view, *Journal of Business Venturing,* **21**(3), 286-305.

Schumpeter, J. (1934) *The Theory of Economic Development. An inquiry into Profits, Capital, Credit, Interest, and the Business Cycle,* Cambridge: Harvard University Press.

Shane, S. and Venkataraman, S. (2000) The promise of entrepreneurship as a field of research, *Academy of Management Review,* **25** (1): 217-226.

Singer, S., Amoros, J. and Moska, D. (2014) *Global Entrepreneurship Monitor 2014 Global Report,* London: Global Entrepreneurship Research Association

Spencer, A., Kirchhoff, B. and White, C. (2008) Entrepreneurship, innovation, and wealth distribution, *International Small Business Journal,* **26** (1), 9-26.

Subway (2015) Explore our World downloaded from https://www.subway.com/subwayroot/default.aspx on 20 June, 2015.

Tourism Alliance (2010) *Tourism: Britain's best opportunity for sustainable economic growth and new employment,* London.

UNWTO (2014) *UNWTO Annual Report,* Spain: UNWTO.

Virgin Galactic (2015) downloaded from http://www.virgingalactic.com/ on 20 June, 2015.

Theme 1: Theoretical Perspectives on Entrepreneurs and Entrepreneurship

In the new millennia, governments, practitioners and academics around the world are seeking ways to foster entrepreneurship as a means of achieving economic development (Chell *et al.*, 2010). Entrepreneurship and innovations are desirable as they create employment opportunities, develop new industries and introduce new business models that address economic and social needs. For instance, the rapid growth of Western economies in the past two decades has been attributed to the Information Technology (IT) revolution spurred by the emergence of innovative, entrepreneurial ventures like Microsoft, Intel and Google (Baumol and Strom, 2007).

There are a number of fundamental perspectives and theories that help our understanding of entrepreneurs and entrepreneurship leading to innovation and making economic and societal impacts. Entrepreneurs bring their individual character traits to bear in their entrepreneurial endeavours, develop innovative ideas and contribute to the economic and social well-being of their communities, societies and countries. Creating economic wealth also requires innovation through engagement in entrepreneurial activities. All these activities are culture-bound and are influenced by cultural factors. In Section 1, we examine entrepreneurial traits, the process of entrepreneurship and innovation and the entrepreneurship and culture interface in order to enable us to understand the complexities of entrepreneurship in the context of the hospitality and tourism industries.

What makes an individual an 'entrepreneur' with his/her character traits has been the focus of an ongoing debate among academics and practitioners. Chapter 1 of this section outlines the distinctive characteristics of entrepreneurs in terms of their personality traits. The chapter reviews some of the key concepts and frameworks relating to entrepreneurial 'trait theory' in order to apply this theory to our knowledge of some specific entrepreneurs in the tourism and hospitality industries. The author also explains the relevance of entrepreneurial traits to tourism and hospitality entrepreneurial activities. Finally, the author acknowledges the importance of risk-taking in entrepreneurial activities and demonstrates the relationship between risk and entrepreneurial behaviour. This chapter also illustrates the exploitation of different entrepreneurial traits in the process of a business start-up and development in Spain. The entrepreneurial motives and traits are extremely important for the initiation and implementation of entrepreneurial change towards economic and social prosperity. In fact, in his early work, Schumpeter (1934) stresses the role of the individual entrepreneur. He elaborates that these are highly motivated individuals who overcome social resistance to change but, if successful, benefit society with greater economic growth. In this regard, Schumpeter (1934) also points to the economic, psychological and social motives of successful entrepreneurs. In terms of economic motives, he suggests that "the dream or will to found a private kingdom or dynasty" for which "industrial or commercial success is still the nearest approach....possible to modern man" (p. 93). The entrepreneur's non-pecuniary motives are stated in Schumpeter's work as "the will to conquer: the impulse to fight, to prove oneself superior to others" and "the joy of creating" (ibid, p. 94).

These motives and ambitions are fulfilled through the process of entrepreneurship; opportunity identification, opportunity evaluation and opportunity exploitation. This process involves the development of creative ideas by the entrepreneurs and/or their teams. These ideas lead to incremental and/or disruptive changes in the organisations or society. Development of new and creative ideas and turning these ideas into a business reality require the mobilisation and exploitation of different forms of capital including financial, social and human. In Chapter 2, we examine how different entrepreneurial traits are exploited in the process of entrepreneurship. This chapter argues that entrepreneurs go through three key stages in the process of entrepreneurship, namely opportunity identification, opportunity evaluation and opportunity exploitation. This process leads to the development of innovative products and services that meet the constantly changing needs and desires of customer groups. Innovation is initiated in the opportunity identification stage; innovation is tested in the opportunity evaluation stage and finally innovation is implemented in the opportunity exploitation stage. The chapter illustrates these with a mini case study explaining how the founder of Holiday Inn, Kemmons Wilson, went through the process of entrepreneurship, exploited his entrepreneurial traits and turned his 'imaginative idea' into a business reality of an international nature. The chapter also argues that the cognitive ability of the entrepreneur is important to both the identification and evaluation stages of entrepreneurship. In the first stage, it helps entrepreneurs to use their prior knowledge and influences the information search activities undertaken. Entrepreneurs' emotions and goal setting behaviour also have influence during opportunity evaluation and in the final stage. It is worth noting that contextual factors and social networks are crucial in the process of entrepreneurship as they play a key role in whether opportunities are exploited. This chapter ends with a very interesting case study of two men who started up and developed Airbnb Company successfully through exploiting their entrepreneurial traits and skills and combining resources effectively. Innovation in the tourism and hospitality industry requires creating an environment for the generation of, and experimentation with, new ideas. Innovation in hospitality and tourism organisations however should not be limited to service and product innovations but also incorporate the adaptation of appropriate 'mental entrepreneurial models'.

Mental entrepreneurial models that drive innovation are culture bound. Understanding the culture and entrepreneurship interface is very important as culture can stimulate entrepreneurship and thus contribute to the business and economic development of a country. Culture and cultural values in particular serve as a mediator that can guide and shape entrepreneurial behaviors, including risk taking, proactiveness and innovativeness (Hayton *et al.*, 2002). In Chapter 3, we examine how culture affects entrepreneurship. This chapter demonstrates that entrepreneurship is culture bound. It explains how entrepreneurship can flourish through the influential role of culture on the psychological characteristics of individuals. The chapter offers a thorough analysis of cultural values as defined by Hofstede, and their influence on entreprencurial activities and entrepreneurial capabilities, including proactiveness, innovativeness and risk taking. Within this chapter, the authors explain various factors, including culture, that may influence an individual's entrepreneurial intention. They further explain cultural differences based on Hofstede's dimensions and discuss the effects of cultural dimensions on entrepreneurial potential, intention and the traits of individuals. They assess whether there may be universal values that can affect an individual's entrepreneurial intention, and compare and contrast models developed to understand the relationship between culture and entrepreneurship. This chapter also offers a case study comparison of the development of entrepreneurship in two globally influential economies, namely the USA and China.

Levent Altinay, Oxford Brookes University

References

Baumol, W. and Strom, R. (2007) 'Entrepreneurship and Economic Growth', *Strategic Entrepreneurship Journal*, **1**(3-4), 233-237.

Chell, E., Nicolopoulou, K. and Karatas-Ozkan, M. (2010) 'Social entrepreneurship and enterprise; International and innovation perspectives', *Entrepreneurship & Regional Development*, **22** (6), 85–493.

Hayton, J., George, G. and Zahra, S. (2002) 'National culture and entrepreneurship: a review of behavioural research', *Entrepreneurship Theory and Practice*, **26** (4), 33-52.

Schumpeter, J. (1934) '*The Theory of Economic Development. An inquiry into Profits, Capital, Credit, Interest, and the Business Cycle*', Cambridge: Harvard University Press.

1 Entrepreneurial Traits

Philip Goulding, Sheffield Hallam University, UK

Introduction

The quest to understand the character traits of entrepreneurs has been an academic preoccupation for the best part of a century. As the study of human psychology rapidly developed during the first half of the 20th century, attention increasingly turned towards what became known as 'entrepreneurial personality'. 'Entrepreneurs' were considered as somehow different from the mass of the population, given their propensity to generate wealth, value and innovation. In the 1930s, the famous Austrian-American economist, Joseph Schumpeter, hailed entrepreneurs as 'great people' in that they possess character attributes not commonly found within the bulk of the population within their society. Therein started the 'great person' school of thought that gave birth to a wealth of scientific study, the purpose of which has been to unlock our understanding of the entrepreneur. Along the way, management scientists, psychologists, behaviouralists and academics from other disciplines developed related approaches such as the study of socio-cultural profiles of entrepreneurs, motivational research, entrepreneurial 'types' and so on. Arguably, the most researched approach, and the most controversial (Stevenson and Sahlman, 1989; Stanworth and Gray 1991; Chell, 2008), has been the study of personality traits (here shortened to 'traits') to understand the entrepreneur.

The rise of the modern hospitality and tourism industries, from the mid-19th century, has produced both 'great persons', i.e. individuals who stand out as internationally renowned entrepreneurial role models, as well as the many unsung 'local heroes' within their domestic or local tourism economies. As Altinay *et al.* (2012) remind us, tourism enterprise plays a significant role in economies, not only in terms of employment and wealth creation, but also in the development of destinations, new tourism products and service innovation. Therefore, an insight into the personality traits of individuals who drive such enterprise and innovation helps us understand the wider processes of entrepreneurship.

The purpose of this chapter, therefore, is to review some of the key concepts and frameworks relating to entrepreneurial trait theory, to apply this to our knowledge of some key individuals in tourism and hospitality and to establish a base from which students can explore further. The chapter aims to establish a knowledge base that can be applied to key contexts of entrepreneurship, that are explored elsewhere in this book, for example social entrepreneurship and franchising.

By the end of this chapter, you should be able to:

■ Explain and critically discuss the relevance of entrepreneurial traits;

■ Identify and critically examine some of the main conceptual approaches and models of entrepreneurial trait theory;

■ Apply your knowledge of entrepreneurial trait theory to individuals within the hospitality and tourism industries.

The chapter begins by examining what we mean by entrepreneurial 'traits' and 'personality'. It will critically examine some of the ways in which empirical studies have attempted to measure 'traits' and appraise some of the entrepreneurial schools of thought. The relationship between risk and entrepreneurial behaviour will then be addressed before a set of conclusions are drawn.

Trait theory within the wider knowledge domains of entrepreneurship

There is no doubt that character or personality traits have been one of the most studied areas of entrepreneurship. However, in order to help us appreciate their role in understanding entrepreneurs, it is useful to position trait theory and concepts within the wider body of knowledge that relates to, or impinges on the character of entrepreneurs.

The 'great person' approach was the first real development of the theory of entrepreneurs. It derived from the study of famous political and military leaders and thus was developed from a leadership perspective (Taylor, 2013). In the 1930s, the economist and political scientist Joseph Schumpeter argued that those individuals who drive forward economic change and wealth creation, essentially through the 'creative destruction' of the existing economic order, possess a particular set of characteristics not found throughout most of the population. His term 'Unternehmergeist' can be translated as 'entrepreneurial spirit' (Chell, 2008).

Some of the major conceptual strands of entrepreneurial theory are illustrated below. While 'great person' theory is very much the antecedent of wider personality trait studies, entrepreneurial character traits cannot be divorced from motivations, socio-demographic, cultural and cognitive approaches. For example, Drucker (1985: 23) believed that decision-making is at the heart of entrepreneurship and thus anyone who can 'face up to decision-making can learn to be an entrepreneur'. Drucker's view supports the cognitive approach, that learning, rather than purely innate personality traits, influences entrepreneurial behaviours. For Drucker, entrepreneurship is about dealing with uncertainty and it is behaviour, which can be learned, rather than personality, that equips an individual to be entrepreneurial.

Conceptual approaches to understanding entrepreneurs

'Great person' approach: The person is seen as 'special', an extraordinary achiever and one of a few, therefore a need to understand his/her qualities. Derived from Schumpeter's characterisation of entrepreneurs as creative destroyers of the existing economic/technological order in order to create new value.

Motivations: Focuses on contextual factors that influence the decision to start a business: entrepreneurial motivators : 'pull' and 'push' factors, opportunity vs necessity-driven entrepreneurship (GEM 2013).

Socio-cultural-demographic profiles: Draws attention to the social and demographic backgrounds of entrepreneurs: eg age, gender, education, ethnicity. Lots of research studies eg on female entrepreneurs, cultural backgrounds, antecedents.

Entrepreneurial 'types': Built up from numerous empirical studies and observations. See Stokes and Wilson, (2006) for a generic list (20 types identified); see Getz et al. (2004) for adaptation to small family business entrepreneur types in hospitality and tourism.

The 'trait' approach: Developed from 'the Great Person' school, examines the nature and role of personality traits; seeks to measure psychological characteristics of entrepreneurs to enhance understanding.

Cognitive or learning: People 'learn' to be entrepreneurs - i.e. are not 'born to be ('nurture vs nature' debate).

What do we mean by 'traits' and 'personality'?

From a psychological perspective, a trait is considered as part of the structure of personality (Chell, 2008). Personality is an amalgam of numerous different traits and as such is a holistic concept, while individual or 'narrow' traits may be either present or absent from the make-up of an individual's personality (Stevenson and Sahlman, 1989). Traits are therefore part of our 'being', while behaviour is clearly associated with 'doing', or taking a course of action in a particular situation. However both, according to Chell (1985), are functions of our personality and this duality complicates the issue of distinguishing between entrepreneurial traits on the one hand and entrepreneurial behaviours on the other.

From the myriad of psychological studies on human personality, evidence suggests that most personality measures can be captured within the umbrella of a five factor model, which has come to be known as the 'Big Five' dimensions. Paraphrasing Nicholson (1998). Judge *et al.* (1999) and Leutner *et al.* (2014), those five factors (or dimensions) of personality include:

- Neuroticism or emotional stability (embracing the specific characteristics of anxiety, vulnerability, self-consciousness, impulsive emotional responsiveness) and often associated with the conditioning of negative life events;

- Extraversion, which is an expression of sociability and outgoing, social orientation, including a dominant, ambitious and assertive personality and associated with active behaviour and lacking in introspection;

- Conscientiousness, a personality type which manifests in achievement orientation, dependability, persistence, self-control and a need for order;

- Openness to experience, a personality type associated with creativity and imagination, adaptivity, unconventionality, autonomy and intellectual orientation;

- Agreeableness, a nurturing personality, where trust, caring, cooperativeness and likeability are dominant traits.

The 'Big Five' personality dimensions indicate that what we recognise as a trait comprises a mix of innate characteristics, cognitions and behaviours. Chell (2008: 83) provides the example of the trait of neuroticism (now often referred to as emotional stability), noting that it is associated not only with the conditions of low self-esteem, anxiety and guilt, but with particular behaviour patterns which can lead to entrepreneurialism. While such broad personality trait bundles provide a starting point for our understanding of the application between personality and entrepreneurial behaviour, it may be more productive to identify what Leutner *et al.* (2014:59) refer to as 'narrow traits': those traits specifically and commonly measured and applied to entrepreneurial behaviours. A discussion of these follows later in this chapter.

Entrepreneurship refers to a set of activities or behaviours. In other words, it's not just the psychological make-up of the individual, but rather this combined with the way he or she behaves that helps us understand entrepreneurial personality (Ahmetoglu *et al.*, 2011). Therefore personality is intrinsically linked to entrepreneurial behaviour in many ways. It has been studied to predict entrepreneurial intent (Correia Santos *et al.*, 2013), future business venture growth (Baum and Locke, 2004), venture success or failure (Zhao and Seibert, 2006; Baron *et al.*, 2007; Dvir *et al.*, 2009; Ahmetoglu *et al.*, 2011) and as a predictor of career outcomes (Judge *et al.*, 1999). Judge *et al.* (1999) conducted a longitudinal intergenerational study of around 350 individuals in the USA over 60 years. Their findings provide evidence of enduring relationships between personality traits and extrinsic career success, i.e. occupational status, income, wealth. They showed that people exhibiting low neuroticism, low agreeableness, high extraversion and high cognitive ability were most associated with extrinsic career success. Links have also been found between levels of emotional intelligence and engagement in entrepreneurial activities. In their study of UK individuals representing all kinds of occupational status, Ahmetoglu *et al.* (2011) found that more emotionally intelligent people are more likely to engage in innovative entrepreneurial activities than those with lower emotional intelligence.

However, the trait approach to understanding entrepreneurship has not been without its criticisms as discussed below.

Critiquing entrepreneurial personality traits

Before we examine personality characteristics commonly associated with entrepreneurship, it is pertinent to acknowledge some of the main criticisms of entrepreneurial trait theory. There are indeed numerous controversies over the role of personality traits in understanding entrepreneurs. The following represent some of the recurrent issues encountered in the literature:

1   Firstly, we have seen that a trait is just one element of personality and that there is a close link between traits and behaviours. Consequently, authors have argued that it is more relevant to understand personality holistically rather than try to isolate the importance of very specific narrow personality components as entrepreneurial 'drivers' (Stanworth and Gray, 1991; Chell, 2008).

2   Socio-demographic variables (age, educational opportunity, learning and achievement, family circumstances, gender, race and social class) cannot be totally isolated from personality characteristics as influencers of entrepreneurial intentions and behaviours (Burns, 2007; Gurel *et al.*, 2010). As an example, Altinay *et al.* (2012) established that family tradition is an influential factor in business start-up intentions within the small hospitality and tourism sectors.

3   Some of the methodologies used to identify and apply traits to entrepreneurs have come under much criticism, not necessarily because of any methodological defect, but rather in the process of ascribing their findings to entrepreneurial behaviour (Kuratko, 2009). A case in point is the application of the Myers Briggs personality test in psychometric tests as a predictor of entrepreneurial personality, given that the test is normally associated with management orientation and leadership skills.

4   The vast body of empirical studies has produced often conflicting results in terms of the relative importance of specific traits. The issue here is how generalisable such studies are, given the broader cultural contexts within which entrepreneurship takes place.

5   The assumption that entrepreneurial behaviour is a function of personality rather than a response to environmental, cultural and political factors within which a business operates should not be unchallenged (Beaver, 2002). According to Sheppardson and Gibson (2011: 128), entrepreneurs "just think in a different way and it is really all about psychology [which] can be provoked by an environment." This argument particularly pertains to the varied market environments within which hospitality and tourism businesses flourish, given the relative low barriers to starting a small business in these sectors in many countries. In other words, entrepreneurial intention might translate more easily into business start-up in places where conditions are more favourable. Entrepreneurial personality traits are therefore not always in themselves totally indicative of entrepreneurial behaviour, rather, entrepreneurs may respond opportunistically to a given business environment.

6   Burns (2007) argues that ascribing personality characteristics to classical entrepreneurs (i.e. business growth-driven individuals) should be distinguished from those who may have entrepreneurial characteristics but whose goals put them more in the owner-manager camp, such as 'lifestyle entrepreneurs'. This is an important consideration in hospitality and tourism, where lifestyle enterprise is particularly prevalent among micro-business owner-managers (Goulding *et al.*, 2005).

7 The role of education and training in influencing entrepreneurial intention should not be underestimated, for example in building confidence and competences such as business planning (Deakins and Freel, 2012).

Despite the criticisms of trait approaches and the movement away from the earlier psychological approaches, there is a consensus that certain character traits are prominent and explanatory in understanding entrepreneurial behaviours within the wider population generally (Beaver, 2002; Burns, 2007; Kuratko, 2009) and among tourism and hospitality specifically (Gurel *et al.*, 2010; Sheppardson and Gibson, 2011; Altinay *et al.*, 2012).

Entrepreneurial traits

In this section we will focus on some of the specific entrepreneurial personality traits that have received recurrent attention in the literature and in the popular media more recently. The 'Big Five' traits, as previously introduced, provide a useful framework of analysis. Given the representation of female entrepreneurs within the hospitality and tourism industries, it is also useful to explore how the literature deals with gender differences in entrepreneurial personality (Carland and Carland, 1991; Hisrich and Peters, 1998; Getz *et al.*, 2004).

Commonly attributed entrepreneurial personality characteristics

Identifying entrepreneurial traits from the literature can read rather like a 'menu' of contributory attributes influencing business start-up behaviour. Hornaday (1982) identified 42 such characteristics that were amassed in the early studies of entrepreneurial personality. Even where such traits have been empirically proven or associated with behaviours that distinguish entrepreneurial individuals from the rest of society, it is notoriously problematic to ascribe behaviour to a particular menu of traits. Indeed, much-heralded entrepreneurs associated with the tourism, travel and hospitality sectors, such as Sir Richard Branson of Virgin group fame, Stelios Haji-Ioannou, founder of easyJet and the easyGroup, the late Mohan Singh Oberoi, founder of the eponymous hotel group and Stephen Kaufer of TripAdvisor fame, are not always identified as having the same bundle of traits as each another.

Figure 1.1 provides a synthesis of entrepreneurial traits positioned in the respective Big Five personality domain with which they are most closely identified.

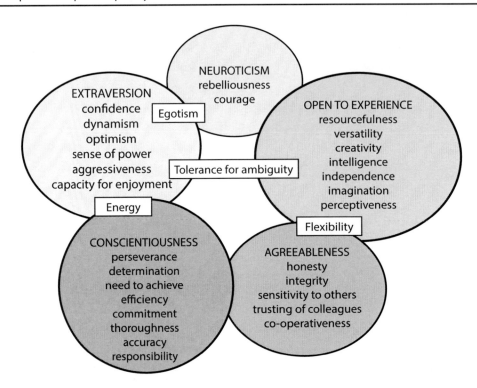

Figure 1.1: The Big Five personality domains and entrepreneurial personality

Leutner *et al.* (2014) examine the relationship between entrepreneurial personality and the 'Big Five' personality traits. They remind us that behaviours commonly identified as indicators of entrepreneurial success include opportunity recognition, opportunity exploitation, innovation and value creation and that such behaviours are a function of personality. Entrepreneurial personality is therefore an expression of those particular character traits most closely associated with entrepreneurial outcomes, i.e. the creation, innovation and growth of business or social enterprise.

Meanwhile, Ahmetoglu *et al.* (2011) developed a self-reporting scale consisting of four dimensions of entrepreneurial personality, namely: entrepreneurial awareness (i.e. ability to spot potentially profitable opportunities); entrepreneurial creativity (innovative ideas); opportunism (i.e. taking advantage, acting upon opportunities) and vision. Each of these can clearly be observed in the accounts of celebrated entrepreneurs.

Stelios Haji-Ioannou

As a self-proclaimed serial entrepreneur with 16 'easy' ventures behind him, Stelios Haji-Ioannou (Stelios as he simply likes to be known) has been passionate about the expansion of the brand since the founding of EasyJet in 1995. Some of his ventures have been financially unsuccessful (e.g., easyMoney, easyCinema) but these forays into non-core travel, tourism and hospitality services demonstrate his innate sense of opportunism, self-belief and self-confidence in his assessment of risk. He remains undeterred by the failures and sees his best business as 'the next one'. He is famously outspoken and intemperate in language if he believes his Board of Management is making bad decisions. He extrovertly courts publicity, most famously distributing free EasyJet tickets on a rival airline's inaugural flight and in his public sparring with low cost airline chief Mike O'Leary of Ryanair. Blackhurst (2010) refers to Stelios as 'an unstoppable force of nature' who would make a hopeless diplomat.

Burns (2007) makes the point that while growth-oriented entrepreneurs share some of the character traits of non-growth or 'lifestyle' oriented owner-managers, (for example the need for independence and achievement, and the ability to live with uncertainty and take measured risks), it is a particular set of personality traits that distinguish them. Drawing on a rich set of empirical studies into entrepreneurial personality, he identifies opportunism, innovativeness, self-confidence, a proactive nature, decisiveness, vision, flair, intrinsic self-motivation and a willingness to take greater risks (in terms of reward opportunities) and to live with the consequences of uncertainty as key personality identifiers that generally distinguish growth-oriented entrepreneurs from the larger pool of small business start-ups. Nicholson (1998) examined personality and entrepreneurial leadership. He set out to test what might make entrepreneurial leaders' personalities different from those of other people. His results suggest there are character differences between entrepreneurial leaders and other managers: an 'emotionally armour-plated single-mindedness' (p. 537), meaning stress-resistant, unselfconscious, assertive, non-experimental in their actions, conscientious, conformist and competitive'. For Leutner *et al.* (2014), the need for achievement, self-confidence, innovativeness, stress tolerance, need for autonomy and a proactive personality are the key 'narrow traits' of entrepreneurial personality.

The argument is that each of these is an essential part of the personality make-up of entrepreneurs, as collectively they explain the behaviours that underlie entrepreneurial success. An opportunistic outlook enables entrepreneurs to see business opportunities where others do not, or indeed where others see challenges or problems. Stelios Haji-Ioannou's innate opportunism for the cause of developing easyJet's route network in order to take advantage of the future growth in EU membership and Schengen mobility gave his airline an early advantage in the European low-cost aviation market. Self-confidence manifests in the ability to take and believe in decisions that are not necessarily based on a rational justification or weighing up of pros and cons. Given the need to network and engage others in a start-up process, self-confidence is a tool of persuasion. Richard Branson's confidence and belief in the Virgin Space tourism project, in spite of its ongoing technical set-backs, is an extreme example of such self-confidence. Finally, self-motivation is the trait most closely associated with what psychologists refer to as 'type A' behaviours: i.e. those that display compulsive behaviours that are driven by a need for achievement (Chell, 2008).

Richard Branson

Crainer and Dearlove (2000) summarise Branson's traits thus:

"Branson is a prospector, panning the multitude of business prospects that Virgin attracts for nuggets of purest gold. He is always on the lookout for new business ventures…..if there is a gleam of an opportunity for a new Virgin company [he] will take a long hard look"…….. He has "the ability to make things happen. He is the catalyst that triggers a chain reaction which transforms potential energy in a project into kinetic energy that sends people scurrying in a thousand directions… His own enthusiasm is contagious, focusing excitement on a goal or destination… Branson has no clearly defined business skill or training" (Crainer and Dearlove, 2000:47-48).

'Locus of control' is another key personality trait which has been much studied and applied to entrepreneurial personality. It refers to the extent to which people believe they have the ability to influence events in their life (Brockhaus and Horowitz, 1986; Chell, 2008; Gurel *et al.*, 2010). The two dimensions are 'external' and 'internal' locus. It is the latter of these, internal locus, that is associated with entrepreneurial personality. Various studies around the world including China, Singapore, Hong Kong and the USA have shown higher internal locus of control among entrepreneurially-inclined individuals and active entrepreneurs (Chell, 2008; Gurel *et al.*, 2010). However, there is an argument that belief in control of one's own destiny (i.e. internal locus of control) might, in some individuals, be a learned behavioural response rather than a personality trait *per se* (Chell, 2008).

Mohan Singh Oberoi

Mohan Singh Oberoi (1898-2002) has been credited as 'the father of the Indian hotel industry' (anon, 2009). In an interview, he claimed to have started out as 'a village boy who left his plague infested village in search of a job' (Rediff, 2005). By the time of his death, he had amassed an empire of luxury hotels, cruise ships, a hotel training school and flight catering businesses bearing his name. As a young man he faced constant adversity, hardship and ill-luck. Accounting for his entry into India's emerging hotel business as a billing clerk, he claimed he suddenly had the urge to go in and try his luck, famously saying 'one becomes bold in the face of difficulties'. Renowned for his compassion, modesty, an emotional disposition, diligence to make a project succeed and his faith, ('I realise it was with God's help that I achieved what the world calls success'), but above all, inner self-belief, he represents an alternative set of personality traits from the more extrovert examples above. Acknowledging that 'nearly every turn in my life has been associated with an epidemic of some sort' (Rediff, 2005), he demonstrates that the line between internal and external locus of control may not always be clear cut.

Another aspect of entrepreneurial personality is its 'deviant' side, famously examined by Kets de Vries (1985). His work identified both negative contextual and motivational factors as drivers for entrepreneurial activity, but also the personality traits that underlie them. Rejection of authority, non-conformity to the social (or work) environment and a need to prove oneself are rooted in the traits of neuroticism. Such traits can be seen as push motivators for entrepreneurial behaviour, as drivers for changing life circumstances. Within a work environment, the non-conformist may be the non-corporate intrapreneurial individual who seeks an escape to start their own business rather than remain shackled to what they see as the deficiencies of their existing employment (Deakins and Freel, 2012).

On the other hand, McClelland's (1961) pioneering work established the importance of positive and nurturing family and social environments with the development of an achievement-seeking personality. It can be argued therefore, that the fundamental entrepreneurial trait of 'need for achievement' arises from very different psychological and contextual circumstances.

Table 1.1 provides a summary of some of the main recurrent trait themes and the key literatures that have contributed to them.

Table 1.1: Key themes in entrepreneurial traits

Need for achievement	Need for autonomy	Self-belief	Risk-taking	Locus of control
Escaping adverse circumstances from childhood; Insecurity; Rejection of others' authority (*Kets de Vries 1985*); Positive parental influences foster 'achievement personality' (*McClelland 1961*)	Desire for independence; Being own boss; Making decisions 'against the flow'; Freedom to create one's own future (*Getz, Carlsen & Morrison 2004*)	Believing in own judgment when assessing business opportunities; Going against criticism, rejection by others (*Stokes and Wilson 2006*)	Risk perception linked to vision of business potential; Opportunism tempered with caution, defining, measuring and trying to minimise risks (*Drucker 1985*)	Belief of controlling one's own destiny and the environment in which we thrive (internal) rather than being subject to the control of external forces or fate (*Brockhaus & Horwitz 1986*)

Adapted and updated from Vecchio (2003) and Kuratko (2009).

Gender and entrepreneurial traits

Hisrich and Peters (1998) drew together findings from numerous empirical studies of male and female entrepreneurs. They noted personality trait similarities and differences between the genders as shown below:

Personality characteristics of male and female entrepreneurs

Male entrepreneurs	Female entrepreneurs
opinionated and persuasive	flexible and tolerant
goal-oriented	goal-oriented
innovative and idealistic	creative and idealistic
high level of self-confidence	medium level of self-confidence
enthusiastic and energetic	enthusiastic and energetic
must be own boss	ability to deal with the social and economic environment

Hisrich and Peters (1998).

On the one hand, goal orientation, the need for achievement, energy and independence are characteristics that cross the gender divide. Conversely, Hisrich and Peters (1998) found the literature points to higher incidence of self-belief and persuasion in male entrepreneurs and lower levels of self-confidence among female entrepreneurs. Beaver (2002) links the latter with findings that suggest that female entrepreneurs are less likely to acknowledge their abilities and to have lower expectations of themselves. The Global Entrepreneurship Monitor (2013) also evidences from their global survey of entrepreneurial intentions that women declare lower self-confidence in their capabilities to start a new business and higher levels of fear of failure than males. Moreover such gender differences in perceptions occur across least developed and highly developed countries and societies. All these factors are seen as barriers to higher levels of female participation in entrepreneurship.

However, various other gender-related research (e.g. Marlow and Patton, 2005; Shelton, 2006) suggests that contextual factors rather than personality traits *per se* play a large role in explaining the gender gap in entrepreneurship. In Shelton's (2006) study, personality traits amongst high-growth-oriented female entrepreneurs – vision, energy and opportunism – drive their ambition and enable them to employ strategies to successfully balance venture performance with reducing any work-family conflict. Marlow and Patton's (2005) study reports that while female entrepreneurs are often more oriented towards greater social fulfilment in their entrepreneurial endeavours, they are more risk averse regarding the pace of growth and investment. However, they found that access to start-up finance is a bigger issue than their personality traits. Moreover, where women do make a name for themselves as successful entrepreneurs, they are likely to field similar traits to men.

Risk-taking

Of all the major traits identified, a propensity for risk-taking or conversely, a risk-averse personality, is perhaps at the forefront of the mind when thinking of entrepreneurial characteristics. Drucker (1985) famously postulated that "entrepreneurship is 'risky' mainly because so few of the so-called entrepreneurs know what they are doing" (p. 26). He had strong views on the propensity for risk-taking as an entrepreneurial personality. He famously stated "I ...know a good many successful innovators and entrepreneurs. Not one of them has a 'propensity for risk-taking'" (pp. 126-127). His view was that innovators are successful to the extent to which they define and confine risks. They systematically analyse sources of innovative opportunities, pinpoint those opportunities and then exploit them, whether small, definable risks or greater but still definable risks. In other words, successful innovators are more opportunity-focused than risk-focused.

Kuratko (2009) agrees, equating risk evaluation behaviour in terms of the level of rewards. Drawing on Monroy and Folger's (1993) typology of entrepreneurial styles, he highlights risk-taking traits in terms of risk avoidance or risk acceptance, depending on the level of personal financial risk and the level of profit motive. Kuratko (2009:39) also notes that not all entrepreneurs are driven solely by monetary gain. Accordingly, the level of financial risk cannot be explained purely by profit opportunity.

Case study: The Geisha Group

Andreea Apetrei, Catholic University of Valencia, Spain
Juan Sapena Bolufer, Catholic University of Valencia, Spain

The story of a travel entrepreneur

This case study reflects the story of a Spanish man whose love of travel encouraged him to seek out entrepreneurial opportunities within the tourism industry. The case is presented below according to the trajectory of his entrepreneurial life and divided according to important time frames.

Discovering the entrepreneurial spirit: 1985-1986

At the beginning of the 1980s, Juan Manuel Baixauli was a young man studying psychology in Spain. At that time, he was really interested in learning more about the field, but it was not easy. As in many other countries, higher education was expensive and Juan Manuel supported himself by giving private lessons to younger people, helping them with their studies. As he enjoyed the experience of meeting new people, he also became involved in different student associations. One of these associations organised humanitarian trips to Africa and Juan Manuel went along. Travelling to the African continent proved to have a crucial impact on his life. Returning from his first trip, Juan Manuel became aware of how important, inspiring and mind-opening travelling can be for a person. He realised that if he could work in the tourism sector, he could also enjoy travelling more often. Travelling, in turn, would enable him to continue to explore and learn about different places. He also realised that at that time, travelling outside of Spain was still uncommon and there were few jobs available. Still needing to work to support his studies, Juan Manuel proposed a collaborative venture to a tourism company from Valencia. He offered to create 'trips' or tourism packages for the company, sell them and earn a commission on the sales. As such, he created a job for himself that would enable him to realise his goals.

In the second year of his university studies, Juan Manuel started to work part-time for the company on this commission basis. He soon realised that this work was not only a great way to fund his studies, but that it was also really enjoyable. Despite the offer of working on a permanent contract, he refused to be 'the employee' of any particular company. Juan Manuel stated, "during the 80s, almost nobody was talking about the concept of 'entrepreneur'. I was not aware either of it either. Everybody was looking for a stable job, or the traditional 'functionary' job for one of the state's institutions. My parents were also encouraging me to follow such a path, but somehow I refused to go on that road. I never wanted to sign a full-time labour contract with the company I was working for. I knew that I was very good at what I was doing, and I wanted to do it by myself."

Discovering the business world: 1987-1990

Over the next few years Juan Manuel kept busy with his studies and his involvement with student associations. At the same time he continued to work for the Valencia tourism firm between 6:00 and 10:00 pm as a territorial representative. It was at this point in time that he made the decision to dedicate his life to tourism, recognising that this was a relatively new sector in Spain. In March 1989 he established his own company called Turisgestión, funded with 100% Spanish capital. His firm realised a turnover of 204,000 Euros (34 million Pesetas) in the first year.

From the beginning Juan Manuel's attention was focused on one thing; creating a sustainable business model. His dream was to develop a business system that could be easily replicated. While his main objective was to develop a strategy suitable for the tourism sector, the daily activities were driven by two main values; client (customer) orientation and competitiveness. Juan Manuel admits that he was, and he still is, obsessed with what the clients look for when they come to a travel agency. He considers that the client focus approach helped him to attract clients, grow and innovate. While many tourism companies were still focusing on the destinations, he tried to adapt to the clients' needs and offer a more personalised service. The success of his company in those early years also stemmed from his fixation to be competitive. As Juan Manuel advises, "one question that any entrepreneur should ask himself every day is: Am I competitive?"

Innovating the tourism business: 1990-2000

Turisgestión and its commercial arm, Gheisa Travel Agencies, continued to grow throughout the 1990s. Juan Manuel continued to work towards the development of a business model. He was interested in creating a strategy based on a commercial methodology that would generate clients and could be easily put into practice. After opening two more offices, he succeeded in developing and implementing this model, testing it with the opening of his fourth agency. He subsequently started to franchise his business model in 1994. At the time, this was an innovative practice in the Spanish tourism sector. However, through franchising, Gheisa Travel became one of the biggest agencies in the Spanish tourism sector, and by the year 2000, network sales had grown to 28.5 million Euros (4,750 million Peseta).

Growing fast and strong: 2000-2005

By 2002, Gheisa Travel comprised 74 agencies, owned and franchised, in Spain and Portugal. Juan Manuel received the national Best Entrepreneur of 2002 Award in recognition of the firm's evolution and development based on new concepts in the world of travel agencies. Further awards followed in 2003 and 2004. In 2003, he received an award from the Valencian Chamber of Commerce for his services to tourism in the Valencian County. The following year, he received another recognition for the best franchise concept for tourism services by the national magazine, *Franquicias Hoy*.

At the same time, Juan Manuel continued to expand his franchise network internationally and registered his brand in 45 countries considered to have potential for development in Europe, North and South America. To each franchisee, Gheisa Travel offered a strong brand, a competitive business system and an efficient operating system. Juan Manuel also opted for a flexible and innovative franchise concept, adapting the standard model according to the experience and ideas of each franchisee. Juan Manuel travelled extensively during this time in search of 'entrepreneurs like me'. However, he found it difficult to find suitable franchise partners with whom he could build trusting relationships. During one meeting in Vancouver, he realised that "any business or company is based on a strong brand and an efficient business model."

Changing reality and cloudy times: 2006-2009

By 2006, the travel market had changed remarkably. In Spain, the travel agency market was saturated, as it was in other international countries. In addition, the world-wide web had created a different type of customer. As a result, Juan Manuel decided to stop international expansion and reinforce the brand and the business model in the local market. Still focusing on value for clients, the company restructured its services for three main segments; holiday, business and golf tourism. However, he subsequently sold his network of agencies to Globalia Halcon. According to Juan Manuel, "too many things were happening at the same time and the sector was not responding to the old business strategy. The traditional model of high street agencies was no longer useful."

Reinvention: New times and a new business model: 2010-2014

Following the sale of Gheisa Travel, Juan Manuel became obsessed with finding a new business model adapted to the new technological era. Recognising the ability of technology to revolutionalise the travel industry, he identified the potential demand for specialised and personalised travel services. He created a new company, Compania Europea de Gestores de Incentivos, focusing his energies on blending tourism and technology. He started to design a system based on Enterprise Resource Planning (ERP) software that could be adapted for the tourism industry and controlled remotely through the Internet. Specialist help was sought to develop Octopus software which assigns each client company a personal travel manager. This manager develops specialist knowledge of the client company and its purchasing and travel policies to ensure that these are always met. It also contains a structured information system (SIS) which allows customers to track travel expenses in real time, by country, destination or employee and receive alerts when consumption levels are exceeded. In 2014, Consultia Travel was launched and presented to the tourism community as an integrated consultancy service for business travellers. The entrepreneur thus shifted his focus from a business-to-consumer (B2C) model to a business-to-business model (B2B). It has since expanded to create a sports travel division, Consultia Travel Sport, specialising in travel to sporting events.

Questions:

1   Explain how Juan Manuel identified his first entrepreneurial opportunity in the travel industry?

2   What traits identified in Chapter 1, did Juan Manuel display when collaborating with the Valencia tourism company?

3   Identify one innovation of Juan Manuel and explain what makes it an innovation.

4   What characteristics or traits, identified in Chapter 1 did Juan Manuel display in his reinvention stage?

5   How do these traits differ, if at all, from his earliest entrepreneurial venture.

Conclusion

The purpose of this chapter was to examine the contribution of personality traits to our understanding of entrepreneurship and to apply this knowledge within a tourism and hospitality context. Trait theory was positioned within the broader framework of approaches to entrepreneurship. It was important to discuss traits from a psychological perspective with particular emphasis on the contribution of the 'Big Five' trait dimensions. It was also important to examine inter-relationships between entrepreneurial traits and behaviours. Trait theory occupies a central place in understanding entrepreneurial behaviours but, as we saw, there are controversies which need to be acknowledged. Moreover, debates continue in terms of differences in entrepreneurial personality between the genders and between growth-oriented versus non-growth or lifestyle entrepreneurs, as was explored. A number of 'narrow traits' are recurrent among entrepreneurs and accordingly were discussed, with reference to some high profile entrepreneurial personalities in hospitality and tourism. From what we know about the personality make-up of entrepreneurs, the relationship between traits and risk-taking propensity is integral to our understanding.

References

Ahmetoglu, G., Leutner, F. and Chamorro-Premuzic, T. (2011) EQ-nomics: Understanding the relationship between individual differences in Trait Emotional Intelligence and entrepreneurship, *Personality and Individual Differences*, **51**, 1028-1033.

Altinay, L., Madanoglu, M., Daniele, R. and Lashley, C. (2012) The influence of family tradition and psychological traits on entrepreneurial intention, *International Journal of Hospitality Management*, **31**, 489-499.

Anon (2009) M.S. Oberoi Profile, iloveindia.com, www.ioveindia.com/indian-heroes/ms-oberoi.html [Retrieved 7th October 2009].

Baron, R.A., Frese, M. and Baum, J.R. (2007) Research Gains: Benefits of closer links between I/O psychology and entrepreneurship, in J.R. Baum, M. Frese and R.A. Baron (eds.), *The Psychology of Entrepreneurship* (pp 347-373), Mahwah NJ: Erlbaum.

Baum, J.R. and Locke, E.A. (2004) The relationship of entrepreneurial traits, skill and motivation to subsequent venture growth, *Journal of Applied Psychology*, **89** (4), 587-598.

Beaver, G. (2002) *Small Business, Entrepreneurship and Enterprise Development*, Harlow: Pearson Education.

Blackhurst, C. (2010) Interview with Sir Stelios Haji-Ioannou, in *Management Today*, 1st June 2010. www.managementtoday.co.uk [Retrieved 26th February 2015].

Brockhaus, R.H. and Horwitz, P.S. (1986) The Psychology of the entrepreneur in D. Sexton and R. Smilor (eds) *The Art and Science of Entrepreneurship* (pp 25-48), Cambridge MA: Ballinger.

Burns, P. (2007) *Entrepreneurship and Small Business*, 2nd edn, Basingstoke: Palgrave Macmillan.

Carland, J.C and Carland, J.W. (1991) An empirical investigation into the distinctions between male and female entrepreneurs and managers, *International Small Business Journal*, **9** (3), 62-72.

Chell, E. (2008) *The Entrepreneurial Personality: a social construction*, 2nd edn, East Sussex: Routledge.

Chell, E. (1985) The entrepreneurial personality: a few ghosts laid to rest?, *International Small Business Journal*, **3** (3), 43-54.

Correia Santos, S., Caetano, A. and Curral, L. (2013) Psychosocial aspects of entrepreneurial potential, *Journal of Small Business and Entrepreneurship*, **26** (6), 661-685.

Crainer, S. and Dearlove, D. (2000) *Generation Entrepreneur*, Harlow: Pearson.

Deakins, D. and Freel, M. (2012) *Entrepreneurship and Small Firms*, 6th edn, Maidenhead: McGraw-Hill.

Drucker, P.F. (1985) *Innovation and Entrepreneurship*, Abingdon: Routledge.

Dvir, D., Sadeh, A., Pines, A.M. and Shenhar, A.J. (2009) Key entrepreneurial traits and their relationship to venture uncertainty and venture success, *PICMET 2009 Proceedings*, August 2-6, Portland, Oregon.

Getz, D., Carlsen, J. and Morrison, A. (2004) *The Family Business in Tourism and Hospitality*, London: CABI International.

Global Entrepreneurship Monitor (2013) *2012 Women's Report*, Global Entrepreneurship Research Association.

Goulding, P., Baum, T. and Morrison, A. (2005) Seasonal trading and lifestyle motivation: experiences of small tourism businesses in Scotland, *Journal of Quality Assurance in Hospitality and Tourism*, **5** (2-4), 209-238.

Gurel, E., Altinay, L. and Daniele, R. (2010) Tourism students' entrepreneurial intentions, *Annals of Tourism Research*, **37** (3), 646-669.

Hisrich, R.D. and Peters, M.P. (1998) *Entrepreneurship*, 4th edn, Boston MA: McGraw-Hill.

Judge T.A., Higgins, C., Thoresen, C.J. and Barrick, M.R. (1999) The Big Five personality traits, general mental ability and career success across the life span, *Personnel Psychology*, **52** (3), 621-652.

Kets de Vries, M.F.R. (1985) The dark side of entrepreneurship, *Harvard Business Review*, November/December, 160-167.

Kuratko, D.F. (2009) *Introduction to Entrepreneurship*, 8th edn, Toronto: Cengage.

Leutner, F., Ahmetoglu, G., Akhtar, R. and Chamorro-Premuzic, T. (2014) The relationship between the entrepreneurial personality and the Big Five personality traits, *Personality and Individual Differences*, **63**, 58-63.

Marlow, S. and Patton, D. (2005) All credit to men? Entrepreneurship, finance and gender, *Entrepreneurship, Theory and Practice*, **29** (6), 717-735.

McClelland, D.C. (1961) *The Achieving Society*, New York: Van Nostrand.

Monroy, T. and Folger, R. (1993) A Typology of Entrepreneurial Paradigm: beyond economic rationality, *Journal of Private Enterprise*, **9** (2), 64-79.

Nicholson, N. (1998) Personality and entrepreneurial leadership: a study of the heads of the UK's most successful independent companies, *European Management Journal*, **16** (5), 529-539.

Rediff (2005), *How M.S. Oberoi Became India's Greatest Hotelier*, Rediff India Abroad, 21 October 2005, http://www.rediff.com/money/2005/oct/21bspec.htm [Retrieved 23 February 2015].

Shelton, L.M. (2006) Female entrepreneurs, work-family conflict and venture performance: new insights into the work-family interface, *Journal of Small Business Management*, **44** (2), 285-297.

Sheppardson, C. and Gibson, H. (2011) *Leadership and Entrepreneurship in the Hospitality Industry*, Oxford: Goodfellow.

Stanworth, J. and Gray, C. (1991) *Bolton 20 Years On: the Small Firm in the 1990s*, London: Paul Chapman.

Stevenson, H.H. and Sahlman, W.A. (1989) The entrepreneurial process in P. Burns and J. Dewhurst (eds), *Small Business and Entrepreneurship*, Basingstoke: Macmillan Education, pp. 94-157.

Stokes, D. and Wilson, N. (2006) *Small Business Management and Entrepreneurship*, 5th edn, London: Thomson Publishing.

Taylor, S. (2013) Leadership in A. Hassanien and C. Dale (eds.), *Facilities Management and Development for Tourism, Hospitality and Events*, Wallingford: CABI, pp. 219-240.

Vecchio, R. (2003) Entrepreneurship and leadership: common trends and common threads, *Human Resource Management Review*, **13** (2), 303-328.

Zhao, H. and Seibert, S.E. (2006) 'The Big Five personality dimensions and entrepreneurial status: a meta-analytical review', *Journal of Applied Psychology*, **91**, 259-271.

2 Entrepreneurship as a Process

Maureen Brookes, Oxford Brookes University, UK

Introduction

As entrepreneurs continue to attract the attention of governments, industrialists and academics, there has been substantial growth in entrepreneurial research. Although researchers have adopted different theoretical perspectives to understand entrepreneurship, Cope (2005) advises that three dominant theoretical perspectives have emerged. The first is the functional perspective which conceptualises entrepreneurs' interaction with their environment and the economic output of that interaction. The second perspective is the personality or traits of the entrepreneur as explored in Chapter 1. The third perspective, which is the focus of this chapter, is the behavioural or process perspective. This perspective focuses on the processes and functions of entrepreneurs and as such it is concerned with what entrepreneurs do, rather than who they are (Gartner, 1988).

As a process, entrepreneurship encompasses the identification, evaluation and exploitation of opportunities (Shane and Venkataraman, 2000). This theoretical perspective reflects the importance of the behaviour of entrepreneurs and the activities they undertake (Bygrave and Hofer, 1991) as well as the critical role of opportunities and innovation (Shane, 2012). It also recognises that an entrepreneur's personality is ancillary to this behaviour. Some academics argue therefore that this perspective provides a more comprehensive base from which to examine entrepreneurship (Cope, 2005). Furthermore, researchers have identified a number of different factors that influence entrepreneurial behaviour. The aim of this chapter therefore, is to develop your understanding of entrepreneurship as a process.

By the end of the chapter you should be able to:

■ Identify the three key stages of the entrepreneurial process;

■ Identify the factors that influence each of the key stages of the entrepreneurship process;

■ Evaluate the central role of innovation throughout the entrepreneurial process.

The chapter explores each of these stages in turn using examples from the Holiday Inn hotel brand to illustrate. A conceptual framework of entrepreneurship as a process is developed and illustrated using another case study of a new lodging concept, Air BnB.

The stages of the entrepreneurship process

Schumpeter (1934) is frequently credited with the original definition of entrepreneurs in a business context, suggesting they are 'individuals whose function is to carry out new combinations of means of production' (cited in Carland *et al.*, 1984:354) and arguing they are distinguishable by type and conduct. However, since Schumpeter's efforts, numerous definitions have subsequently emerged within the literature that suggest entrepreneurs are involved in a range of activities in the process of entrepreneurship. Despite these different interpretations, it is generally agreed that this range of activities can be clustered within three key stages around opportunities. As such, the process of entrepreneurship involves opportunity identification, opportunity evaluation, and opportunity exploitation (Shane and Venkataraman, 2000; Ucbasaran *et al.*, 2008, Nasution *et al.*, 2011). Furthermore, research suggests that innovation plays a fundamental role throughout the process, and that there are a number of different factors which influence the activities undertaken within each entrepreneurial stage.

As this textbook demonstrates, entrepreneurship can be considered from both a commercial and social perspective. This chapter considers it from a purely commercial perspective and from the perspective of the individual, rather than from an organisational viewpoint. By doing so, it incorporates what Shane (2012) describes as the nexus of two entrepreneurial phenomenon; opportunities and enterprising individuals. Each stage of the entrepreneurial process is considered, in turn, in the following sections.

Opportunity identification

The identification of an opportunity is considered the first key step in the entrepreneurial process (Baron, 2006). An opportunity is a 'future situation which is deemed desirable and feasible' (Stevenson and Jarillo, 1990:23). Within a business context however, opportunities are considered as 'situations in which new goods, services, raw materials and organizing methods can be introduced and sold for greater than their cost of production' (Shane and Venkataraman, 2000:220). In other words, opportunities can generate economic value, although this is not always guaranteed (Baron, 2006).

There are conflicting theories as to whether opportunities are discovered or created (Edelman and Yli-Renko, 2010). Discovery theorists maintain that opportunities arise from macro environmental dynamics, whereas the creative view considers that opportunities are created through entrepreneurs' perceptions and interactions with the environment (Shane and Venkataraman, 2000). However, some researchers argue that opportunities can be made as well as found (Venkataraman *et al.*, 2012) and whichever is the case, individual entrepreneurs are needed to identify opportunities (Ucbasaran *et al.*,2008) through their perception of market inefficiencies. Changing demographics, government regulations or socio-cultural norms may yield new markets or new market segments (Ireland *et al.*, 2003). Recognising these changes, entrepreneurs identify a need in the market or underemployed resources that could be used, and determine a fit between these needs and the resources available (Ardchivelli *et al.*, 2003). As such, they require the recombination of resources to create a new means-end resource relationship (Shane and Venkataraman, 2000). These relationships could be slight modifications of existing ones or fundamentally new relationships in new markets or markets not yet saturated (Smith *et al.*, 2009; Shane, 2012).

The concept of innovation is central to the process of opportunity identification. Indeed, Schumpeter (1934) defined innovation as the novel combination of resources brought about by the vision of the entrepreneur. This combination can yield new products, services, methods of production or markets, or incorporate new technology into new products, processes and services (McDermott and O'Connor, 2002). Innovations therefore differ according to their degree of 'newness'. Innovations can be radically new, incrementally new, or even imitative innovations that can be introduced to new markets that are not saturated by competition. Innovation 'newness' therefore depends on the particular recombination of resources and the type of market where inefficiencies are addressed (Gaglio and Katz, 2001). Whatever the type of innovation however, entrepreneurs are the creative force behind innovation and during the stage of opportunity identification, innovations are considered to be initiated (Garud *et al.*, 2013) as illustrated in Text Box 1.

Text box 1: Opportunity identification

In 1951, Kemmons Wilson, a builder, was travelling with his family by car to Washington DC from his home in Memphis. Throughout the journey, he was frustrated by the poor quality of accommodation available and the cost of accommodating his children even though they slept in sleeping bags on the floor of the room he shared with his wife. As family 'road trips' were becoming increasingly popular in the US as car ownership grew, Wilson spotted a clear gap in the market and an opportunity to develop a motel that offered clean, quality accommodation in accessible locations where kids could stay free in their parents' room.

There are three inter-related factors which influence opportunity identification; prior knowledge, cognitive ability and the search for information (Corbett, 2005; Baron, 2006). Prior knowledge of markets and customers and ways to serve them are important to opportunity identification (Shane, 2000) as it enables entrepreneurs to make connections between resources and market inefficiencies (Baron, 2006). The cognitive ability of individuals is also important therefore to direct the opportunity identification process (Gaglio and Katz, 2001) but this can be shaped through prior experience by facilitating pattern recognition (Mitchell *et al.*, 2004). In other words, it helps entrepreneurs to be more alert to opportunities (Ardichvili *et al.*, 2003). Research suggests that individuals with no prior business experience detect fewer entrepreneurial opportunities (Haynie *et al.*, 2009).

Cognitive ability also influences the information search process (Keh *et al.*, 2002). Entrepreneurs access to publication-based information (Ucbasaran *et al.*, 2007 and access to information through social and professional networks (Ozgen and Baron, 2007) also facilitate opportunity identification. Social ties, in particular, have been shown to serve as a conduit for new information and be particularly important when there are weak or inefficient formal institutions to provide information in a business environment (Batjargal *et al.*, 2013).

Researchers also identify that entrepreneurs' alertness to opportunities is also shaped by particular personality traits such as optimism, self-efficacy and proactivity (Ardichvili *et al.*, 2003; Nasution *et al.*, 2011). Entrepreneurs who are optimistic and believe in their own capabilities are more likely to identify opportunities, as are those who are proactive in searching for information related to opportunities. As such, an entrepreneurial trait or personality is ancillary to the entrepreneurial process as researchers argue (Bygrave and Hofer, 1991).

Opportunity evaluation

Having identified an opportunity, entrepreneurs must undertake the process of evaluation to determine whether it is worth pursuing. In other words, they seek to determine whether the opportunity will lead to a viable business outcome. The evaluation process is therefore reflective of the due diligence undertaken by the entrepreneur (Bishop and Nixon, 2006). Innovation researchers suggest that this is when innovations are tested for their feasibility using different criteria, labelling it the innovation development stage (Garud *et al.*, 2013). Entrepreneur researchers have identified that this stage is also influenced by a number of inter-related factors.

As with opportunity identification, the cognition or the cognitive ability of the entrepreneur influences the process of opportunity evaluation (Mitchell *et al.*, 2004; Haynie *et al.*, 2009). Cognition influences how information is used and what criteria are used to evaluate the opportunity. However research findings are mixed and wide ranging criteria have been identified. A simple way to distinguish between these criteria is to categorise them as those that are external to the firm and those that are internal. Baker *et al.* (2005) refer to these as objective criteria and demand criteria. Objective criteria comprise the external criteria related to the market, for example market size, potential for market growth and level of competition. Demand criteria, on the other hand, reflect the internal resources demanded from the entrepreneur, such as the financial and technological resources, tasks and behaviours required to pursue the opportunity. Baker *et al.* (2005) advise that the evaluation process is influenced by the criteria used by entrepreneurs; for example the use of more criteria would require more, potentially different sources of information and lengthen the evaluation process. Some criteria might also be given different weighting during evaluation. For example, Haynie *et al.* (2009) examined evaluation criteria including value, rarity, imitability, and limits on competition. The researchers identified that opportunities relating to existing knowledge and skills were rated as more attractive, although entrepreneurs were attracted to those outside their skill set if rarity was high and competition limited. However, these type of opportunities are likely to reflect radically new innovations and their performance in the market may be difficult to determine. As such, radical new innovations are unpredictable and thus considered risky.

The entrepreneur's goal setting behaviour (Bishop and Nixon, 2006) is the second factor which influences the evaluation process. Entrepreneurs must consider whether the opportunity fits in with their core objectives, not just when starting up the new enterprise but also in the subsequent stages of developing the business. Bryant (2006) suggests that entrepreneurs therefore evaluate the strategic fit of the opportunity in relation to their goals. These goals could reflect both financial and market aspirations of the entrepreneur. For example, an entrepreneur's goals may be focussed purely on realising first-mover advantages in the marketplace, but not necessarily on subsequently growing the business.

The third factor that influences entrepreneurs' evaluation of opportunities is emotion (Baron, 2006). Emotions impact on risk perceptions and risk preferences (Foo, 2009). Entrepreneurs can use their emotions as a source of information (Ellsworth and Scherer, 2003). Positive emotions trigger the recall of positive information and optimistic assessments, whereas negative emotions trigger the opposite (Foo, 2009). Positive emotions can therefore encourage entrepreneurs to try new things and negative ones can encourage them to process information very carefully before making decisions. Entrepreneurs often rely on 'gut feelings' during opportunity evaluation (Lindsay and Craig, 2002), although Bryant (2006) suggests that these feelings are self-regulated and used to confirm or disconfirm evaluation decisions. Nonetheless, entrepreneurial downfall has been linked to idea infatuation because it may cause entrepreneurs to reject negative information that does not support the viability of pursuing the opportunity and developing the innovation. Foo (2009) argues therefore that emotion directly influences the process of opportunity evaluation through the entrepreneur's information recall, processing of information and through seeking new or additional information if deemed necessary.

An entrepreneur's willingness to undertake risks, also referred to as risk appetite or risk preference, is a further factor that influences the evaluation process (Gilmore *et al.*, 2004). Keh et al. (2002) contend that as evaluation is usually made under conditions of uncertainty, perceptions of risk are also important. Whereas risk preference may be a trait of the entrepreneur, risk perception is related entrepreneurial cognition (Gilmore *et al.*, 2004) and the criteria used by entrepreneurs to evaluate opportunities as discussed above. Text Box 2 explores the evaluation stage of entrepreneurship for Holiday Inn.

Text box 2: Opportunity evaluation

Wilson sought the help of one of the architects at his building firm, Eddie Bluestein to design the first motel. They found a location on one of the main roads into Memphis, Tennessee and the first Holiday Inn was opened in August, 1952. It was Bluestein who thought of the name Holiday Inn for the motel that offered air conditioning and a swimming pool and did not charge additional fees for children. That motel served as a test bed for the Holiday Inn concept and it proved to be popular with customers. While there were other hotel brands available for customers to choose from, the accommodation offered in Holiday Inn Motels for the price offered superior value for money. To fully develop the business, however, Wilson needed a partner, and with Wallace E Johnson, they developed three further Holiday Inns on the other major roads into Memphis in 1953.

Opportunity exploitation

The final stage in the entrepreneurial process is opportunity exploitation. While some researchers consider the evaluation and exploitation stages together, others argue it is a process in its own right (Johnson *et al.*, 2006). Opportunity exploitation reflects the series of activities focussed on the creation of value from the opportunity identified (Block *et al.*, 2011). During exploitation, entrepreneurs must access and organise the resources and competencies required in order to realise economic gains (Choi *et al.*, 2007). For entrepreneurs, this step involves building the operations and systems necessary to develop new or altered products and services and making them available in new or less-than-saturated markets. Innovation researchers argue that this stage is reflective of innovation implementation, where the entrepreneur transforms existing resources into value-added outputs (Garud *et al.*, 2013). At this stage, innovation creates value for the entrepreneur as well as the wider community.

Not all opportunities however, are exploited for their potential value. A logical assumption would be that decisions to exploit opportunities are dependent on the evaluation process. Indeed, Choi and Shepherd (2004) argue that those opportunities deemed viable, or considered to have a high expected value, tend to be exploited. They also argue that when evaluation decisions are not positive, entrepreneurs are likely to return to the first stage of the entrepreneurial process to seek out new opportunities. However, it is recognised in the literature that further research is needed to better understand opportunity exploitation and in particular, why some entrepreneurs make the transition into business, when others do not. Given the contribution entrepreneurship makes to economic growth, and that only about 50% of entrepreneurs succeed in creating new organisations (Johnson *et al.*, 2006), developing this understanding is important. Accordingly, researchers have so far focused on the nature of the opportunity (Venkataraman, 1997); the contextual factors surrounding the opportunity (Welter, 2010); the role of networks (Pinho and de Sa, 2013) and entrepreneurs as individuals (Venkataraman, 1997; Shane and Venkataraman, 2000).

The nature of the opportunity is reflected in its degree of novelty, or the degree to which the innovation associated with the opportunity is radical, rather than incremental. Novel opportunities and radical innovations are likely to lead to economic rewards associated with being the first to market, or in other words, the realisation of first-mover benefits. However, the timing of exploitation is important for the entrepreneur to maximise revenue gains. Choi *et al.* (2007) argue therefore that entrepreneurs must trade off the need to gather more information about what is required for exploitation against the potential to achieve these first-mover advantages. When the opportunity reflects a high degree of novelty, entrepreneurs also need to educate potential stakeholders to speed up the exploitation process. Furthermore, the researchers suggest that when opportunities are reflective of lower levels of novelty, then exploitation should be expedited as competitors could enter the market quickly and erode profit potential. More recently, Choi *et al.* (2007) identified that when there are more fully developed technologies associated with opportunities and greater stakeholder support, entrepreneurs are more likely to exploit them.

Contextual factors surrounding the opportunity can serve to facilitate or to create barriers to exploitation (Jack and Anderson, 2002). Welter (2010:167) defines context as "the circumstances, conditions, situations or environments that are external to the respective phenomenon and enable or constrain it". Mueller (2006) found that markets with established entrepreneurs provide a good breeding ground for other entrepreneurs as they serve as role models and encourage them to start up their own businesses. As such, they are enablers of entrepreneurial exploitation. In contrast, environments where entrepreneurs may be unable to access resources required to start the new enterprise constrain the exploitation process. In particular, entrepreneurs need to access financial, social and human capital in order to exploit opportunities.

Because of the need for capital, access to networks is critical in the exploitation stage. Kim *et al.'s* (2006) research suggests that the entrepreneur's possession of financial resources is not correlated with exploitation. What is more important is the access to financial capital which is a key challenge for entrepreneurs. As such, social and professional networks play an important role in helping entrepreneurs access financial resources for exploitation. Other means by which entrepreneurs can access financial capital are discussed further within Chapter 9.

These same networks can also be a source of human and social capital. Social capital reflects the ability of actors to extract benefits from their social structures (Davidsson and Honig, 2003). Altinay *et al.*(2013) found that when influenced by social networks, entrepreneurs frequently made decisions to enter into a new business quickly, based on the trust of friends and family, rather than taking sufficient time to fully research and evaluate opportunities. In their Swedish study, Davidsson and Honig (2003) also found that social capital positively influenced entrepreneurs to advance the start-up process. Bonding social capital, or strong ties with family and friends who own businesses, facilitates the procurement and utilisation of resources necessary for exploitation. Bridging social capital, or the weak ties between entrepreneurs and their networks was also found to be a good predictor of start-up activities. The importance of social capital to tourism entrepreneurs is discussed further in Chapter 10.

According to Davidsson and Honig (2003), human capital reflects an entrepreneur's formal education or training, previous business and/or start-up experience. Davidsson and Hong (2003) found that entrepreneurs' human capital only weakly influences their decision to follow the start-up process towards a successful completion, yet Kim *et al.* (2006) found that advanced education and managerial experience are positively associated with entrepreneurial start-up. Other studies have also yielded mixed results on the importance of different elements of human capital to exploitation (Mueller, 2006; Block *et al.*, 2011), suggesting the need for further empirical research. However, it is generally agreed that networking helps entrepreneurs to make more informed decisions as they can tap into the network's knowledge to solicit advice (Gilmore *et al.*, 2004). Likewise Ardichivili *et al.* (2003) advise that entrepreneurs seek the advice of parents, mentors and friends when making exploitation decisions. Networks can therefore complement or enhance the entrepreneur's personal human capital (Block *et al.*, 2011).

Opportunity exploitation is also reported to be influenced by the entrepreneurs themselves, or that traits of the individuals making decisions (Venkataraman, 1997). These individual traits include risk taking, autonomy, proactivity, self-efficacy, tolerance for ambiguity and a high need for achievement (Shane and Venkataraman, 2000). Many of these traits are therefore the same as those required for opportunity identification. Text Box 3 explores the exploitation process for Holiday Inn.

Text box 3: Opportunity exploitation

By 1956, the entrepreneurs had built 23 Holiday Inn Motels and demand in the US was growing for clean, predictable, family-friendly, and readily accessible accommodation. In order to continue to grow their brand however, Wilson and Wallace needed access to both financial and human capital. In 1957, the duo therefore decided to franchise the Holiday Inn brand to realise their desired growth and fully exploit the opportunity. They developed a franchise manual to ensure standardisation and consistency and that the brand remained true to the original concept. By 1958, there were 50 Holiday Inns in operation, and by 1968, there were 1,000 Holiday Inn Motels. This growth was also helped through the innovations that Wilson and Wallace introduced along the way. They were the first to negotiate a venture with Gulf Oil to accept their credit cards at Holiday Inn properties in 1963 and in 1965, they introduced the first centralised reservation system, Holidex.

Entrepreneurship as a process

The preceding sections have identified that entrepreneurship, as a process, can be broken down into three key stages, and each of these can be considered a process in its own right where a number of activities are undertaken by entrepreneurs. In addition, several factors influence the behaviour and activities of entrepreneurs throughout the entrepreneurial process. The preceding discussion reveals that many of these factors are inter-related and relevant at more than one stage. The personal traits of the entrepreneur have also been shown to influence these entrepreneurial activities. Entrepreneurship as a process is depicted in Figure 2.1.

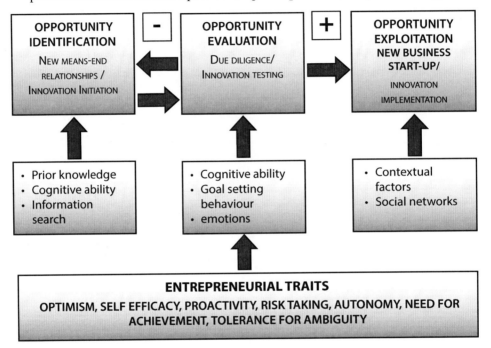

Figure 2.1: The entrepreneurial process

Conclusion

This chapter set out to explain entrepreneurship as a process and in doing so, develop your understanding of the activities that entrepreneurs undertake to identify, evaluate and exploit opportunities. Innovation is central to each of these stages as it develops from the initiation, through testing and to the implementation phase. However, the innovation itself could range from being imitative to radical. In each stage of the entrepreneurship process, the chapter identified a number of factors that influence the activities entrepreneurs undertake. The cognitive ability of the entrepreneur is important to both the identification and evaluation stages of entrepreneurship. In the first stage, it helps entrepreneurs to use their prior knowledge and influences the information search activities undertaken. Entrepreneurs' emotions and goal-setting behaviour also influence opportunity evaluation and in the final stage, contextual factors and social networks play a key role in whether opportunities are exploited. While there is clearly a need for further research, particularly in relation to exploitation, this chapter reveals that the traits of individual entrepreneurs are also very important to the entrepreneurial process. The following case study of AirBnB, provides further insight into the entrepreneurial process to help develop your understanding of this theoretical perspective.

The Case of AirBnB

In 2007, two 27 year-old men named Joe Gebbia and Brian Chesky, who had previously met as design students, were living in San Francisco in the USA. When a large design conference was hosted in that city, they realised that many of the hotels were fully booked and conference delegates were struggling to find accommodation. As Gebbia and Chesky were struggling to pay their rent, the enterprising individuals decided to rent out three air mattresses on the floor of their apartment to desperate conference delegates. In addition to providing the sleeping accommodation, they also decided to provide their guests with breakfast. They quickly created a website, airbedandbreakfast.com and within a week, they had bookings from three guests who were willing to pay $80.00 each night.

Following this first successful venture into the accommodation industry, Gebbia and Chesky thought their idea had more potential and was worth pursuing. Furthermore, these budding entrepreneurs liked the idea of not creating something new, but using something that was already in existence. In other words, they liked the idea of using accommodation that people had and were willing to share. Drawing on their San Francisco experience, they decided to target festivals and conferences throughout the USA and ask local people to accommodate attendees at these events.

To get their venture off the ground, they contacted one of Gebbia's old roommates, who was a computer programmer, to help develop their website. In the summer of 2008, they identified a Democratic National Convention with 80,000 delegates in Denver as the venue to launch their new venture. Two weeks before the convention they launched their website and within a week they had 800 local listings for accommodation in homes and apartments. The problem was, they were not actually making any money from their efforts. They also struggled to raise financial capital for their start-up.

The entrepreneurs themselves report that potential backers were very sceptical of their idea. The concept of the sharing economy was just emerging at that time. When people began to dismiss the idea of owning things in favour of borrowing or renting them, the sharing economy was born. Products and services not in use 100% of the time were recognised as having wasted value and as such could be used more collaboratively to avoid this waste. With the sharing economy, access to goods and services is shared amongst participants often through an online marketplace. For Airbnb, the entrepreneurs envisaged sharing space through accommodation rental made available through a central website. However, potential investors were not convinced in the initial stages and the entrepreneurs struggled to find sufficient capital to exploit their opportunity.

To get the initial financial capital, the entrepreneurs diversified into a short-term breakfast cereal enterprise which raised $30,000 for them. It wasn't until 2009 that they received funding to support their efforts from an 'angel' investor who reportedly offered them sound advice about developing their business. Subsequently, larger cash injections followed from venture capitalists. This funding enabled the entrepreneurs to develop the necessary software to handle payments and charge a commission of 15% of the booking fee. The capital injections also enabled the entrepreneurs to hire suitable premises for the venture and employ staff to ensure the business could grow.

The company went from strength to strength, although it was not all trouble-free growth. Reports of guests' damaging property raised questions about trust. The entrepreneurs recognised a weakness in their original business model and started to insure guest premises. At the beginning of 2011, Airbnb had 1 million bookings; 2 million by July, 2011 and 5 million at the end of the year. By June, 2012 the company had booked over 10 million nights of accommodation through their website and was valued at $1.3 billion. Airbnb offices were opened in Europe, South America and India and accommodation was available in more than 19,000 cities worldwide and 192 countries. By 2014, Airbnb was valued at $10 billion. By 2015, guests could book accommodation in more than 34,000 cities around the world. Guests choose from a wide range of accommodation in over 1 million listings, over an equally-wide price range including a spare room in someone's home, a cave, a boat, a treehouse, a castle or a private island. With over 10 million nights booked through the Airbnb website, various press reports put the current valuation of Airbnb at $20 billion. Anyone, anywhere in the world can list an accommodation option and anyone, anywhere in the world, can log onto the website and book a room.

Airbnb continues to develop its services, trying to make it simpler for guests to book accommodation and trying to encourage quicker response times from those who let property. The entrepreneurial founders are reported to want to make every trip as meaningful as possible for guests and to popularise the sharing economy, so that anyone who wants to let accommodation, has the opportunity to become an entrepreneur.

Questions

1 Drawing on the information provided in the chapter, explain how the two entrepreneurs identified their opportunity.

2 Did the entrepreneurs undertake due diligence in evaluating the viability of the opportunity? What were the consequences of their actions?

3 How were the entrepreneurs' goals important in their decision to pursue the opportunity?

4 Did the environmental context at the time enable or constrain the exploitation of the opportunity?

5 How were networks used to provide access to capital and what specific type of capital was accessed through their networking?

References

Altinay, L. Brookes, M. and Aktas, G. (2013) Selecting franchise partners: Franchisee perspectives, processes and criteria, *Tourism Management*, **37**,176-185.

Ardichvili, A., Cardozo, R. and Ray, S. (2003) A theory of entrepreneurial opportunity identification and development, *Journal of Business Venturing*, **18** (1), 105-123.

Baker, T., Gadajlovic, E. and Lubatkin, M. (2005) A framework for comparing entrepreneurship processes across nations, *Journal of International Business Studies*, **36** (5): 492-504.

Baron, R. (2006) Opportunity recognition as pattern recognition: How entrepreneurs 'connect the dots' to identify new business opportunities, *Academy of Management Perspectives*, **20** (1): 104-119.

Batjargal, B., Hitt, A., Tsui, A., Arregle, J., Webb, W. and Miller, T, (2013) Institutional polycentrism, entrepreneurs' social networks, and new venture growth, *Academy of Management Journal*, **56** (4): 1024-1049.

Bishop, K. and Nixon, R. (2006) Venture opportunity evaluations: Comparisons between venture capitalists and inexperienced pre-nascent entrepreneurs, *Journal of Developmental Entrepreneurship*, **11**(1): 19-33.

Block, J., Gruber, M. and Petty, J. (2011) The exploitation of business opportunities: patterns, biases and processes, *Frontiers of Entrepreneurship Research*, **31** (4): 28.

Bryant, P. (2006) Self-regulation and decision heuristics in entrepreneurial opportunity evaluation and exploitation, *Management Decision*, **45**(4): 732-748.

Bygrave, W. and Hofer, C. (1991) Theorizing about entrepreneurship, *Entrepreneurship Theory & Practice*, **16** (2): 13-22.

Carland, J., Hoy, F., Boulton, W., and Carland, J. (1984) Differentiating entrepreneurs from small business owners: A conceptualization, *Academy of management review*, **9**(2), 354-359.

Choi, Y. and Shepherd, D. (2004) Entrepreneurs' decisions to exploit opportunities, *Journal of Management*, **30**, 377-395.

Choi, Y., Levesque, M. and Shepherd, D. (2007) When should entrepreneurs expedite or delay opportunity exploitation?, *Journal of Business Venturing*, **23** (3): 333-355.

Cope, J. (2005) Toward a dynamic learning perspective of entrepreneurship, *Entrepreneurship Theory and Practice*, **29** (4): 373-397.

Corbett, A. (2005) Experiential learning within the process of opportunity identification and exploitation, *Entrepreneurship Theory and Practice*, **29** (4): 473-491.

Davidsson, P. and Honig, B. (2003) The role of social and human capital among nascent entrepreneurs, *Journal of Business Venturing*, **18** (3):301-331.

Edelman, L. and Yli-Renko, H. (2010) The impact of environment and entrepreneurial perceptions on venture-creation efforts: Bridging the discovery and creation views of entrepreneurship, *Entrepreneurship Theory and Practice*, **34** (5): 833-856.

Ellsworth,P. and Scherer, K. (2003) Appraisal processes in emotion, in Davidson, R., Scherer, K. and Goldsmith, H. (eds). *Handbook of Effective Sciences*, New York: Oxford University Press.

Foo, M. (2009) Emotions and entrepreneurial opportunity evaluation, *Entrepreneurship Theory and Practice*, **33** (2): 375-393.

Gaglio, C. and Katz, J. (2001) The psychological basis of opportunity identification: Entrepreneurial alterness, *Small Business Economics*, **16** (2): 95-111.

Gartner, W. (1988) 'Who is an entrepreneur?' Is the wrong question, *American Journal of Small Business*, **12** (4): 11-32.

Garud, R., Tuertscher, P. and Van de Ven, A. (2013) Perspectives on innovation processes, *The Academy of Management Annals*, **7** (1), 775-819.

Gilmore, A., Carson, D. and O'Donnell, A. (2004) Small business owner-managers and their attitude to risk, *Marketing Intelligence & Planning*, **22** (3): 349-360.

Haynie, M., Shepherd, D. and McMullen, J. (2009) An opportunity for me? The role of resources in opportunity evaluation decisions, *Journal of Management Studies*, **46**(3): 337-361.

Ireland, R., Reutzel, C. and Webb, J. (2005) Entrepreneurship research in AMJ: What has been published, and what might the future hold?, *Academy of Management Journal*, **48** (4): 556-564.

Jack, S. and Anderson, A. (2002) The effects of embeddedness on the entrepreneurial process, *Journal of business Venturing*, **17**(5): 467-487.

Johnson, P., Parker, S. and Wijbenga, F. (2006) Nascent entrepreneurship research: achievements and opportunities, *Small Business Economics,* **27**: 1-4.

Keh, H., Foo, M. and Lim, B. (2002) Opportunity evaluation under risky conditions: The cognitive processes of entrepreneurs, *Entrepreneurship Theory and Practice,* **27** (2): 125-148.

Kim, P., Aldrich, H. and Keister, L. (2006) Access (not) denied: the impact of financial, human, and cultural capital on entrepreneurial entry in the United States, *Small Business Economics,* **27**: 5-22.

Lindsay, N. and Craig, J. (2002) A framework for understanding opportunity recognition, *The Journal of Private Equity,* **6** (1): 13-24.

Mcdermott, C. and O'Connor, G. (2002) Managing radical innovation, *Journal of Product Innovation Management,* **19** (6): 424-438.

Mitchell, R., Busenitz, L., Lant, T., McDougall, P., Morse, E. and Smith, J. (2004) The distinctive and inclusive domain of entrepreneurial cognition research, *Entrepreneurship Theory & Practice,* **28** (6):505-518.

Mueller, P. (2006) Entrepreneurship in the Region: Breeding Ground for Nascent Entrepreneurs?, *Small Business Economics* **27**, 41-58.

Nasution, H., Mavondo, F., Matanda, M. and Ndubisi, N. (2011) Entrepreneurship: Its relationship with market orientation and learning orientation and as antecedents to innovation and customer value, *Industrial Marketing Management,* **40** (3): 336-345.

Ozgen, E. and Baron, R. (2007) Social sources of information in opportunity recognition: Effects of mentors, industry networks and professional forums, *Journal of Business Venturing,* **22** (2): 174-192.

Pinho, C. and de Sa, S. (2013) Entrepreneurial performance and stakeholders' relationships: A social network analysis perspective, *International Journal of Entrepreneurship* **17** (1): 1-19.

Shane, S. (2000) Prior knowledge and the discovery of entrepreneurial opportunities, *Organization Science,* **11** (4): 448-469.

Shane, S. (2012) Reflections on the 2010 AMR decade award: Delivering on the promise of entrepreneurship as a field of research, *Academy of Management Review,* **37** (1): 10-20.

Shane, S. and Venkataraman, S. (2000) The promise of entrepreneurship as a field of research, *Academy of Management Review,* **25** (1): 217-226.

Smith, B., Matthews, C. and Schenkel, M. (2009) Differences in entrepreneurial opportunities: The role of tacitness and codification in opportunity identification, *Journal of Small Business Management,* **47** (1): 38-57.

Stevenson, H. and Jarillo, J. (1990) 'A paradigm of entrepreneurship: Entrepreneurial management', *Strategic Management Journal,* **11** (4): 17-27.

Ucbasaran, D., Wright, M. and Westhead, P. (2008) Opportunity identification and pursuit: Does an entrepreneur's human capital matter?, *Small Business Economics*, **30**(2): 153-170.

Venkataraman, S., Dew, N. and Forster, W. (2012) Reflections on the 2010 AMR decade award: Wither the promise? Moving forward with entrepreneurship as a science of the artificial, *Academy of Management Review*, **37** (1): 21-22.

Venkataraman, S. (1997) The distinctive domain of entrepreneurship research, *Advances in Entrepreneurship, Firm Emergence and Growth*, **3**:119-13.

Welter, F. (2010) Contextualizing entrepreneurship – conceptual challenges and ways forward, *Entrepreneurship Theory & Practice*, **35** (1): 165-184.

3 Culture and Entrepreneurship

ZI Ertung, Bilkent University, Turkey
Levent Altinay, Oxford Brookes University, UK
Eda Gurel, Bilkent University, Turkey

Introduction

Entrepreneurial activities have a great impact on the economy as a whole. They are crucial to the economic growth and employment opportunities in any country, but particularly in developing countries. According to Guasch *et al.* (2002), a lack of strong entrepreneurial culture could be the source of macroeconomic and even institutional instability in these countries. As culture influences business development (Etzioni, 1987), investigating the influence of culture on entrepreneurship has received much attention from researchers. Culture may also influence the psychological characteristics of individuals in a society; therefore it influences the supply of individuals with entrepreneurial potential. Consequently, several studies have investigated the relationship between national culture and entrepreneurial characteristics and traits (Hayton *et al.*, 2002).

In this chapter, previous research, discussions and models on entrepreneurship and culture are reviewed and new avenues for future research are explored. The chapter aims to contribute to the advancement of the body of knowledge in the area within the context of hospitality and tourism.

The objective of this chapter is to develop your understanding of the relationship between culture and entrepreneurship. More specifically, by the end of this chapter, you should be able to:

■ Explain various factors, including culture, that may influence an individual's entrepreneurial intention;

- Explain cultural differences based on Hofstede's dimensions;

- Explain the effect of cultural dimensions on entrepreneurial potential, intention and the traits of an individual;

- Assess whether there may be universal values that can affect an individual's entrepreneurial intention;

- Compare and contrast models developed to understand the relationship between culture and entrepreneurship.

The chapter begins by defining entrepreneurship and culture. Famous frameworks with a special emphasis on Hofstede's Theory of Cultural Dimensions proposed to evaluate the impact of culture on entrepreneurship are explained and then universal values that may motivate entrepreneurial behaviour and attitudes are explored. Finally, the chapter concludes with important conceptual models offered to analyse venture formation by tapping into the influence of culture.

Entrepreneurship and culture

There are many definitions of entrepreneurship. However, as various authors (e.g. Cunningham and Lischeron, 1991; Steward and Roth, 2001; Kirby, 2005; Zhao *et al.*, 2011) point out, there is no universally accepted definition of entrepreneurship. Gartner (1990) identifies eight themes repeatedly utilised in defining entrepreneurship in the literature: the entrepreneur (personality traits), innovation, organisation creation, creating value, profit or non-profit, growth, uniqueness and the owner-manager. Gartner (1988: 26) argues that organisation creation separates entrepreneurship from other disciplines and therefore defines entrepreneurship as "the creation of new organizations". In essence, entrepreneurship is the initiation of change through creation or innovation that usually involves risk (Zhao *et al.*, 2011). As Morrison (2000) states, this initiation has its foundations not only in persons and institutions, but also in society and culture.

Accordingly, when the literature on entry into entrepreneurship is reviewed, two streams of enquiry emerge. While the first stream of research focuses on 'the person', the second highlights the importance of 'the environment' in stimulating entrepreneurial initiatives. Research that focuses on the individual is primarily concerned with the psychological characteristics of the enterprising individual (Zhao *et al.*, 2011). According to Mueller (2004: 200), a potential entrepreneur is an individual (male or female) "within a given population or society that possesses a particular set of personal traits, skills, aptitudes and desires believed to motivate entrepreneurial behaviour or at least increase its likelihood". According to this stream of research, entrepreneurs possess innate, genetic entrepreneurial traits which cannot be learned or taught (Martinez, 2014). As stated by Zhao *et al.* (2011), this stream of research also emphasises the importance of human capital and availability of required resources. However, this topic has not been adequately addressed within a tourism context.

The second stream of research investigates the effect of the social and cultural environment upon entrepreneurial formation (Martinez, 2014). Culture is defined as a set of shared values and beliefs (Hofstede, 1980). These values shape the development of certain personality traits, and therefore motivate individuals in a specific group or society to engage in behaviours that may not be evident in others (Mueller and Thomas, 2001). Cultures that value and reward entrepreneurial behaviours such as risk-taking and independent thinking, promote a propensity to develop innovative entrepreneurial individuals, whereas cultures that reinforce values like conformity, group interests and control over the future do not promote risk-taking and entrepreneurial behaviour (Hayton *et al.*, 2002). By cultivating the mind and character of the potential entrepreneur, a supportive national culture increases the entrepreneurial potential of a country (Mueller and Thomas, 2001).

Cultural differences and their implications for organisations have been investigated by many previous researchers and several frameworks or models have been proposed to evaluate the impact of culture. The most widely used models are those which have been developed by Kluckhohn and Strodbeck (1961), Hall (1977), Hofstede (1980), Laurent (1983) and Trompenaars (1993). These models can all be used to make cross-cultural comparisons on a range of dimensions, although their limitations have been identified. Kluckhohn and Strodbeck (1961) think that cultures can be compared on the basis of their different, but constant orientation towards the world and other human beings, although their research does not consider the implications for management. Hall's (1977) research emphasises that members' experiences of context influence how they communicate and therefore different cultural groups respond to their contexts in dissimilar ways. Hall's model is built on qualitative insights rather than quantitative data and does not rank different countries. Laurent (1983) uses the concepts of culture, status and function to examine how far status is carried outside the workplace to assess managers' capacity to avoid hierarchical levels and to explain managerial roles. Trompenaars (1993) has attempted to draw together and apply the ideas developed by previous researchers to develop a model which is considered to meet practical needs of business people and consultants rather than academic needs. However, the lack of detail and homogeneity of the informants, resulting in inaccurate comparisons between cultures, is considered to be the main weakness of his research.

Hofstede's (1980) research, one of the most cited cultural studies, goes further in showing how national culture affects the values of the workplace by comparing work-related values across a range of cultures in much detail. Although Hofstede's (1980) research has been criticised for ignoring the existence of different cultural groups within a nation, most behavioural studies have been skewed toward cultural values and entrepreneurial behaviour that stem from Hofstede's research. Hofstede's (1980) work has proven valuable as it presents a concise cultural taxonomy for explaining behaviours of people at work (Hayton et al., 2002). Hofstede identifies five cultural dimensions to explain behavioural differences among individuals from different nations as individualism-collectivism, uncertainty avoidance, power distance, masculinity-femininity, and long-short term orientation.

Although Hofstede (1980) did not define the relationship between culture and entrepreneurial activity, his cultural dimensions have been utilised by researchers to investigate individual entrepreneurial characteristics conceptually (Hofstede, 1980; Morrison, 2000; Hayton et al., 2002) and empirically. Empirical studies have employed Hofstede's five dimensions to extensively examine entry mode (Kogut and Singh, 1988), entrepreneurial propensity (Chelariu et al., 2008), entrepreneurial activity (Pinillos and Reyes, 2011), entrepreneurial perceptions and intentions (Shinnar et al., 2012), tourism students' entrepreneurial intentions (Gurel et al., 2010), rates of innovation (Morris et al., 1993; Mueller and Thomas, 2001), entrepreneurial differences between countries (McGrath et al., 1992), behavioural differences between entrepreneurs and non-entrepreneurs (McGrath et al., 1992; Shane, 1993; Morris et al., 1994) and entrepreneurial orientation (Saeed et al., 2014). In the following section, the cultural dimensions of Hofstede (1980) will be reviewed in relation to their effect on entrepreneurial potential, intention and traits of an individual.

Cultural dimensions and entrepreneurship

Individualism

According to Hofstede (2003), individualism represents the preference of people to put themselves and their immediate families first, as opposed to collectivism, which puts the extended family or social group first. While social identity is based on individual contribution in individualistic cultures, it is based on group membership in collectivist ones (Mueller and Thomas, 2000). In an individualistic society, freedom and personal achievement prevail and these lead to innovation (Hofstede, 1980; Herbig and Dunphy, 1998). Individualism facilitates the initiation of new ideas because it triggers creativity and entrepreneurism (Shane, 1993; Sivakumar and Nakata, 2003). Mueller and Thomas (2001) found that innovativeness was prevalent in cultures high in individualism. In a study of small manufacturing firms, Laforet and Tann (2006) also found that innovative firm behaviour is closely associated with the individualistic assertive behaviour of the owners.

In addition to innovativeness, high individualism in small business owners leads to higher tolerance for ambiguity and more proactive firm behaviour (Chen and McQueen, 2008). Moreover, managers in individualistic cultures view the uncertainty in the external environment more optimistically than collectivist managers and they are more likely to involve themselves in situations that collectivist managers perceive as being extremely risky (Morris *et al.*, 1994). Their individualist values and the strong leadership attributions which accompany them may well exacerbate their sense of confidence (Geletkanycz, 1997) leading to risk-taking behaviour. Risk-taking is associated with a willingness to commit to high-risk and high-return business and implies potentially large resource commitments to projects where the outcomes are unknown (Lee *et al.*, 2001; Runyan *et al.*, 2006; Madsen, 2007). As entrepreneurship is regarded as an ability of the entrepreneur to continually renew and innovate by constructively taking risks in the market and channelling these creative innovations into ventures with value, it is regarded as critical to firm survival and performance (Tajeddini, 2010).

Entrepreneurs are also frequently characterised with an internal locus of control. As 'internals', they believe in their own abilities to achieve and therefore give little credit to external forces such as destiny, luck or powerful others. Since highly individualistic cultures assign importance to individual freedom of action and independence, internal locus of control is more prevalent in individualistic cultures than in collectivist societies (Mueller and Thomas, 2000). Thus there are more individuals with entrepreneurial intentions in individualistic cultures.

Uncertainty avoidance

Uncertainty avoidance refers to the extent to which people within a culture are made nervous by ambiguous situations and the extent to which they seek to adopt strict codes of behaviour to avoid these situations. Cultures with high uncertainty avoidance are security-seeking and intolerant whereas cultures with low uncertainty avoidance are accepting of personal risk and relatively tolerant (Hofstede, 1984). A positive perception of the issues in the external environment held by managers in uncertainty accepting societies make their firms more willing to act as first movers when identifying opportunities and entering new markets (Lieberman and Montgomery, 1988). Competitive aggression is seen as the crucial element of proactive behaviour and the greater willingness of entrepreneurs in uncertainty accepting societies to engage in change and competition naturally increases their firms' abilities to act proactively (Covin and Slevin, 1989; Mueller and Thomas, 2001). In particular, managers with a high tolerance for uncertainty are thought to be more innovative than managers with a low tolerance for uncertainty (Shane, 1995). Innovative behaviour is demonstrated by those firms whose managers are tolerant of uncertainty, willing to take unknown risks and therefore open and supportive of change (Kleinschmidt, 1994; Kale, 1995; Karande *et al.*, 2002; Ritchie and Brindley, 2005; Zhao, 2005).

Power distance

Power distance refers to "the extent to which the less powerful person in a society accepts inequality in power and considers it as normal" (Hofstede, 1984: 389). In high power-distant societies, people in the lower classes may view venturing as something that only the elite do (Mitchell *et al.*, 2000) and they might not have the tolerance for commitment and motivation. In addition, they might not have the confidence and the ability to recognise opportunities. In particular, power distance leads business owners to low self-efficacy and lack of belief in themselves and their businesses (Kumar, 2007). It affects business owners' intentions to develop their businesses by influencing their perspectives on the availability of opportunities (Mitchell *et al.*, 2000; Dodd and Patra, 2002; Hayton *et al.*, 2002). Managers in high power distance cultures are also inherently more anxious about taking risks than those in low power distance ones (Hofstede, 2003; Shane, 1993).

Masculinity

Masculine cultures define very different sex roles for men and women. In societies with high masculinity, men are expected to be assertive, ambitious, and competitive to gain material success, whereas women are expected to serve and to care for the non-material quality of life – for children, and for the weak. In contrast, feminine cultures support relatively overlapping social roles for the sexes (Hofstede, 1984). Since masculine societies place emphasis on achievement and advancement, the development of new and novel products in the market place to demonstrate individual achievements is highly regarded (Yalcinkaya, 2008). In addition, business owners in masculine societies will be more likely to pursue proactive strategies aimed at exploiting opportunities in the market and weakening competition (Everdingen and Waarts, 2003). Motivational factors such as the need for achievement (McCleland, 1965) in high masculine cultures predispose small business owners to proactiveness (Hurmenrinta, 2001; Swierczek and Ha, 2003). As a result, they actively seek potential opportunities to develop their businesses. Garland *et al.* (1984) and Steward *et al.* (1998) argue that entrepreneurs who have higher achievement motivation are more inclined to lead their firms to innovation and change.

Managers in masculine cultures also display their willingness to strive for prestige and recognition at the expense of potential risks and failure (Hofstede, 2003). They have a low perception of risk and consider handling uncertainty as a route to large strategic payoffs and thus a prerequisite for the achievement of superior materialistic conditions (Petrakis, 2005) both for themselves and their firms (Karande *et al.*, 2002).

3

Long-term vs short-term orientation

Long-term versus short-term orientation, also known as Confucian Dynamism, describes a society's time horizon in terms of the importance attached to the future relative to the past and present. In long-term oriented societies, values such as persistence (perseverance), ordering relationships by status, and thrift are highly regarded, whereas in short-term oriented societies, the relative importance of values such as normative statements, personal steadiness and stability, saving one's face and respect for tradition are high (Hofstede, 2003).

Long-term orientation has positive effects on the work values of self-enhancement, commitment and openness to change (Hofstede and Bond, 1988; Jaw *et al.*, 2007). In particular, the combined effects of two dimensions of long-term oriented culture, namely strong work ethics and future orientation lead to long-term commitment to getting involved in different endeavours and bringing them to successful fruition (Nakata and Sivaskumar, 1996). Decision makers are favourably disposed towards action or proactiveness in competing and getting things done (Heunks, 1998; Miller and Lee, 2001). Siu and Kirby (1999) found that small businesses run with a long-term orientation are more customer-oriented and proactive.

In summary, research suggests that while entrepreneurship is facilitated by cultures that are high in individualism, low in uncertainty avoidance, low in power distance and high in masculinity, it is hindered by cultures distant from this ideal type (Scheinberg and MacMillan, 1988; Shane *et al.*, 1991; Hayton *et al.*, 2002). Research findings also suggest that cultural values such as individualism and uncertainty avoidance are significantly related to the entrepreneurial traits of internal locus of control, risk taking and innovativeness (Mueller and Thomas, 2000; Thomas and Mueller, 2000; Gurel *et al.*, 2010).

Universal values

From the review above, it is evident that most behavioural studies use Hofstede's (1980) conceptualisation of national culture. George and Zahra (2002) state that culture is manifest in various forms and as a result its characteristics can be measured at the national, regional or societal level. Yet most of the studies emphasise national characteristics over other distinguishing characteristics. In order to fully capture the rich variety of the dimensions of culture, alternative measures of culture and entrepreneurship should be considered. These measures can help validate prior findings of those studies using Hofstede's measures.

Tayeb (1988) points out that not all individuals in a society follow all the dimensions of their cultures in every aspect of their lives. There will be individuals who deviate from their cultural norms. This perspective of culture recognises that most human beings do not see the world through the same rationale. Their world is shaped and interpreted through their own attitudes, attributes, behaviours and values (Morrison, 2000).

Rokeach (1973) defines values as "the result of all the cultural, institutional and personal forces that act upon an individual throughout his lifetime" (Martinez, 2014: 51). Schwartz (1992) advises "values are relatively stable yet changeable cognitive structures that transcend specific actions and situations and serve as guiding principles in people's lives" (quoted in Holland and Shepherd, 2013:332). Although the role of values in decision making has been investigated in cross-cultural studies (such as Hosftede, 1980; Schwartz, 2004), the influence of personal values as opposed to cultural values has been insufficiently investigated in entrepreneurship (Holland and Shepherd, 2013). According to Schwartz (2012), values are critical motivators of behaviour and attitudes and some are likely to be universal.

Schwartz (2012) argues that there are basic values that people in all cultures recognise. They are motivational constructs that are used by individuals to understand and judge the world and act on it. He identifies 10 motivationally distinct types of universal values and specifies the dynamic relations among them. These 10 values include power, achievement, hedonism, stimulation, self-direction, universalism, benevolence, tradition, conformity and security. Identifying similarities and differences among these value structures, he describes four higher order value types as self-enhancement, openness to change, self-transcendence and conservation. He presents his theoretical model in a circular structure in which adjacent values are more likely to share commonalities in motivations, whereas values on opposite ends of the structure are more likely to produce incompatible motivations. Holland and Shepherd (2013) note that Schwartz's values theory has been found to be reliable and generalisable across a number of samples. Therefore, as an alternative measure, Schwartz's values theory appears to be useful to advance understanding of the association between culture and entrepreneurship. In the following section, the value types of Schwartz (2012) are introduced in brief to understand how they can affect an individual's entrepreneurial intention.

Self-enhancement

Self-enhancement consists of the values of achievement, power and hedonism. Entrepreneurs who place high importance on self-enhancement focus on their personal interests and success of their new venture in order to obtain recognition and social status. By running a business, these individuals enjoy the power of control over employees. In business, individuals with high levels of power and achievement look for and are likely to achieve financial success (Holland and Shepherd, 2013).

Openness to change

Openness to change includes the values of stimulation, self-direction and hedonism. Individuals who value openness enjoy independent thought and action and new ways of doing things and are not afraid of the challenges and obstacles in life. They have the intellectual capacity to create new products and services. They are motivated by learning and seek self-realisation and advancement toward their ideal selves. Individuals who place high importance on self-enhancement and openness to change share the value of hedonism but differ in their source of pleasure-seeking. While individuals who value self-enhancement are delighted by power and achievement, individuals with openness to change enjoy novel experiences and the autonomy of the entrepreneurial role. These individuals enjoy non-financial benefits like freedom to control their own time and work approach (Holland and Shepherd, 2013).

Self-transcendence

Self-transcendence involves values of universalism and benevolence. Although universalism and benevolence are similar in nature, they are different in the way they are exercised. While benevolence applies to people inside an individual's close environment, universalism applies to people outside an individual's immediate environment. Individuals who place high importance on self-transcendence may be more inclined to exercise social entrepreneurship since they look beyond self-interests but seek to enrich the lives of others such as associates or those within the wider society. Therefore, they may create ventures that deal with social concerns such as promoting equal opportunity for all, protection of the environment, or improving standards of living in the third world. In return, they enjoy personal psychological benefits. These individuals also value honesty and loyalty in their interactions with others (Holland and Shepherd, 2013).

Conservation

Conservation consists of the values of tradition, conformity and security. Individuals with these values give importance to ideals, standards, traditions and norms in society. Entrepreneurs who value conservation give high priority to stability and security, therefore they may be more inclined to protect the status quo rather than make changes. As a result, they may place greater weight on the potential costs rather than benefits of new opportunities that would lead to negative outcomes (Holland and Shepherd, 2013).

Conceptual models

Four notable conceptual models proposed to understand the influence of culture on entrepreneurship are addressed here. The first model is offered by Busenitz and Lau (1997) in order to explore why some cultures produce more entrepreneurs than others. These researchers argue that an individual's cognition significantly affects the intention to start a business. Accordingly, their cross-cultural cognitive model builds on the fact that entrepreneurial cognition is affected by not only cultural values but also by the social environment and some personal variables. Under the social context, these researchers emphasise the influence of social networks. The social ties and networks the entrepreneur has may have a great impact on his/her entrepreneurial cognition as these networks directly affect the exposure to potential opportunities.

The second, a dynamic entrepreneurial cultural model, is offered by Morrison who considers the impact of culture, industry setting and organisational context together within the tourism industry. Morrison (2000, 2006) summarises the key features associated with culture which may impact upon the degree to which entrepreneurship is initiated and sustained. His model identifies a range of inputs, societal constructs and evidence as being significant elements of entrepreneurship. At the basic level, he recognises entrepreneurship as a highly personalised activity. Accordingly, his selected inputs include personal motivations and characteristics, formal education system, family background, regional history and characteristics, and inter-generational role models. The unique personal motivations and characteristics of the entrepreneurs, interacting with their specific host society and business environment, are translated into entrepreneurial activities and behaviour. In other words, the entrepreneurial process is influenced by an individual's evaluation of social legitimacy, desirability and feasibility shaped by cultural values, economic factors and the relationship between the entrepreneur and his/her host environment. The degree to which an entrepreneurial culture has been embedded in a country results in the variance in the responses of individuals to entrepreneurship.

The third model is offered by Hayton *et al.* (2002) to explain the influence of national culture on entrepreneurship. These researchers review past empirical research, illustrate the relationships among these studies in a model and suggest some future directions for research. By capturing national culture in different forms in behavioural research, they depict culture as a moderating variable in the relationship between contextual factors and entrepreneurial outcomes. In this way, the influence of national culture is highlighted as a catalyst rather than a causal agent of entrepreneurship. Cultural characteristics transform and complement the institutional and economic contexts and influence entrepreneurial outcomes in return.

The fourth model is proposed by Siu and Lo (2013) to advance the body of knowledge in the area of entrepreneurial cognition. Drawing together the major cognitive research approaches, these researchers examine and test cultural-contingent influences on entrepreneurial intention in Chinese cultures. Introducing the individualism and collectivism dimension of culture as a moderating variable, these researchers aim to develop a sound theory to explain the cultural contingency in the cognitive model of entrepreneurial intention. Their findings showed that "for Chinese who place more value on their connectedness with others, their perceptions of what the influential people (e.g., family, close friends, partners, colleagues) in their lives think about their new venture creation have very significant influence on their entrepreneurial intentions. Conversely, for Chinese who place less value on their connectedness with others, their perceptions of what influential people think become less influential". This result verifies the importance of social factors on the entrepreneurial intentions of individuals (Siu and Lo, 2013: 167).

Conclusion

In conclusion, this chapter set out to develop your understanding of the relationship between culture and entrepreneurship. Based on those research findings using the Hofstede's (1980) conceptualisation of national culture, entrepreneurship seems to be facilitated by cultures that are high in individualism, low in uncertainty avoidance, low in power distance and high in masculinity (Kolvereid and Westhead, 1991; Scheinberg and MacMillan, 1988; Hayton *et al.*, 2002).

Research findings also suggest that cultural values such as individualism and uncertainty avoidance are significantly related to the entrepreneurial traits of internal locus of control, risk taking and innovativeness (Mueller and Thomas, 2000; Thomas and Mueller, 2000; Gurel et al., 2010).

However, from the foregoing discussions, conceptual models and studies reviewed, it is evident that investigating the relationship between culture and entrepreneurship is complex. More cross-cultural studies are needed to understand the effect of different cultures and values on entrepreneurship. Indeed, in their review of the literature on small firms in tourism, Thomas et al., (2011) identify social and cultural perspectives as emerging research areas and that international comparative studies are generally absent from tourism research.

It is evident from the conceptual models covered in the chapter that not only cultural, but also societal, institutional and personal factors play an important part in the initiation of entrepreneurship. Therefore, a holistic and systematic approach should be employed when studying and understanding culture on entrepreneurship. As culture is recognised in many forms in the literature, it can be measured at the national, regional or societal level (George and Hayton, 2002). Nevertheless, most studies emphasise national characteristics over other distinguishing characteristics.

Our review in this chapter highlighted that Schwartz's (2012) values might be an alternative to measure the influence of culture. Values present a useful construct within the psychological traits and behavioural schools of entrepreneurship, since values are defined as an inner and outer construct. Utilising a values construct, entrepreneurship can be studied by integrating internal and external factors (Martinez, 2014).

Nevertheless, in recent research on the cultural aspects of entrepreneurship conducted by the OECD, it was found that positive foundation-related attitudes depend to a great extent on the personality traits of the person and his or her integration into social networks and to a lesser degree on cultural background (Bergmann, 2009). This lays an important foundation for those policy makers who are trying to encourage more entrepreneurship within their cultures (Busenitz and Lau, 1996). Since the environment is subject to the influence of group norms and cultural networks, policy makers who aim to influence entrepreneurial intentions should take into account these relationships and be aware that entrepreneurial initiation is greatly dependent on the characteristics of the person and his/her regional environment (Bergmann, 2009).

The following case study describes the cultural characteristics of different countries according to Hofstede's cultural framework.

Case study: Cultural characteristics

USA

USA is a described as a low power distance and a high individualist country. The society is loosely-knit in which the expectation is that people look after themselves and their immediate families only and should not rely (too much) on authorities for support. Americans are accustomed to doing business or interacting with people they don't know well. Consequently, Americans are not shy about approaching their prospective counterparts in order to obtain or seek information. In the business world, employees are expected to be self-reliant and display initiative.

The score of the US on masculinity is high. Behaviour in school, work, and play is based on the shared values that people should "strive to be the best they can be" and that "the winner takes all". As a result, Americans will tend to display and talk freely about their 'successes' and achievements in life. Being successful per se is not the great motivator in American society, but being able to show one's success. There exists a 'can-do' mentality which creates a lot of dynamism in the society, as it is believed that there is always the possibility to do things in a better way.

The US scores below average on the uncertainty avoidance dimension. This cultural pattern reflects itself thus: there is a fair degree of acceptance for new ideas, innovative products and a willingness to try something new or different, whether it pertains to technology, business practices or food. Americans tend to be more tolerant of ideas or opinions from anyone and allow the freedom of expression.

The US scores low on the long-term orientation dimension of culture. This is reflected by the following: Americans are prone to analyse new information to check whether it is true. Thus, the culture doesn't make most Americans pragmatic, but this should not be confused with the fact that Americans are very practical, being reflected by the 'can-do' mentality mentioned above. Many Americans have very strong ideas about what is 'good' and 'evil'. American businesses measure their performance on a short-term basis, with profit and loss statements being issued on a quarterly basis. This dimension also drives individuals to strive for quick results within the work place.

China

China is one of the highest power distance countries. This dimension suggests that individuals are influenced by formal authority and sanctions and are in general optimistic about people's capacity for leadership and initiative.

China is a highly collectivist society. In a highly collectivist society people act in the interests of the group and not necessarily for themselves. In-group considerations affect hiring and promotions, with closer in-groups (such as family) getting preferential treatment. Personal relationships prevail over task and company.

A high score on the masculine dimension indicates that the society will be driven by competition, achievement and success, with success being defined by the winner / best in field – a value system that starts in school and continues throughout organisational life. China is a masculine society – success-oriented and driven. The need to ensure success can be exemplified by the fact that many Chinese will sacrifice family and leisure priorities to work.

China has a low score on uncertainty avoidance. This suggests that adherence to laws and rules may be flexible to suit the actual situation and pragmatism is a fact of life. The Chinese are comfortable with ambiguity and they are adaptable.

China scores high on long-term orientation, which means that it is a very pragmatic culture. In societies with a pragmatic orientation, people believe that truth depends very much on situation, context and time. They show an ability to adapt traditions easily to changed conditions, a strong propensity to save and invest, thriftiness, and perseverance in achieving results.

(Source: http://geert-hofstede.com/countries.html, Retrieved on the 7th of June, 2015).

Case study questions

1   How do the US and China compare in terms of the Hostede's cultural dimensions?

2   How do you think the cultural characteristics outlined above influence entrepreneurship in the US?

3   How could the US stimulate entrepreneurship further?

4   How do you think the cultural characteristics outlined above influence entrepreneurship in China?

5   How could China stimulate entrepreneurship further?

References

Anderson, A., Park, J. and Jack, S. (2007) Entrepreneurial social capital, *International Small Business Journal*, **25**, 245-272.

Bergmann, H. (2009) Cultural aspects of entrepreneurship, report prepared for *OECD - Local Entrepreneurship Reviews – Strengthening Entrepreneurship and Economic Development in East Germany: Lessons from Local Approaches Final Report*. Retrieved on 10th February from http://www.oecd.org/site/cfecpr/42367462.pdf

Busenitz, L. W. and Lau, C. (1996) A cross-cultural cognitive model of new venture creation, *Entrepreneurship Theory and Practice*, **20** (4), 25-39.

Chelariu, C., Brashear, T. G., Osmonbekov, T. and Zait, A. (2008) Entrepreneurial propensity in a transition economy: Exploring micro-level and meso-level cultural antecedents, *Journal of Business and Industrial Marketing*, **23** (6), 405-415.

Chen, J., and McQueen, R. J. (2008) Factors affecting e-commerce stages of growth in small Chinese firms in New Zealand, *Journal of Global Information Management*, **16** (1), 26-60.

Covin, J. G. and Slevin, D. P. (1989) Strategic management of small firms in hostile and benign environments, *Strategic Management Journal*, **10** (1), 75-87.

Cunnigham, J. B. and Lischeron, J. (1991) Defining entrepreneurship, *Journal of Small Business Management*, **29**, 45-61.

Dakhli, M. and De Clercq, D. (2004) Human capital, social capital and innovation: A multi-country study, *Entrepreneurship and Regional Development*, **16**, 107-128.

Dodd, S. D. and Patra, E. (2002) National differences in entrepreneurial networking, *Entrepreneurship and Regional Development*, **14**, 117-134.

Etzioni, A. (1987) Entrepreneurship, adaptation and legitimation: A macro-behavioral perspective, *Journal of Economic Behavior and Organization*, **8**, 175-189.

Everdingen Y. and Waarts E. (2003) The effect of national culture in the adoption of innovation, *Marketing Letters*, **14**, 217 – 232.

Garland, J. W., Hoy, B., Boulton, W. R. and Garand, J. C. (1984) Differentiating entrepreneurs from small business owners: a conceptualisation, *Academy of Management Review*, **9** (2), 354-359.

Gartner, W. B. (1988) Who is an entrepreneur? Is the wrong question, *American Journal of Small Business*, **12** (4), 11-32.

Gartner, W. B. (1990) What are we talking about when we talk about entrepreneurship?, *Journal of Business Venturing*, **5**, 15-28.

Geletkanycz, M. A. (1997) The salience of 'culture's consequences: The effects of cultural values on top executive commitment on the status quo, *Strategic Management Journal*, **18**, 615-634.

3

George, G. and Zahra, S. A. (2002) Culture and its consequences for entrepreneurship, *Entrepreneurship Theory and Practice*, **26** (4), 5-8.

Guasch, J. L., Kuznetsov, Y. N., and Sanchez, S. M. (2002) *Small and Medium Sized Enterprises in Argentins: A Potential Engine for Economic Growth and Employment*. World Bank Sector Rep. No. 22803-AR. Washington, D.C.: World Bank.

Gurel, E., Altinay, L. and Daniele, R. (2010) Tourism students' entrepreneurial intentions, *Annals of Tourism Research*, **37** (3), 646-669.

Hall, E. T. (1977) *Beyond Culture*. Garden City, New York: Anchor Books.

Hayton, J. C., George, G. and Zahra, S. A. (2002) National culture and entrepreneurship: A review of behaviour research, *Entrepreneurship Theory and Practice*, **26** (4), 33-52.

Herbig, P. and Dunphy, S. (1998) Culture and innovation, *Cross Cultural Management: An International Journal*, **5** (4), 13-21.

Heunks, F. J. (1998) Innovation, creativity and success, *Small Business Economics*, **10** (3), 363-372.

Hofstede, G. (1980) *Culture's Consequences: International Differences in Work Related Values*, Beverly Hills, CA: Sage Publications.

Hofstede, G. (2003) *Culture's Consequences, International Differences in Work Related Values*, Beverly Hills, CA: Sage Publications.

Hofstede, G. (1984) The cultural relativity of the quality of life concept, *Academy of Management Review*, **9**, 389–398.

Hofstede, G. and M. Bond (1988) The Confucius connection: from cultural roots to economic growth, *Organizational Dynamics*, **16** (4), 4-21.

Holland, D. V. and Shepherd, D. A. (2013) Deciding to persist: Adversity, values, and entrepreneurs' decision policies, *Entrepreneurship Theory and Practice*, **37** (2), 331-358.

Hurmentrinta, L. P. (2001) The innovation and internationalisation of small businesses: Applying an innovation concept in an export context, *Academy of Entrepreneurship Journal*, **2** (1), 21-33.

Jaw, B., Ling, Y., Wang, Y. and Chang, W. (2007) The impact of culture on Chinese employees' work values, *Personnel Review*, **36** (5), 763-780.

Johannesson, G., Skaptadottir, U. D. and Benediktsson, K. (2003) Coping with social capital? The cultural economy of tourism in the North, *Sociologia Ruralis*, **43** (1), 3-16.

Jones, s. (2005) Community-based ecotourism – The significance of social capital, *Annals of Tourism Research*, **32** (2), 303-324.

Kale, H. S. (1995) Grouping euroconsumers: a cultural based clustering approach, *Journal of International Marketing*, **3** (3), 35-49.

Karande, K., Rao, P. C. and Singhapakdi, A. (2002) Moral philosophies of marketing managers, *European Journal of Marketing*, **36** (7/8), 768-791.

Kirby, D. A. (2005) Entrepreneurship Education: Can Business Schools Meet the Challenge, in the Proceedings of the 2005 San Francisco-Silicon Valley Global Entrepreneurship Research Conference, San Francisco, California, March 9-12, 2005, pp. 173-193.

Kleinschmidt, E. J. (1994) A comparative analysis of new product programmes: European versus North American companies, *European Journal of Marketing*, **28** (7), 5-29.

Kluckhohn, F. R. and Strodtbeck, F. L. (1961) *Variations in Value Orientations*, Westport, CT: Greenwood Press.

Kogut, B. and Singh, H. (1988) The effect of national culture on the choice of entry mode, *Journal of International Business Studies*, **19**, 411-432.

Kumar, M. (2007) Explaining entrepreneurial success: A conceptual model, *Academy of Entrepreneurship Journal*, **13** (1), 57-77.

Laforet, S. and Tann, J. (2006) Innovative characteristics of small manufacturing firms, *Journal of Small Business and Enterprise Development*, **13** (3), 363-380.

Laurent, A. (1983) The cultural diversity of western conceptions of management, *International Studies of Management and Organisations*, **13** (1), 75-96.

Lee, C., Lee, K. and Pennings, J. M. (2001) Internal capabilities, external networks, and performance: a study on technology-based ventures, *Strategic Management Journal*, **22**, 615-640.

Lieberman, M. B. and Montgomery, D. B. (1988) First mover advantages, *Strategic Management Journal*, **9** (1/2), 41-58.

Madsen, E. L. (2007) The significance of sustained entrepreneurial orientation on performance of firms – a longitudinal analysis, *Entrepreneurship and Regional Development*, **19**, 185-204.

Martinez, N. (2014) *Social and entrepreneurial values profiles*. MPGI Dissertation, Escola de Administração de Empresas de São Paulo. Retrieved on the 10th of February from http://bibliotecadigital.fgv.br/dspace/bitstream/handle/10438/11508/NAYLIA%20 MARTINEZ.pdf

McClelland, D. (1965) Need achievement and entrepreneurship: A longitudinal study, *Journal of Personality and Social Psychology*, **1**, 389-392.

McGrath, R. G., MacMillan, I. C., and Scheinberg, S. (1992) Elitists, risk-takers, and rugged individualists? An exploratory analysis of cultural differences between entrepreneurs and non-entrepreneurs, *Journal of Business Venturing*, **7** (2), 115–135.

Miles, M. P., Covin, J. G. and Heeley, M. B. (2000) The relationship between environmental dynamism and small firm structure, strategy and performance, *Journal of Marketing Theory and Practice*, **8** (2), 63-74.

Miller, D and Lee, J. (2001) The people make the process, *Journal of Management*, **27**(2), 163-189.

Mitchell, R. K., Smith, B., Seawright, K. W. and Morse, E. A. (2000) Cross-cultural cognitions and the venture creation decision, *Academy of Management Journal*, **43**, 974-993.

Morris, M. H., Avila, R. A. and Allen, J. (1993) Individualism and the modern corporation: Implications for innovation and entrepreneurship, *Journal of Management*, **19**(3), 595-612.

Morris, M. H., Davis, D. L. and Allen, J. W. (1994) Fostering corporate entrepreneurship: Cross-cultural comparisons of the importance of Individualism versus Collectivism, *Journal of International Business Studies*, **25**, 65–89.

Morrison, A. (2000) Entrepreneurship: what triggers it?, *International Journal of Entrepreneurial Behaviour and Research*, **6** (2), 59-71.

Morrison, A. (2006) A contextualisation of entrepreneurship, *International Journal of Entrepreneurial Behaviour and Research*, **12** (4), 192-211.

Mueller, S. L. (2004) Gender gaps in potential for entrepreneurship across countries and cultures, *Journal of Developmental Entrepreneurship*, **9** (3), 199-220.

Mueller, S. L. and Thomas, A. S. (2001) Culture and entrepreneurial potential: A nine country study of locus of control and innovativeness, *Journal of Business Venturing*, **16**, 51-75.

Nahapiet, J. and Ghoshal, S. (1998) Social capital, intellectual capital, and the organizational advantage *Academy of Management Review*, **23**, 242-266.

Nakata, C. and Sivakumar, K. (1996) National culture and new product development: An integrative review, *Journal of Marketing*, **60** (January), 61-72.

Petrakis, P. E. (2005) Risk perception, risk propensity and entrepreneurial behaviour: The Greek case, *Journal of American Academy of Business*, **7** (1), 233-243.

Pinillos, M. and Reyes, L. (2011) Relationship between individualist-collectivist culture and entrepreneurial activity: Evidence from Global Entrepreneurship Monitor data, *Small Business Economics*, **37**, 23-37.

Ritchie, B. and Brindley, C. (2005) Cultural determinants of competitiveness within SMEs, *Journal of Small Business and Enterprise Development*, **12** (1), 104-119.

Rokeach, M. (1973) *The Nature of Human Values*, New York: The Free Press.

Runyan, R. C., Huddleston, P. and Swinney, J. (2006) Entrepreneurial orientation and social capital as small firm strategies: A study of gender differences from a resource-based view, *Entrepreneurship Management*, **2**, 455-477.

Saeed, S., Yousafzai, S. Y. and Engelen, A. (2014) On cultural and macroeconomic contingencies of the entrepreneurial orientation – performance relationship, *Entrepreneurship Theory and Practice*, **38** (2), 255-290.

Scheinberg, S. and MacMillan, I. C. (1988) An 11-country study of motivations to start a business, in Kirchoff, B.A., Long, W.A., McMullan, W.E., Vesper, K.E., Wetzel, W.E. (Eds.), *Frontiers of Entrepreneurship Research*, Wellesley, MA: Babson College, pp. 669-687.

Schwartz, S. H. (1992) Universals in the content and structure of values: theoretical advances and empirical tests in 20 countries, in M. Zanna (Ed.), *Advances in Experimental Social Psychology*, New York: Academic Press, pp. 1-65.

Schwartz, S. H. (2004) Mapping and interpreting cultural differences around the world, in H. Vinken, J. Soeter, and P. Ester (Eds.), *Comparing cultures, dimensions of culture in a comparative perspective*, Leiden, The Netherlands: Brill, pp. 43-73.

Schwartz, S. H. (2012) An overview of the Schwartz Theory of Basic Values, Online Readings in Psychology and Culture, **2** (1), 1-20. Retrieved on the 10th of February from http://http://scholarworks.gvsu.edu/cgi/viewcontent.cgi?article=1116&context=orpc

Shane, S. (1993) Cultural influences on national rates of innovation, *Journal of Business Venturing*, **8**, 59–73.

Shane, S. (1995) Uncertainty Avoidance and the preference for innovation championing roles, *Journal of International Business Studies*, First Quarter, 47-67.

Shane, S., Kolvereid, L. and Westhead, P. (1991) An exploratory examination of reasons leading to new firm formation across country and gender, *Journal of Business Venturing*, **6**, 431-446.

Shinnar, R. S., Giacomin, O. and Janssen, F. (2012) 'Entrepreneurial perceptions and intentions: The role of gender and culture', *Entrepreneurship Theory and Practice*, **36** (3), 465-493.

Siu, W. and Kirby, D. (1999) Small firm marketing in China: a comparative study of Chinese and British Marketing Practices . Research into Entrepreneurship (RENT) Proceedings of the Thirteenth RENT Conference. London, England: November 25-26.

Siu, W. and Lo, E. S. (2013) Cultural contingency in the cognitive model of entrepreneurial intention, *Entrepreneurship Theory and Practice*, **37** (2), 147-173.

Sivakumar, K. and Cheryl Nakata (2003) Designing global new product teams: Optimizing the effects of national culture on new product development, *International Marketing Review*, **20** (4), 397-445.

Steward, W. H. and Roth, P. L. (2001) Risk propensity differences between entrepreneurs and managers: A meta-analytic review, *Journal of Applied Psychology*, **86** (1), 145-153.

Steward, W. H., Watson, W. E., Garland, J. C. and Garland, J. W. (1998) A proclivity for entrepreneurship: a comparison of entrepreneurs, small business owners and corporate managers, *Journal of Business Venturing*, **14** (2), 189-214.

Swierczek, F and Ha, T. T. (2003) Motivation, entrepreneurship and the performance of SMEs in Vietnam, *Journal of Enterprising Culture*, **11** (1), 47-68.

3

Tajeddini, K. (2010) Effect of customer orientation and entrepreneurial orientation on innovativeness: Evidence from the hotel industry in Switzerland, *Tourism Management*, **31**, 221-231.

Tayeb, M. (1988) *Organisations and National Culture*. London: Sage.

Thomas, A. S., and Mueller, S. L. (2000) A case for comparative entrepreneurship: Assessing the relevance of culture, *Journal of International Business Studies*, **31**, 287–301.

Thomas, R., Shaw, G. and Page, S. J. (2011) Understanding small firms in tourism: A perspective on research trends and challenges, *Tourism Management*, **32**, 963-976.

Trompenaars, F. (1993) *Riding the Waves of Culture*, London: The Economist Books.

Yalcinkaya, G. (2008) A culture-based approach to understanding the adoption and diffusion of new products across countries, *International Marketing Review*, **25** (2), 202 – 214.

Zhao, F. (2005) Exploring the synergy between entrepreneurship and innovation, *International Journal of Entrepreneurial Behaviour and Research*, **11** (1), 25-41.

Zhao, W., Ritchie, J. R. B. and Echtner, C. M. (2011) Social capital and tourism entrepreneurship, *Annals of Tourism Research*, **38** (4), 1570-1593.

Theme 2: Types of Entrepreneurship

The benefits of entrepreneurship and entrepreneurial endeavours are far reaching. The economic benefits yielded to regional or national economies are generated through the creation of new businesses to bring entrepreneurial innovations to market, the creation of new jobs and the profits generated through these business endeavours. As a result, the concept of entrepreneurship has been embraced in different ways by different types of organisations. In Section 2, we examine 5 distinct types of entrepreneurship that have great relevance within the hospitality and tourism industries.

In Chapter 4, we examine social entrepreneurship, a type of entrepreneurship that is growing in popularity and attracting the attention of aspiring entrepreneurs, governments, non-government organisations (NGOs), charities and socially-minded organisations. Social entrepreneurship is quite simply the use of new and innovative products, services or approaches to address societal problems or challenges. In other words, the benefits of the entrepreneurial activity are realised socially, culturally or environmentally, rather than purely economically. There are numerous foundations or associations around the globe that support social entrepreneurship such as Ashoka, SKOLL and the Schwab Foundation for Social Enterprise. There is even a school for social entrepreneurs with locations across the UK, Canada and Australia. Social enterprises have been developed across numerous industry sectors, including hospitality and tourism. For example the Art & Woonhotel in Rotterdam provides employment for some of the most marginalised people in Dutch society. It also provides temporary, affordable accommodation for the staff. The Solidarity Restaurant in Nice feeds locals who cannot afford to eat, for free on its proceeds from paying customers. The Koto (Know One Teach One) social enterprise provides training and employment opportunities for disadvantaged youth through its training centres, restaurants, online bakery, and catering service in Vietnam. Research on social enterprises however, is at an early stage. Within Chapter 5, the author identifies the three major research streams of social entrepreneurship but questions the value of these in shedding insight into how social entrepreneurs identify and exploit opportunities for generating social value and transformation. Accordingly, the author proposes a new theoretical approach of learning with the market, an adaptive process that results in several learning outcomes that change three market-level properties: network structure, market practices and market pictures. Using a case study of a social enterprise in Greece, the author clearly demonstrates how this learning can be applied to co-create social value and transformation.

The social contribution of entrepreneurship is also recognised in ethnic minority entrepreneurship, the topic of Chapter 5. Within Europe, as in other areas around the globe, the contribution of ethnic entrepreneurial activities has been steadily increasing (European Commission, 2008). As ethnic entrepreneurs contribute to the economic growth of their local area and create employment, they also help to integrate ethnic migrants into employment and tackle illegal employment. Across Europe, there are numerous policies and programmes therefore designed to promote and support ethnic entrepreneurship. Ethnic minority entrepreneurs are dominant in the hospitality industry, particularly in the independent restaurant sector. Despite this prevalence, Li (2008) argues that our knowledge of the nature and extent of ethnic minority entrepreneurship is limited within the hospitality sector and that more research is needed. This chapter addresses this deficiency in the literature by exploring the theories that underpin ethnic entrepreneurship as well as the motivations of ethnic minority entrepreneurs. The authors identify a number of relationship development strategies adopted by ethnic minority entrepreneurs, arguing they must have a strong market orientation and penetrate mainstream markets to remain competitive and survive in the long-term. The authors embed their arguments into a conceptual framework comprising motive, socio-cultural environments, co-ethnic resources and competitive strategies.

A very different type of entrepreneurship is explored within Chapter 6; that of corporate entrepreneurship (CE). Often referred to as intrapreneurship, this particular type of entrepreneurship sees employees within companies use their initiative to identify new and innovative products, services or processes to improve company performance. Many hospitality and tourism firms have adopted the practice of empowerment to give employees a chance to use their initiative. However, as this chapter identifies, empowering employees may not be sufficient to realise CE. Previous research suggests that managers have an important role to play in encouraging entrepreneurial thinking in employees (Kilroy, 2015). In this chapter, the critical role of middle managers in realising CE in the hotel industry is examined. As these managers possess a high degree of expertise and understanding of the business, they are in strong position to identify opportunities to improve business performance. The chapter identifies the different, but inter-dependent roles that middle managers must adopt to realise corporate entrepreneurship. In order to fulfil these roles effectively however, a number of antecedents must be in place within the organisation. The chapter identifies middle manager roles and these antecedents, how they are inter-related and how they can create an appropriate environment for CE to flourish.

Chapter 7 also examines entrepreneurship in larger organisations, but this time within the context of franchise networks. Franchising and business format franchising in particular, has long been popular within the hospitality and the fast-food industry, particularly in developed markets. However, franchising is now increasingly used to support international expansion across a wide range of industry sectors. It is therefore considered by some as important to the growth of global entrepreneurship. However, there is ongoing debate in the academic literature on the relationship between franchising and entrepreneurship. While the majority of academics accept that franchisors are entrepreneurs, many argue that this is not the case for franchisees. This chapter therefore explores this debate to consider franchising as an entrepreneurial partnership. It examines the growth of franchising within hospitality and tourism, and identifies the benefits realised through franchising for national economies, franchisors and franchisees. These benefits are explained through the popular theoretical explanations of franchising: resource scarcity, agency and plural form theories. The entrepreneurial role of franchisors and franchisees within a network to identify and exploit opportunities are examined as an entrepreneurial partnership to help networks to remain competitive within local and global markets. While achieving an effective entrepreneurial partnership is not without its challenges, the case study of the Little Sheep restaurant chain, demonstrates the benefits of an entrepreneurial partnership.

A number of challenges facing franchise networks are also identified in Chapter 8, albeit within the context of social franchising. As with the other types of social enterprises explored in Chapter 5, social franchising is considered a way to address some of society's current social inequalities or ills. Social franchising is in its emergent stages and to date, there is limited research undertaken from either a practical or academic perspective. This chapter therefore offers a welcome insight into this relatively new phenomenon. The European Social Franchise Network (2015) reports 63 social franchisors in 12 European countries with 80% established within the last 10 years and 40% within the last 5 years. This same report estimates that social franchising has created 10,000 jobs with 65% of these filled by those considered disadvantaged in the labour market. The majority of these franchises are within the service sectors, including hospitality, leisure, and tourism. However, research reports on the total number of social franchises across Europe vary widely, which may be a result of the different interpretations of social franchising, which vary depending on the industry sector and country context. Broadly, "social franchising encompasses the potential for commercial franchising to be socialised and utilised to achieve social, rather than purely commercial ends" (Richardson and Berlowitz, 2012:3). However there are different models of social franchises in operation. Some operate using a 'for profit model' and some are supported through financial grants which enable franchisors to support franchisees. Within this chapter, the authors consider social franchising as an entrepreneurial business model which adds economic and social value, thus offering a different perspective on franchising than that presented in Chapter 7. By comparing the purely commercial and social franchise models, the challenges facing social franchisors are identified. The challenges are explored through the examination of social franchise organisations such as Le Mat which is expanding through Europe with hotels, hostels and B&Bs from its Italian origins.

Maureen Brookes, Oxford Brookes University

References

European Commission (2008) *Entrepreneurial Diversity in a Unified Europe*, Brussels: European Commission.

European Social Franchise Network (2015), *Social Franchise. Growing More than Business and Social Economies*, downloaded from http://www.socialfranchising.coop/ on March 15, 2015.

Kilroy, T. (2015) Do the best employees think like entrepreneurs? *Social Brand Communications in Hospitality*, downloaded from https://www.linkedin.com/ on March 23, 2015.

Li, L. (2008) A review of entrepreneurship published in the hospitality and tourism management journals, *Tourism Management,* **29**, 1013-1022.

Richardson, M. and Berlowitz, D. (2012) *Investing in Social Franchising*, London: International Centre for Social Franchising.

4 Social Entrepreneurship and Social Value Co-creation:

the case of Mageires (a social restaurant)

Marianna Sigala, University of South Australia

Introduction

Although addressing social problems is at the heart of social entrepreneurship (Dees and Economy, 2001; Mair and Marti, 2006; Zahra *et al.*, 2009; Peredo and McLean, 2006), there is still limited research on how social entrepreneurs can generate social value and transformation (Ormiston and Seymour, 2013; Seymour, 2013). In tourism, the development of social entrepreneurship is booming (Kline *et al.*, 2014; Mody and Day, 2014; Sloan *et al.*, 2014), since it is viewed as a good way to support sustainable and community-based tourism that can alleviate many social problems (Kravva, 2014). However, research about social entrepreneurship in tourism simply replicates existing knowledge by examining the operations and motives of social entrepreneurs (e.g. Tetzschner and Herlau, 2003; von der Weppen and Cochrane, 2012) rather than adds to our understanding on how social value and transformation can be created.

Moreover, although market failures are widely recognised as the driving force of social entrepreneurship, the conventional economic approaches examining social entrepreneurship provide limited understanding into the functioning and formation of the markets (Dean and McMullen, 2007) and so, of the processes and the capabilities enabling social entrepreneurs to engage with and shape (new) markets that can solve these market failures. On the other hand, advances in marketing thinking (Kjellberg and Helgesson, 2007; Storbacka and Nenonen, 2011a; Vargo and Lusch, 2011) explaining the nature of markets and the factors influencing their becoming and formation, provide a useful theoretical lens for understanding how social entrepreneurs can identify and create market opportunities for achieving their social goals. Consequently, Sigala (in press) proposes a market-based framework advocating three market capabilities explaining how social entrepreneurs can generate social value and transformation.

This chapter aims to enhance your understanding of how social entrepreneurs can generate social value and transformation by applying this framework in a case study of a social restaurant called *Mageires* (meaning 'Chefs' in Greek). Thus, by the end of this chapter you should be able to explain:

■ The role and the importance of the three market capabilities enabling the social enterprises to form markets in which social value and transformation can be co-created;

■ How social entrepreneurs access and mobilise resources by building social networks (market structure capabilities);

■ How social entrepreneurs enable and motivate market actors to exchange and integrate resources in different ways and contexts (market practices capabilities);

■ How social entrepreneurs nurture and diffuse a new mind-set and language for interpreting and understanding the markets that, in turn, can drive and support social transformation (market pictures capabilities).

The chapter first critically reviews and discusses the limitations of the current literature in explaining social entrepreneurship. It then presents and advocates the three market capabilities and their importance in generating social value and transformation. Finally, the case study of Mageires is analysed by applying this framework and showing its implications.

Social entrepreneurship and social value and transformation: research approaches and limitations

Social entrepreneurship is heavily researched from three major streams: research examining the entrepreneurial behavior and goals of social ventures (Dees and Economy, 2001; Mort et al., 2003); research primarily focusing on the personality and distinctive characteristics, traits and competencies of the social venture founder (e.g. Dees, 1998); and research on social enterprises concentrating on the tangible outcomes of social entrepreneurship. However, the directions of existing research have been accused (e.g. Mair and Marti, 2006) for our limited understanding and consensus on what social entrepreneurship is, and how it can generate social value and transformation. For example, Ormiston and Seymour (2013) claimed that research has been asking the wrong questions: i.e. inquiring "who is and can be characterised as a social entrepreneur" and "what are the social entrepreneurship motives, goals, drivers and impacts", instead of examining how social entrepreneurs and enterprises act and create social value. Indeed, the entrepreneurial and environmental/sustainable entrepreneurship approaches investigating social entrepreneurship provide limited and abstract insight into how social entrepreneurs can recognise and exploit opportunities for generating social value and transformation.

First, the entrepreneurship literature is heavily used for defining the social 'entrepreneur', since social entrepreneurs are one species of entrepreneurs (Dees, 1998), who apply the principles and tenets of entrepreneurship for developing social ventures that aim to alleviate socio-economic and/or environmental problems and catalyse social change (Dees, 1998; Mort *et al.*, 2003; Ormiston and Seymour, 2013). However, this approach entails a very deterministic role of social entrepreneurs in continually sensing the market environment for identifying and satisfying social needs (Dees, 2001; Mort *et al.*, 2003; Haugh, 2005), while it also limits the conceptions of social entrepreneurship to those that capture opportunities through superior alertness. On the other hand, the entrepreneurship literature (Buchanan and Vanberg, 1991; Venkataraman, 1997) identifies three approaches for generating entrepreneurial opportunities: the allocative view (opportunity recognition); the discovery view (opportunity discovery); and the creative view (opportunity creation). Moreover, entrepreneurship viewed as 'creative destruction' (Schumpeter, 1934), requires social entrepreneurs to not only identify and meet existing social gaps, but also to initiate societal transformations by shaping and/or creating new and better markets and institutions that can address both social needs and generate economic value (Cohen and Winn, 2007). Hence, although from an entrepreneurial approach, the social enterprises have to be both reactive and proactive in order to address social needs and drive social change by creating new institutions (e.g. Dees, 1998; Peredo and McLean, 2010), the literature in (social/sustainable) entrepreneurship, that is reviewed below, provides limited insight on how this can be achieved.

In creating a typology of social entrepreneurs, Zahra *et al.* (2009) identified three types of social entrepreneurs based on: how they discover and define social opportunities and social needs (i.e. search processes); the scope and scale of their social value and impact on the broader social system; and the ways they use the market for assembling resources to pursue social opportunities.

- *Social bricoleurs* utilise and depend on their own local knowledge and resources for discovering and addressing small-scale local social needs by developing, maintaining and reconfiguring relations with various market actors (e.g. volunteers, employees, institutions, governmental agents) that give them access to resources and knowledge.

- *Social constructionists* cater for those social needs and market failures, that are inadequately addressed by existing institutions, by introducing reforms and innovations that fill in holes in the social system.

- *Social engineers* act as prime movers of innovation and revolutionary change, because they identify systemic problems within existing social structures and address them by destroying existing/dated institutions and replacing them with newer and more suitable ones.

Thus, although this typology recognises that social entrepreneurs need to challenge and influence the formation of market equilibriums for generating social value and transformation, the study does not provide specific guidelines and understanding on how social entrepreneurs can engage and interact with the market for influencing its formation, institutions and operations. In addition, the literature has failed to explain what social entrepreneurs have to do for identifying, forming and institutionalising (new) market equilibriums that deliver social value and transformation.

Social entrepreneurship is also studied from an environmental/sustainable entrepreneurship approach (i.e. based on environmental and welfare economics), because of the commonalities in entrepreneurial goals and processes. This literature also highlights that sustainable entrepreneurs have to adopt both a reactive and proactive (transformational market role) for identifying and creating new market opportunities or responding to/restructuring existing market forces, conditions or new regulations respectively (Cohen and Winn, 2007; Dean and McMullen, 2007; Hall *et al.*, 2010; Schaltegger and Wagner, 2011). Environmental entrepreneurship is the only approach using the concept of market failures and equilibrium for explaining how environmental entrepreneurial opportunities are created and exploited (Hall *et al.*, 2010). It is generally recognised (e.g. Cohen and Winn, 2007; Dean and McMullen, 2007; Hall *et al.*, 2010) that environmentally-relevant market failures create entrepreneurial opportunities, because they represent 'problems' that people would pay to have removed if given a cost-effective solution. By creating and/or improving the markets for environmental resources (e.g. biofuels, fair trade food and tourism), environmental entrepreneurs profit from the economic value, while simultaneously reducing environmental degradation and enhancing ecological sustainability (Dean and McMullen, 2007).

However, despite their contribution in identifying environmental opportunities, neoclassical economists cannot efficiently elaborate either normatively or descriptively on the existence, exploitation or (mainly) on the proactive creation of (new) entrepreneurial opportunities. Rather, they adopt a deterministic and market reactive approach to environmental entrepreneurship that limits conceptions of entrepreneurship to those individuals and organisations that capture opportunities through superior alertness (Dean and McMullen, 2007). On the other hand, many authors (e.g. Cohen and Winn, 2007; Dean and McMullen, 2007; Hall *et al.*, 2010) also advocate that environmental entrepreneurs need to interpret market failures and equilibrium-seeking in a more proactive approach that enables them to understand how to develop new economic institutions and forces that are necessary to overcome market failures and allow markets to function properly. Moreover, neoclassical economics conceptualises markets and market failures from an over-materialised and an under-socialised view of what is a market and how it evolves, because: markets are viewed as solely price-market institutions that create failures when desirable activities cannot be sustained or when undesirable activities cannot be stopped (Dean and McMullen, 2007); and market failures are created when entrepreneurs do not consider the social costs of production in their private costs of production (Schaltegger and Wagner, 2011). Thus, traditional economic theories perceive markets as economic/cost regulating mechanisms and overlook the impact of social issues (e.g. customs, traditions, norms and culture) on the functioning of the markets (Williamson, 2000). According to the social embeddedness concept and structuration theory (Giddens, 1979), this approach critically limits our understanding of markets' formation and evolution, because one cannot separate the market actors from the market structure and so, the impacts and inter-relations amongst these two elements.

Overall, all approaches identify the dual role of social entrepreneurs to continually sense and be alert to market needs and conditions, while simultaneously being creative and constructing new opportunities for shaping new market conditions and change. However, research is not specific, detailed and analytical enough on how (new) markets are formed/changed, and how social entrepreneurs can identify and create new market opportunities and initiate market change. This is because the traditional approaches to social entrepreneurship make the following assumption about the nature and operations of markets (Schaltegger and Wagner, 2011): social institutions and markets simply exist, are given and function effectively at a given equilibrium point, and so, when gaps and failures create market imbalances (malfunctions and failures), social enterprises aim to correct them by bringing societies and markets back to the given and desired equilibrium point. This conventional rationale also entails that in order to deliver social value, social entrepreneurs need to conduct market sensing for learning 'about the market' so that they can identify and exploit 'already existing' market gaps and opportunities. Economic and welfare economics also adopt a narrow economic understanding of the markets that do not challenge how the market equilibrium point is set, why it is fixed, whether market actors can challenge/

change its position and whether markets can also effectively work at another market equilibrium. The implications of the traditional approaches echo debates of market-driven (reactive strategies responding to market forces) versus market-driving entrepreneurial strategies (proactive strategies changing the market equilibrium point).

Hence, in order to develop a more holistic understanding about the creation of social value and transformation, research should adopt an approach expanding the conceptualisation of markets from the dominant economic view to a wider social perspective. Investigating social entrepreneurship from a new market approach also demands new thinking on how social enterprises can engage with and shape markets for creating new equilibriums, social value and transformation. So, instead of only learning *about* the market, social entrepreneurs should also learn *with* the market (Day, 2011; Storbacka and Nenonen, 2011b) in order to both respond to and change markets by influencing their becoming and formation.

Learning with the market: a market-based approach for creating social value

The nature of the markets

Given the limitations identified in the preceding section, a better theoretical lens is required to unravel how the market enables and constrains the appearance of social entrepreneurship (i.e. by creating and/or defining entrepreneurial opportunities) and how social entrepreneurs as market actors can initiate and institutionalise social change (Mair and Marti, 2006). Current marketing advances in conceptualising markets, their dynamics and evolution provide a useful approach to achieve this.

The marketing literature increasingly recognises that markets do not simply exist, but rather they are formed and are continuously evolving, as markets are malleable, dynamic, subjective, and subject to change efforts of multiple actors (Rosa *et al.*, 1999; Storbacka and Nenonen, 2011a; Kjellberg *et al.*, 2012). Consequently, marketing research is migrating from developing process-based models that describe market changes (e.g. product life-cycle models) to understanding the processes of market construction and transformation, by trying to identify the characteristics of the markets and the various socio-cultural and technical factors that can enable market dynamics (Geiger *et al.*, 2012; Nenonen *et al.*, 2013).

To that end, the current marketing thinking adopts a middle ground approach for defining markets and explaining their formation. It takes an embeddedness position highlighting how ongoing social relations shape the goals of market actors, the market actions they undertake and the relevant market institutions. This middle-ground approach provides a more pragmatic and accurate understanding of market creation, because it assumes a balance between the two extreme approaches to market conceptualisation (Granovetter, 1985; Geiger *et al.*, 2012): the traditional economic approaches that are characterised as under-socialised and highly materialised, as they assume that market devices (e.g. characteristics of technical resources and products/services, costs) significantly influence market co-ordination, shape market agents and determine markets (Callon, 2007); and the classic structural sociology approaches (emphasising the importance of dialogues and linguistics in market formation) that are characterised as 'over-socialised', because they attribute so much power to the socio-cultural context in which a market is situated that specific ongoing social relations have a minimal impact on the way the market works (Granovetter, 1992). Moreover, this synthesised impact of the middle-ground approach can better explain market emergence, construction and maintenance/change, because (Geiger *et al.*, 2012): the social and material aspects of markets are interwoven; the highly materialised and socialisation approaches treat change as exogenous (caused by technical conditions or social developments taking place independently of the market under study); while the middle-ground approach treats change as endogenous demonstrating how markets possess internal capabilities, dynamics and mechanisms to continually create and retain forms.

Thus, markets are increasingly viewed as self-empowered ever changing 'socio-technical arrangements' (Kjellberg and Helgesson, 2007; Callon, 2007) or 'on-going socio-material enactments that organise economised exchanges' (Nenonen *et al.*, 2013); and performative, since they can form and retain form, and give form to other market entities (Kjellberg and Helgesson, 2006; Geiger *et al.*, 2012).

'Learning with the market': three market capabilities

Creating markets requires firms to engage in processes that aim to influence the market practices undertaken by the market actors (Kjellberg and Helgesson, 2006). These "conscious activities conducted by a single market actor in order to alter the current market configuration" define market-driving strategies that are also termed as 'market scripting' (Storbacka and Nenonen, 2011b: 251) in contrast to 'market sensing' that supports market-driven strategies. Nenonen *et al.* (2013) also recognised that markets 'take form' intentionally (as a result of intentional efforts of a market actor or an external party) or are emergent (without intentional market shaping efforts from any actor). For markets to retain form, actors should engage with processes related to formalisation, institutionalisation, routinisation, and materialisation (Nenonen *et al.*, 2013).

Learning is also associated with the firms' capability to improve their market-driving strategies (Storbacka, 2011), as learning increases the firms' power to form markets (Knight, 2002; Storbacka, 2011; Geiger *et al.*, 2012; Nenonen *et al.*, 2013). Storbacka (2011: 22) termed this as 'learning with the market' and defined it as learning that requires "reciprocal adaptive processes, involving several market actors in a network, and resulting in learning outcomes that change market-level properties such as: network structure; market practices; or interpretations of the market (market pictures)". Thus, the 'learning with the market' approach identifies three learning outcomes and capabilities (Table 4.1) that organisations have to develop for shaping and forming (new) markets to generate social value and transformation: network structure referring to the firms' ability to develop and maintain networks and ties with other market actors in order to exchange resources and co-create value; market practices referring to the ways and the institutions that support and frame the actors' interactions and resource exchanges; and the market pictures representing the actors' interpretation and understanding of the market, which in turn influence their market practices. These capabilities enable the market actors to initiate change and form (new) markets by influencing the market practices of all the other market elements that constitute and shape markets (Nenonen *et al.*, 2013); and engaging in (collaborative) sense-making processes that change the actors' mental models/understanding of the markets (i.e. market pictures) and so, their market practices.

Overall, 'learning with the market' builds on network learning (Knight and Pye, 2005), i.e. not learning 'within networks' but learning 'as networks' or a group of organisations, that aims to construct inter-subjectivity or shared meanings. Consequently, 'learning with the market' recognises that market-shaping strategies entail the nurturing and pursuit of longitudinal, collaborative and reciprocal activities among the various market actors for creating shared market meanings, forming markets, and co-creating social value and transformation.

Table 4.1: Learning with the market: market capabilities and outcomes

Outcomes of 'learning with the market'	Dimensions of learning outcomes	Learning capabilities required for 'learning with the market' in order to form/change markets:
Network structure: Actors and their ties in the network	Inclusion or exclusion of actors in a network Access to networks and creation of network ties for controlling and accessing strategic information or resources	Ability to develop, maintain and manage a network structure by identifying and connecting with other market actors Ability to actively engage in tie formation with other market actors
Market practices that happen between actors in the market network Three interconnected market practices: • Exchange practices: through which value propositions are being communicated, refined and agreed upon • Normalised practices: (reciprocity, trust and overt rules) that influence the behaviour of actors • Representational practices: common language to describe markets and actions within them. They portray markets and the way they work, and thus, they produce shared images of the market	Exchange practices: • Financial transactions • Commonly agreed sales item definition • Price formation mechanisms • Customer readiness (e.g. to participate in the market and to use the product/service) • Network readiness (e.g. to participate in the market) • Competitive alternatives Normalised practices: • Technological standards (agreed or established) • Legislation • Official rules and regulations • Social and relational norms Representational practices: • Commonly agreed terminology • Market research • Coverage in media • Official statistics • Market/industry associations	Ability to format exchange practices: • Ability to reconfigure resources within a network in order to actualise value proposition and economic exchanges Ability to format normalised practices: • Ability to use normalisation practices for stabilising the business models and social norms Ability to format representational practices: • Ability to create knowledge and to engage in dialogues for creating inter-subjective meanings or consensus
Market pictures (Interpretations of the market): • How actors interpret the market network (where it starts and where it ends)	Idiosyncratic sense-making processes of managers that create the managers' subjective mental representations of their market. Subjective representations of markets are influenced by assumptions, labeled dominating ideas, dominating logic, commonly accepted dominant designs and business models	Ability to change the existing mental models and institutionalise new ones (cognitive market learning) Ability to overcome the institutions, e.g. existing understandings and patterns of actions

Mageires: the three market capabilities of the social restaurant for co-creating social value and transformation

Social vision and social value definition

Mageires is a social restaurant; its foundation and operations are based upon a business model (explained below according to the three market capabilities) that enables the organisation to generate sufficient revenues in order to support the achievement of its mission, which is the production and provision of healthy, good quality, Greek food at reasonable prices and in a sustainable way in order to help the Greek economy and society during the difficult times of the economic crisis. In other words, Mageires represents a social enterprise, since the creation of economic value is a means-to-a-social-end and is sought to ensure sustainability of the social enterprise (Dees, 1998; Mair and Marti, 2006; Ormiston and Seymour, 2013) so that social value is co-created in the following ways and for the following market actors.

The restaurant is located in Thessaloniki, Greece and it is heavily used by locals, tourists and people with economic problems. Mageires also does free food delivery to people with mobility problems.

Market structure

Market structure is a 'learning with the market' capability that enables the social entrepreneurs to generate social value in the markets by developing networks and inter-relations/ties with various market actors in order to access, exchange and integrate resources; and/or influence the market practices of other actors through mimetic behaviour and/or peer pressure (Storbacka, 2011; Sigala, in press).

Mageires network with the following market actors in order to exchange resources and co-create social value:

- *Social support institutions* (such as unemployment agents, centers of social rehabilitation and family support centers): Mageires employs exclusively people that have social problems (e.g. domestic violence, ex-drug addicts, ex-prisoners). They are stigmatised and facing difficulties to be socially accepted again. Thus, instead of reproducing ineffective ways of rehabilitating people (e.g. charities, donations, volunteer work) that result in stigmatisation and passivity undermining human advocacy, Mageires aims to give a second chance to their staff and give them the power and the responsibility to rebuild their lives. In this way, Mageires aims to provide a sustainable solution, and not a sustainable advantage, based on the logic of people's empowerment rather than on the logic of control (Santos, 2009), i.e. disadvantaged people are supported to take action to solve their problems rather than being registered under a charity programme in order to receive (financial or food) support based on their profile, conditions or status that can control and stigmatise them.

- *Greek food and beverages suppliers*: Mageires procures exclusively from Greek producers as its mission is to produce and maintain the tradition of Greek food/cuisine as well as to support Greek companies during the economic crisis.

- *Animal-friendly associations, churches and social markets*: Mageires does not want to throw away and waste any type of food. Mageires pays a member of staff to separate 'meat from vegetables' and provide food remaining to associations that feed stray animals, while edible food is given to charities for free re-distri-bution to people in need. Hence, it aims to help address the problems of food insecurity and the abandonment of animals, assisting to solve the problems of food insecurity which have escalated during the economic crisis in Greece.

- *One nutritionist and one expert in gerontology*: Mageires sought the cooperation of these two experts in order to gain the knowledge and expertise in designing a dietary programme called 'Taste and Life'. 'Taste and Life' is based on the Greek gastronomy, includes food-assisting wellness and memory and targets senior citizens. 'Taste and life' is reasonably priced at 50 or 100 euros (for 15 days or a month programme respectively) and it can be delivered at home for people with mobility problems.

- *An online social network built on Facebook* (https://www.facebook.com/mageire-speople): Mageires cannot and does not wish to spend funds for promotion and marketing. Thus, Mageires heavily depends on the Facebook online com-munity and user-generated-content for: enhancing awareness; promoting its social vision and values; generating and attracting more market actors into its social ventures (e.g. customers, associations etc.). Consequently, after just a few months of operation, Mageires experiences: seat occupancies of around 80-90% every day; a Facebook community of about 5000 fans; publicity in numerous national and local TV channels, radio stations and newspapers. This result is not surprising since previous studies have already shown the affordable opportunities that social media provides to fledgling (food/social) entrepreneurs (Kline *et al.*, 2014; Sigala, in press).

The market actors enabling Mageires to co-create social value confirms research findings in food entrepreneurship and innovation (Kline *et al.*, 2014) that advocate the role of ecosystems in supporting food entrepreneurs to innovate and create value in areas such as: sourcing; new product development; production processes; markets; and ways of organising business. Findings also confirm research in social entrepreneurship highlighting the importance of networks to access resources, which in turn can significantly boost or prevent the ability of social entrepreneurs to: identify and exploit social entrepreneurship opportunities (Mair and Marti,

2006; Zahra *et al.*, 2009;); mobilise different organisations to share and exchange resources within these networks (Ormiston and Seymour, 2013); and enlarge/escalate their social impact in the market by creating spill-over effects to other market actors and so, increase their marketability (Schaltegger and Wagner, 2011).

Market practices

Market practices represent exchange, normalised and representational practices that happen between actors in market exchanges (Storbacka, 2011: Table 1). The exchange practices supported by Mageires are characterised by the following. All menu items are priced and transacted at nearly cost prices (prices ranges between 3-5 euros), as the primary goal of the social restaurant is not to maximise profits but to generate social value and transformation by: promoting Greek cuisine and gastronomic traditions; supporting the Greek suppliers and producers; and empowering people in need. In terms of the definition of sales items, all menu items include Greek dishes and materials and the menu is fully written in Greek (no foreign language/words are used).

The market practices of Mageires are not regulated by official rules and regulations, but the restaurant has developed its own informal operating standards, norms and procedures. For example, the daily menu also includes dishes that follow the Greek tradition and customs, e.g. fasting menu 40 days before Easter and Christmas, traditional dishes on national days such as the 25th of March. The restaurant has 50 seats and although it achieves very high daily occupancies, the rule and the agreed practice of the four co-founders and co-owners is that they do not wish to expand the restaurant in order to commercialise and profiteer from this social ventures. Mageires also aims to develop its social and relational norms with its market actors. For example, the servicescape of the restaurant includes a communal long table whereby everyone can enjoy his/her meal by joining and networking with other people irrespective of their social and economic profile. The communal table has proved to be a great way to enable people to get to know each other, develop relational ties and friendship so that they can give social and psychological support to each other. The restaurant has also developed a 'loyalty' card for its friends/repeat customers called "the Mageires friends' card". Members of this card get special prices and offers.

In terms of representational practices (i.e. a common language that portrays the way markets work so they create a shared image/interpretation of what the market is and how it works), there is a specific terminology that is used in the restaurant such as, all staff are called associates, customers are called guests. The social values and mission of the restaurant are written and displayed in several locations; on the menu, on restaurant decorations and in press releases published on mass media. Indeed, Mageires is continually featured in numerous TV series, newspapers and radio stations, where its social mission, values and initiatives are promoted and explained.

Market pictures

The simple development of a social venture and its use/support by citizens are not sufficient for solving the causes and roots of social problems. Instead, a social problem is better solved when a new mindset is nurtured, that is guided by a renewed sense of caring for the self, community and nature, and a redefinition of what is well-being and good life (Sheth *et al.*, 2011). In this vein, social enterprises should develop and inspire a philosophy whereby the market actors understand the co-creation of social value not as an act of sacrifice, but as a normal element in their daily life that can be a key to greater happiness, meaning in life and a better socially-oriented way of everyday life. Consequently, *market pictures* is the third 'learning with the market' capability that social entrepreneurs should develop to influence their and the other actors' idiosyncratic sense-making processes and cognitive schema, so that they can in turn adopt and ultimately institutionalise social value co-creation behaviours as normal, daily market practices. To change mindsets, the 'learning with the market' approach advocates that social entrepreneurs should engage in cognitive market learning, because it can influence the formation of subjective mental representations by challenging and modifying the assumptions and the commonly accepted dominant ideas, logics and business models that the various market actors hold about the functioning of the market.

To that end, Mageires adopt the following activities for creating and forming market pictures:

- Organisation of workshops and seminars (e.g. seminars about 'food and social anthropology') that aim to educate people as well as instill in the market a healthy lifestyle that is based on the healthy, authentic, local and traditional Greek gastronomy;

- Organisation of 'meet the local suppliers' marketplaces whereby local producers are offered the opportunity to exhibit their products in the restaurant so that people get to know about them and learn how to access and use local food materials;

- 'Eat-and-learn' sessions for various groups such as schools, that aim to educate and motivate people to take home what they have learnt;

- Revival, promotion and diffusion of the Greek traditional dishes and food culture by the design of a fully Greek menu that follows the Greek gastronomical traditions; education of guests on menu items, e.g. how to cook them, their meaning for the Greek culture and their role in a healthy life;

■ Use of Facebook for posting messages relating to Greek food and culture, cooking recipes, food seminars, motivational messages for adopting a healthy diet. Messages have an informative and educational role that aim to nurture and diffuse a healthy Greek food/diet culture.

Findings from the activities of Mageires which form the market pictures also support Santos' (2009) claim that the distinctive domain of social entrepreneurs is to address 'neglected positive externalities' (NPE), which are the positive impacts that could be generated from a business beyond profit, but are neglected by the public and private sector. One type of NPE is the invisible public goods for which the social enterprises play a major role in raising awareness regarding their importance for society (Santos, 2009). Kline *et al.* (2014) identified some examples of potential NPEs generated by food entrepreneurs that also coincide with the market pictures formed by Mageires including:

■ Healthier lifestyles from eating local food;

■ Farm to table initiatives;

■ More natural and local products (less processed and more nutritious);

■ Education of consumers (and stakeholders of food system);

■ Increased community cohesion by fostering a sense of community; a healthier, more productive community;

■ Assistance to local food producers;

■ Customer empowerment to be able to recreate a healthy meal;

■ Empowerment of disadvantaged people to take control of their lives ;

■ Citizens' empowerment to propose a new market system of organising economic activities.

Overall, Mageires do not simply provide meals that someone can buy in order to feel as a good citizen. In other words, Mageires do not aim to create the understanding (market picture) that when confronted with a social problem, someone can buy a meal in order to support disadvantaged people and support the Greek economy. The latter can create the wrong message: "for the price of a meal, you can continue in your ignorance and pleasurable life, not only feeling any guilt, but even feeling good for having participated in the struggle against suffering" (Zizek, 2011: 117). Instead, Mageires strongly believe in educating, empowering and supporting their customers by teaching them why and how to make the food at home themselves. According to practice theory (Schatzki, 1996), Mageires aim to influence the following three elements that determine market practices and people's behaviors: *material things* (marketing offerings and material infrastructures, such as menu design, dishes, procurement), *know-how* (implying the importance of learning, e.g. educational sessions, cooking classes, explanations of food production), and *meanings* (e.g. social awareness, acceptability, appreciation and respect of a healthy, traditional/local food and gastronomical values and culture).

Customer empowerment was also found as an important aim of food social entrepreneurs in the USA (Kline *et al.*, 2014). Research has also shown (McGehee *et al.*, 2014) that the conscious-raising of the community, the development of networks that work to mobilise scare resources and the improvement of individual self-efficacy through empowerment can drive economic and social change within social movements. These three factors can also be catalysts of change for social enterprises. Citizen empowerment is also compatible with arguments related to food activism (Rakopoulos, 2014), whereby economic activities are taken over by citizens themselves, who have produced a model of a more humane, supportive economy based on mutuality, community participation and exchange. Under these circumstances, people are not seen as passive victims of capitalist infrastructures but active creators of their own lives and thus, economic and social agents that can drive social transformation (Kravva, 2014).

Because of these, Mageires can be characterised as social engineers (Zahra *et al.*, 2009), as they aim to replace existing market institutions and practices with a new proposition of social value co-creation in the food market.

Conclusion

This chapter aimed to unravel how social enterprises can co-create social value and transformation by adopting a market-based approach. To that end, a three market capabilities framework was proposed and analysed, and later applied to a social restaurant (Mageires) to demonstrate its applicability and implications. The case study of Mageires showed that for co-creating social value and transformation, social entrepreneurs should develop the following three market capabilities:

- **Market structure**, because it enables them to network with various actors for accessing, exchanging and aggregating resources;
- **Market practices** for enabling new ways, contexts, rules, norms and institutions that the market actors can use for interacting and exchanging resources; and
- **Market pictures** for nurturing and instilling in the market actors a new mindset and mental model of living and behaviour that is favourable towards the social values and mission of the social enterprise.

Questions

1 What was the social value created by the founders of Mageires?

2 How were resources accessed and mobilised in the case of Mageires?

3 Explain how market practice capabilities were developed in the case of Mageires.

4 Explain whether and how a new mind-set and language for interpreting and understanding the markets was developed in the case of Mageires.

5 What is meant by the term social transformation?

6 Compare and contrast the three different capabilities needed by social entrepreneurs.

References

Buchanan, J.M. and Vanberg, V.J., (1991) The market as a creative process, *Economics and Philosophy*, **7**, 167– 186.

Callon, M. (2007) What does it mean to say that economics is performative?, in D. MacKenzie, F., Muniesa, and L. Siu (Eds.) *Do Economists Make Markets: On the performativity of economics*, Princeton University Press Princeton, NJ, pp. 311–57.

Cohen, B. and Winn, M. (2007) Market imperfections, opportunity and sustainable entrepreneurship, *Journal of Business Venturing*, **22**, 29– 49.

Day, G.S. (2011) Closing the marketing capabilities gap, *Journal of Marketing*, **75**(4),183-195.

Dean, T. and McMullen, J. (2007) Toward a theory of sustainable entrepreneurship: Reducing environmental degradation through entrepreneurial action, *Journal of Business Venturing*, **22**, 50– 76.

Dees, J. G. (1998) *The meaning of 'social entrepreneurship*, Stanford University: Draft Report for the Kauffman Center for Entrepreneurial Leadership.

Dees, J. G., & Economy, P. (2001) *Social Entrepreneurship. Enterprising Nonprofits: A Toolkit for Social Entrepreneurs*, New York: John Wiley & Sons, 1-18.

Geiger, S., Kjellberg, H., and Spencer, R. (2012) Shaping exchanges, building markets, *Consumption Markets & Culture*, **15**(2), 133-147.

Giddens, A. (1979) *Central Problems in Social Theory*, Berkeley, CA: University of California Press.

Giddens, A. (1984) *The Constitution of Society*, Cambridge: Polity Press.

Granovetter, M. (1985) Economic action and social structure: The problem of embeddedness, *American Journal of Sociology*, **91**(3), 481–510.

Granovetter, M. (1992) Problems of explanation in economic sociology, in N. Nohria & R. Eccles (Eds) *Networks and Organizations*, Harvard Business School Press, Boston, MA, pp. 25–56.

Hall, J., Daneke, G. and Lenox, M. (2010) Sustainable development and entrepreneurship: Past contributions and future directions, *Journal of Business Venturing*, **25**, 439–448.

Haugh, H. (2005) A research agenda for social entrepreneurship, *Social Enterprise Journal*, **1**(1): 1-12.

Kjellberg, H. and Helgesson, C.F. (2006) Multiple versions of markets: Multiplicity and performativity in market practice, *Industrial Marketing Management*, **35**(7), 839-855.

Kjellberg, H. and Helgesson, C.F. (2007) On the nature of markets and their practices, *Marketing Theory*, **7**(2), 137-162.

Kjellberg, H., Storbacka, K., Akaka, M., Chandler, J., Finch, J., Lindeman, S., Löbler, H., Mason, K., McColl-Kennedy, J. and Nenonen, S. (2012) Market futures/future markets: Commentary on future research directions in the study of markets, *Marketing Theory*, **12**(2), 219-223.

Kline, C., Shah, N. and Rubright, H. (2014) Applying the positive theory of social entrepreneurship to understand food entrepreneurs and their operations, *Tourism Planning & Development*, **11**(3), 330-342.

Knight, L. (2002) Network learning: exploring learning by interorganizational networks, *Human Relations*, **55**(4), 427-454.

Knight, L. and Pye, A. (2005) Network learning: an empirically derived model of learning by groups of organizations, *Human Relations*, **58**(3), 369-392.

Kravva, V. (2014) Politicizing hospitality: the emergency food assistance landscape in Thessaloniki, *Hospitality & Society*, **4**(3), 249 – 274.

Mair, J. and Marti. I. (2006) Social entrepreneurship research: A source of explanation, prediction, and delight, *Journal of World Business* **41**, 36–44.

McGehee, N.G., Kline, C. and Knollenberg, W. (2014) Social movements and tourism-related local action, *Annals of Tourism Research*, **48**, 140–155.

Mody, M. and Day, J. (2014) Rationality of social entrepreneurs in tourism: Max Weber and the sociology of tourism development, *International Journal of Tourism Anthropology*, **3**(3), 227–244.

Mort, G.S., Weerawardena, J. and Carnegie, K. (2003), Social entrepreneurship: towards conceptualisation, *International Journal of Nonprofit and Voluntary Sector Marketing*, **8**(1), 76–88.

Nenonen, S., Cheung, L., Kjellberg, H., Lindeman, S., Mele, C., Pels, J., Sajtos, L. and Storbacka, K. (2013) Understanding market plasticity: the dialectic dynamics between stability and fluidity, The 2013 Naples Forum on *Service Dominant logic, Network &*

Systems Theory and Service Science: integrating three perspectives for a new service agenda, 18 - 21 June, Iscia, Italy.

Ormiston, J. and Seymour, R. (2013) Understanding value creation in social entrepreneurship: the importance of aligning mission, strategy and impact measurement, *Journal of Social Entrepreneurship*, **2**(2), 125 – 150.

Peredo, A. M. and McLean, M. (2006) Social entrepreneurship: A critical review of the concept, *Journal of World Business*, **41**, 56–65.

Rakopoulos, T. (2014) Food activism and antimafia cooperatives in contemporary Sicily, in C. Counihan and V. Siniscaechi (eds), *Food Activism: Agency, Democracy and Economy*, Bloomsbury, London, pp. 113 – 128.

Rosa, J.A., Porac, J.F., Runser-Spanjol, J. and Saxon, M.S. (1999) Sociocognitive dynamics in a product market, *Journal of Marketing*, **63**, 64-77.

Santos, F. (2009) A positive theory of social entrepreneurship, (INSEAD Working Paper Series). Fontainebleau, France, INSEAD Social Innovation Centre.

Schaltegger, S. and Wagner, M. (2011) Sustainable entrepreneurship and sustainability innovation: categories and interactions, *Business strategy and the Environment*, **20**, 222 – 237.

Schatzki, T.R. (1996) *Social Practices: A Wittgensteinian approach to human activity and the social*. Cambridge University Press, Cambridge, England.

Schumpeter, J. A. (1934) *The Theory of Economic Development: An inquiry into profits, capital, credit, interest, and the business cycle* (Vol. 55). Transaction publishers.

Seymour, R.S. (2013) *Handbook of Research Methods on Social Entrepreneurship*, Cheltenham: Edward Elgar.

Sheth, J., Sethia, N. and Srinivas, S. (2011) Mindful consumption: a customer-centric approach to sustainability, *Journal of Academy of Marketing Science*, **39**, 21 – 39.

Sigala, M. (in press) Learning with the market: a market framework for developing social entrepreneurship in tourism, *International Journal of Contemporary Hospitality Management*.

Sloan, P., Legrand, W. and Simons-Kaufmann, C. (2014) A survey of social entrepreneurial community-based hospitality and tourism initiatives in developing economies: A new business approach for industry, *Worldwide Hospitality and Tourism Themes*, **6**(1), 51 – 61.

Storbacka, K. (2011) Learning with the market: business model alignment in networks, Otago Forum - 3 - Academic Papers.

Storbacka, K. and Nenonen S. (2011a) Markets as configurations, *European Journal of Marketing*, **45**(1/2), 241-258.

Storbacka, K. and Nenonen S. (2011b) Scripting markets: from value propositions to market propositions, *Industrial Marketing Management*, **40**, 255-266.

4

Tetzschner, H. and Herlau, H. (2003) *Innovation and Social Entrepreneurship in Tourism. A Potential for Local Business Development*, Working Paper, Department of Environmental and Business Economics, University of Southern Denmark, No. 49.

Vargo, S. L. and Lusch, R. F. (2004) Evolving to a new dominant logic for marketing, *Journal of Marketing*, **68**, 1–17.

Venkataraman, S. (1997) The distinctive domain of entrepreneurship research: an editor's perspective, in, Katz, J.,Brockhaus, J. (Eds.), *Advances in Entrepreneurship, Firm Emergence, and Growth.* JAI Press, Greenwich, CT.

von der Weppen, J. and Cochrane, J. (2012) Social enterprises in tourism: an exploratory study of operational models and success factors, *Journal of Sustainable Tourism*, **20**(3), 497-511.

Williamson, O.E., (2000) The new institutional economics: taking stock, looking ahead, *Journal of Economic Literature*, **38**(3), 595–613.

Zahra, S.A., Gedajlovic, E., Neubaum, D.O. and Shulman, J.M. (2009) A typology of social entrepreneurs: motives, search processes and ethical challenges, *Journal of Business Venturing*, **24**(5), 519 – 532.

Zizek, S. (2011) *Living the End Times*, London: Verso.

5 Hotel Middle Managers and Corporate Entrepreneurship

Cathy Burgess, Oxford Brookes University, UK

Introduction

Hotels are very complex in structure and organisation, with differing ownership patterns as well as a variety of styles, sizes and locations. With several operating departments and differing guest profiles and behaviours, the inter-relationship of products and services require individual approaches to management, even if branded and part of a chain (Burgess, 2007). In hotels, middle managers are those reporting to the General Manager within the operating unit. Often known as the Executive team, their key responsibilities are to follow senior management directives in managing their areas to optimise profitability (Burgess, 2007). Therefore, they need to have a thorough knowledge of the business and the various factors that impact on sales, costs and profitability to meet the needs of stakeholders.

These expectations have driven organisations to find new ways of doing business (Kuratko *et al.*, 2007), and corporate entrepreneurship (CE) has emerged as key strategy for management to improve innovation in products and services. CE is a `cascading yet integrated set of entrepreneurial activities at different levels' of the organisation (Hornsby *et al.*, 2009), improving performance (Kuratko *et al.*, 2007; Sebora *et al.*, 2010), profitability and thereby market value (Nicolau and Santa-Maria, 2013) to meet stakeholder expectations. It is a proactive whole-organisation approach of `organisational renewal' (Ribeiro-Soriano and Urbano, 2010) that, to be effective, requires the commitment of all levels of management. Although senior management (those in senior positions based at a corporate office) instigate innovation at a strategic level, it is middle managers' expertise and understanding of the business that enables them to identify opportunities for improvements and innovation, which may be in systems and processes, customer service or by increasing revenues or reducing costs (Hancer *et al.*, 2009). They undertake various roles as part of this entrepreneurial activity, as shown in Figure 5.1.

In CE, the industry context is important (Zahra *et al.*, 2014), with factors relevant in one industry not appropriate in others. Within hotels, the service elements are paramount for all managers, dominating all aspects of the business. Although there is extensive generic literature in the area of CE, there is only limited evidence of the importance of hotel middle managers to the implementation of CE in this complex, inter-linked industry.

The overall purpose of this chapter is to identify the key factors that encourage or inhibit CE, so you will be able to:

■ Identify the inter-related antecedents needed for effective implementation of CE;

■ Identify the key roles of middle managers in undertaking CE;

■ Comprehend the role of senior management in facilitating these antecedents.

Antecedents and barriers of CE and the influence of senior management

Profitability is a key driver of entrepreneurial activities but, in order for middle managers to undertake these, certain antecedents must be enabled by senior management. A range of authors (Ireland *et al.*, 2009, for instance) discuss different antecedents and emphasise their inter-dependence (Goodale *et al.*, 2011). Figure 5.1 demonstrates these antecedents.

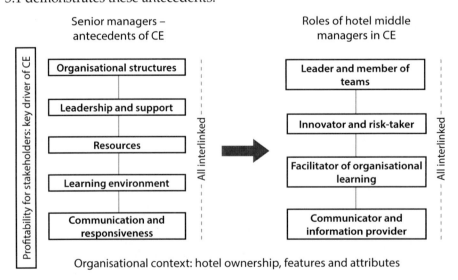

Figure 5.1: Factors affecting middle managers' ability to contribute to corporate entrepreneurship. Adapted from Burgess (2015)

The influence of organisational structures on CE

Changes in hotel ownership structures, with the separation of property, operating company and brand, have resulted in complex reporting networks and multiple stakeholders (Whittaker, 2006). These stakeholders all have different levels of interest and power (salience) within the organisation, requiring various amounts of interaction with both senior and middle management (Altinay and Miles, 2006). When very profitable, there may well be little contact from stakeholders, such as owners, banks and senior management, and managers will be allowed to take decisions themselves. However, stakeholders' involvement in the operation and expectations of information increases in times of economic difficulty (Burgess, 2012). Their demand for information requires much time and effort from middle managers and impacts on their other activities, including CE (Boesso and Kumar, 2009). These relationships can be made more difficult if stakeholders lack comprehension of the inter-relationship of different aspects of hotel operations (Burgess, 2012), resulting in a lack of effective decision-making from owners that can impact on future investment in the property.

Within hotel units, the growth of branding (Whitla *et al.*, 2007) has enabled more standardisation of products, services and systems to meet the needs of customers, managers and owners. A consequence has been increased centralisation of many functions, facilitated by improvements in technology (Burgess, 2012). This has reinforced traditional, hierarchical management structures with top-down decision-making by senior management. Although centralisation and standardisation can minimise the potential for errors (Burgess, 2012), they can also 'stifle' innovation (Hisrich *et al,*.2005:58). Middle managers in such structures may have less opportunity to be innovative, despite the expectations of senior management (Burgess, 2012). Therefore senior managers need to find ways of encouraging a more entrepreneurial culture within the confines of standard structures and systems, and of removing potential barriers to CE.

Senior management leadership and support

Senior management need to demonstrate leadership (Goosen *et al.*, 2002), not just in decision-making but also in ensuring that the various antecedents are established to facilitate the effective implementation of CE. The role of senior managers is to take decisions and give directives (Ireland *et al.*, 2009; Mongiello and Harris, 2006) but there have been criticisms that they can be `very short-termist' (Burgess, 2011), with a lack of strategic planning and an emphasis on short-term cost-cutting to boost profitability. Senior management need to have vision and to understand the impact of their decisions, taking advice from unit-based middle management.

5

They should recognise that CE can take time to show benefits (Hornsby *et al.*, 2002) and so demonstrate strategic awareness (Li *et al.*, 2009) of the impact of their decisions.

Hotel senior management want middle managers to be more entrepreneurial (Burgess, 2012). An entrepreneurial culture requires an empowering environment that encourages innovation and allows job discretion (Sebora *et al.*, 2010). Middle managers should be allowed to manage their own team activities, but top-down approaches to management mean a lack of freedom for them to do this. Middle managers must be positively encouraged to take risks and have the opportunity to test new ideas (Hancer *et al.*, 2009). They should, therefore, be able to take their own decisions even where there is a possibility of failure. However, centralised approaches to decision-making, with strong corporate controls, can result in a lack of empowerment and trust (Qiao and Wang, 2009) by senior management, resulting in middle managers being unable to take decisions. Hence this situation presents contradictions that can inhibit managers' ability to be entrepreneurial.

Resources

Senior managers need to provide the resources (Hancer *et al.*, 2009) such as systems, time and rewards, to ensure that middle managers can fulfil their own roles, including entrepreneurial activity. These resources allow middle managers to make effective decisions to control sales and costs, thereby increasing profits.

- *Systems*: Hotels rely on good systems for control of revenue generation, costs and working capital. If efficient, these can reduce the day-to-day control activities in the unit (Espino-Rodriguez and Taylor, 2006), freeing up staff to focus on customer service and innovation. For effective decision-making, managers need good information, and for this the systems must be fit for purpose and able to generate accurate data and reports as required by managers. However, the accuracy and effectiveness of systems has been of deep concern to managers in the past. For example, Burgess (2007) found that there were still huge gaps in technological systems that took time and effort deal with, and impacted on profitability.

- *Time*: Hotels are seven-day, 24-hour operations, and a long-hours culture (Brizek and Khan, 2007) is a feature of the industry, as are the complex stakeholder relationships identified above. Managers need to have time to identify opportunities and explore innovative ideas with their teams, but their responsibilities may mean that they may have insufficient time to undertake entrepreneurial – or developmental – activities (Burgess, 2011).

■ *Rewards* are cited as a key antecedent of CE by several authors (Ireland *et al.,* 2006, for example). These may be financial (Brizek and Khan, 2007), but job satisfaction, motivation and respect (Wood *et al.,* 2008) are all important to middle managers, as is professional development and the ability to learn new skills (Burgess, 2011). These opportunities can all result in career progression, also leading to increased financial rewards.

A learning environment

Middle managers need learn the skills to undertake their activities, through both informal and formal learning. Organisational learning means that all levels of staff and management learn from their experiences (Berends and Lammers, 2010) with managers encouraging members of their teams to share their knowledge and learn from each other (Yang, 2009). This learning is also known as `collective intelligence' (Goosen *et al.,* 2002), and the improved knowledge gained from learning leads to innovation (Kalyar and Rafi, 2013), which has been shown to improve products and services and therefore profits and competitive advantage (Garcia-Morales *et al.,* 2006). To be effective, organisational learning requires a culture of learning throughout the organisation (Berends and Lammers, 2010), with senior managers also required to learn from the experiences of their middle managers, reinforcing the need for effective feedback processes and communication. However, if the processes for feedback are inadequate then the learning is incomplete (Okumus, 2004).

A learning environment also requires a commitment to training and development, but there have been ongoing criticisms of the industry's attitude towards this (Burgess, 2007). Middle managers need senior management to recognise the links between improved skills and business needs, particularly in the finance area, and to provide the investment in resources and time to aid development. A lack of skills results in inadequate decision-making, with a consequent negative impact on profitability. Senior managers, therefore, must provide opportunities for learning, being informed by middle managers of the resources required, and then taking action which demonstrates that they themselves are learning from the experience.

Communication and responsiveness

Underpinning all the antecedents of CE is communication, which may be between organisational levels, within the same level, or between managers and other stakeholders. Senior management must communicate their vision (Whitla *et al.,* 2007; Ireland *et al.,* 2009) and the reasons for their strategic decisions, so that middle managers can implement these in their operational areas.

Mantere (2008) emphasises the importance of two-way communication for all organisations, and senior managers are expected to respond to feedback from middle managers; for instance on the impact of specific changes or lack of resources (Li *et al.*, 2009). Listening to feedback enables senior managers to identify what is working, and what is not, and where action needs to be taken to resolve issues (Mantere, 2008). A lack of communication, however, can result in a level of frustration amongst unit-based middle management (Burgess, 2011, 2012). If managers feel that they are not being listened to, then the sense of cohesiveness and trust of the team (Zahra *et al.*, 2012) can be compromised. Senior management, therefore, must ensure that they optimise two-way communication and minimise the factors that might inhibit communication, for CE to be effective.

The roles of hotel middle managers in CE

Middle managers undertake various roles in CE, all of which are inter-linked as shown in Figure 5.1. This section will explore these roles and identify the links between them.

Leader and member of teams

All members of the hotel management team work together to operationalise senior management decisions, manage their areas and generate profits for stakeholders, but they need to be empowered to make day-to-day decisions (Hales, 2001). Leadership of their teams is a principal attribute of middle managers (Harrington and Williams, 2004) and this teamwork means that they have a major role in encouraging entrepreneurial activities within the unit. Ribeiro-Soriano and Urbano (2010) call this 'collective entrepreneurship', but this requires them to be able to take action where needed. However, the top-down, centralised decision-making discussed earlier may mean that they have little autonomy, constraining their activities and potentially compromising their leadership roles (Burgess, 2007, 2012).

Innovator and risk-taker

As middle managers' responsibilities include profitability (Burgess, 2007), they have an incentive to find new ways of working that will enhance performance (Kuratko *et al.*, 2007). Senior management want their middle managers to be entrepreneurial (Burgess, 2012). Middle managers' comprehensive knowledge of the business means that they can work with their teams to identify opportunities for innovation, whether in cost management, customer service or generating new revenue streams. However, the conservative approach, resistance to change and lack of long-term perspectives found in hotels (Okumus, 2004), combined with standardised systems, mean that it may be difficult for them to be innovative (Costa, 2008).

Hornsby *et al.* (2009) stressed the need for managers to be able to take risks, and their knowledge enables them to identify potential risks for themselves and their teams, but the strong controls that exist in centralised hotels can counteract this need for risk-taking. Additionally, as managers are measured on their results (Burgess, 2012) on a short-term basis, and much entrepreneurial activity can take some time to show results (Hornsby *et al.*, 2002), middle managers need reassurance from senior management that they can take risks without reprisals. Therefore the need for a culture of trust is reinforced (Qiao and Wang, 2009) so managers can feel empowered to take risks and be innovative.

Facilitator of organisational learning

There are two aspects of the middle manager role in organisational learning: a critical competence of CE – the learning in teams from the experience of innovation and risk; and the personal learning to improve their skills and competencies for the benefit of the organisation and themselves (Qiao and Wang, 2009). Managers encourage their teams to learn from each other (Harrington and Williams, 2004) to identify new ways of working, and the resources that are needed to achieve this. They should then be able to report these to senior managers for action, so that all learn from the experience, which is enabled by the effective two-way communication discussed earlier.

A key feature of successful managers is a willingness to constantly learn and develop, informally and formally (Kay and Moncarz, 2007). As well as learning from each other, middle managers want to be trained and developed (Burgess, 2011). They therefore need active support at senior level, not just for skills training to enhance standards, but also for management skills to help them make better decisions and identify innovative ways of working to improve profitability.

Communicator and information provider

Middle managers receive communications from senior management on their visions and directives (Mongiello and Harris, 2006), and are then expected to communicate these to their reporting staff, converting these directives into day-to-day activities. They also communicate with their own teams in identifying opportunities to improve products, services and processes by discussing ideas and finding solutions, again facilitated by their knowledge of the business and the shared organisational learning discussed above. Managers communicate with other managers in providing, interpreting and explaining information (Burgess, 2012), hereby facilitating the planning and control processes, whether on forecasting customer volumes, identifying staffing levels or potential control issues.

Communication may be verbal or in the form of management reports generated by the systems available. To be effective in aiding decision-making and innovation, however, this information must be accurate and timely. The hotel financial controller, for instance, both provides information and acts as a 'business advisor' (Burgess, 2007) to other managers, available to give advice, analyse and interpret results and to assist in accurate forecasting. This assistance allows other managers to focus on the customer-related aspects of the business and encourages them to be more entrepreneurial.

Middle managers also communicate upwards, to both senior management and external stakeholders (deFranco, 2006), providing information about hotel performance on a regular basis (de Franco, 2006). Some stakeholders, particularly owners and banks, may have a high level of salience and be very demanding of information regarding profitability and cash flow (Burgess, 2012). If they do not understand the information provided, then they expect explanations from managers, a time-consuming task that could potentially hinder their entrepreneurial activities.

It is also beneficial for middle managers to be proactive in giving feedback to senior managers on their innovative ideas, and the resources required to achieve their objectives. In return, they need to have the confidence that they will be listened to when reporting the issues that impact on their ability to be entrepreneurial, further evidence of the need for two-way communication (Mantere, 2008), essential to CE. If this communication is limited, then a lack of support can result, seriously impacting on their ability to do their jobs, and to be innovative within their areas. Therefore, the middle manager has a role in communicating and explaining information to many constituents.

Conclusion

There is no single factor that impacts on the ability of the middle manager to be entrepreneurial. A range of antecedents are required to enable CE which must all work together to produce an appropriate environment for CE, as shown in Figure 5.1. Senior managers should recognise the antecedents relevant for their particular environment, and their inter-relationships, and that many innovative activities take time to mature. The middle manager has various inter-dependant roles to fulfil if CE is to be effective. These roles all demand considerable commitment in their relationships with other managers, senior management and external stakeholders.

In summary, therefore:

- A range of antecedents impact on the middle manager's ability to be entrepreneurial.

- Complex ownership structures result in multiple stakeholders with varied expectations, reducing the time middle managers have for innovation.

- Senior management must recognise the issues that impact on the middle managers ability to be entrepreneurial. They should take a long-term strategic approach that would ensure that the relevant antecedents are in place, rather than a short-term perspective that focuses on cost-reduction.

- Middle managers undertake a variety of roles in enabling CE.

- Senior management need to invest in systems, processes, time and professional development to optimise entrepreneurial activity and thence profitability.

- The most important factor, at all levels, is that of communication – a lack of which impacts on innovation and thence on performance and profitability.

5

Questions

1 Identify the key drivers of CE in a particular industry context.

2 Identify the antecedents of CE, and how senior management can facilitate these.

3 Identify the barriers that can inhibit CE, in a hospitality or tourism industry context.

4 Identify the various roles of middle managers in CE, and consider whether these can be viewed separately.

References

Altinay, L. and Miles, S. (2006) International franchise decision-making: an application of stakeholder theory. *The Service Industries Journal*, **26**(7), 421-436.

Berends, H. and Lammers, I. (2010) Explaining discontinuity in organizational learning: a process analysis, *Organization Studies*, **31**(8), 1045-1068.

Boesso, G. and Kumar, K. (2009) An investigation of stakeholder prioritization and engagement: who or what really counts, *Journal of Accounting and Organizational Change*, **5**(1), 62-80.

Brizek, M. and Khan, M. (2007) An empirical investigation of corporate entrepreneurship intensity in the casual dining sector, *International Journal of Hospitality Management*, **26**, 871-885.

Burgess, C. (2007). Do managers have sufficient financial skills to help them manage their areas. *International Journal of Contemporary Hospitality Management*, **19**(3), 188-200.

Burgess, C. (2011). Are hotel managers becoming more professional – the case of hotel financial controllers? *International Journal of Contemporary Hospitality Management*. June/July, **23**(5), 681-695.

Burgess, C (2012). Multiple stakeholders and middle managers: the role of the hotel financial controller. *Service Industries Journal*. **32**(1), 151-170.

Burgess, C. (2015) *Factors impacting on the ability of unit-based middle-managers to contribute to corporate entrepreneurship.* PhD thesis: Oxford Brookes University.

Costa, J. (2008) Scanning the business environment, in M. Olsen and J. Zhao (eds.), *Handbook of Hospitality Strategic Management*, Oxford: Butterworth-Heinemann, pp. 15-40.

deFranco, A. (2006) Benchmarking: measuring financial success in the hotel industry, in P. Harris and M. Mongiello (eds.), *Accounting and financial management: developments in the international hospitality industry*, Oxford: Butterworth-Heinemann, pp. 87-104.

Espino-Rodriguez, T. and Taylor, S. (2006) The perceived influence of centralising operations in chain hotels. *Tourism and Hospitality Research*, **6**(4), 251-266.

Garcia-Morales, V., Llorens-Montes, F. and Verdu-Jover, A. (2006) Antecedents and consequences of organizational innovation and organizational learning in entrepreneurship. *Industrial Management and Data Systems*, **106**(1), 21-42.

Goodale, J., Kuratko, D., Hornsby, J. and Covin, J. (2011) Operations management and corporate entrepreneurship: the moderating effect of operations control on the antecedents of corporate entrepreneurial activity in relation to innovation performance. *Journal of Operations Management*, **29**, 116-127.

Goosen, C., De Coning, T. and Smit, E. (2002) Corporate entrepreneurship and financial performance: the role of management. *South African Journal of Business Management*, **33**(4), 21-27.

Hales, C. (2001) Does it matter what do managers do? *Business Strategy Review*, 12(2), 50-58.

Hancer, M., Ozturk, A. and Ayyildiz, T. (2009) Middle-level hotel managers' corporate entrepreneurial behaviour and risk-taking propensities: a case of Didim, Turkey. *Journal of Hospitality Marketing and Management*, **18**, 523-537.

Harrington, D. and Williams, B. (2004) Moving the quality effort forward – the emerging role of the middle manager. *Managing Service Quality*, **14**(4), 297-306.

Hisrich, R., Peters, M. and Shepherd, D. (2005) *Entrepreneurship*. 6th ed., Boston: McGraw-Hill Irvine.

Hornsby, J., Kuratko, D. and Zahra, S. (2002) Middle managers' perception of the internal environment for corporate entrepreneurship: assessing a measurement scale. *Journal of Business Venturing*, **17**(2002), 253-273.

Hornsby, J., Kuratko, D., Shepherd, D. and Bott, J. (2009) Managers' corporate entrepreneurial actions: examining perception and position. *Journal of Business Venturing*, **24**(3), 236-247.

Ireland, R., Covin, J. and Kuratko, D. (2009) Conceptualising corporate entrepreneurship strategy. *Entrepreneurship Theory and Practice*, **33**(1), 19-46.

Ireland, R., Kuratko, D. and Morris, M. (2006) A health audit for corporate entrepreneurship: innovation at all levels: part I. *Journal of Business Strategy*, **27**(1), 10-17.

Kalyar, M. and Rafi, N. (2013) Organizational learning culture: an ingenious device for promoting a firm's innovativeness. *Service Industries Journal*, **33**(12), 1135-1147.

Kay, C. and Moncarz, E. (2007) Lodging management success: personal antecedents, achievements, KSAs and situational influencers. *International Journal of Hospitality Management*, **26**, 33-48.

Kuratko, D., Hornsby, J. and Goldsby, M. (2007) The relationship of stakeholder salience, organizational posture and entrepreneurial intensity to corporate entrepreneurship'. *Journal of Leadership and Organizational Studies*, **13**(4), 56-72.

Li, L., Tse, E. and Zhao, J-L. (2009) An empirical study of corporate entrepreneurship in hospitality companies. *International Journal of Hospitality and Tourism Administration*, **10**, 213-231.

Mantere, S. (2008) Role expectations and middle manager strategic agency. *Journal of Management Studies*, **45**(2), 294-316.

Mongiello, M. and Harris, P. (2006) Autonomy and control in managing network organizations: the case of multinational hotel companies, in P. Harris and M. Mongiello (eds.), *Accounting and Financial Management: Developments in the International Hospitality Industry*, Oxford: Butterworth-Heinemann, pp. 423-445.

Nicolau, J and Santa-Maria, M. (2013) The effect of innovation on hotel market value. *International Journal of Hospitality Management*, **32** (2013), 71-79.

Okumus, F. (2004) Implementation of yield management practices in service organisations: empirical findings from a major hotel group. *Service Industries Journal*, **24**(6), 65-89.

Qiao, J. and Wang, W. (2009) Managerial competencies for middle managers: some empirical findings from China. *Journal of European Industrial Training*, **33**(1), 69-80.

5

Ribeiro-Soriano, D. and Urbano, D. (2010) Employee-organization relationship in collective entrepreneurship: an overview. *Journal of Organizational Change Management*, **23**(4), 349-359.

Sebora, T., Theerapatvong, T. and Lee, S. (2010) Corporate entrepreneurship in the face of changing competition. *Journal of Organizational Change Management*, 23(4), 453-470.

Whitla, P., Walters, P. and Davies, H. (2007) Global strategies in the international hotel industry. *International Journal of Hospitality Management*, **26**, 777-792.

Whittaker, C. (2006) Sale and leaseback transactions in the hospitality industry, in P. Harris and M. Mongiello (eds.), *Accounting and Financial Management: Developments in the International Hospitality Industry* , Oxford: Butterworth-Heinemann, pp. 362–382.

Wood, C., Holt, D., Reed, T. and Hudgens, B. (2008) Perceptions of corporate entrepreneurship in air force organizations: Antecedents and outcomes. *Journal of Small Business and Entrepreneurship*, **21**(1), 117-131.

Yang, J-T, (2009) Individual attitudes to learning and sharing individual and organisational knowledge in the hospitality industry. *The Service Industries Journal*, **29**(12), 1723-1743.

Zahra, S. (2012) Organizational learning and entrepreneurship in family firms: exploring the moderating effect of ownership and cohesion. *Small Business Economics*, **38**, 51-65.

Zahra, S., Wright, M. and Abdelgawad, S. (2014) Contextualisation and the advancement of entrepreneurial research. *International Small Business Journal*, **32**(5), 479-500.

Corporate entrepreneurship through a centralised organisational structure?

Levent Altinay, Oxford Brookes University, UK

Having recognised market opportunities for growth, Hotel Group Global set itself the target of becoming established as a major force in Europe without incurring significant mid-market investment by using franchise and management contract arrangements. However, markets in this geographic region tended to lack a 'franchising culture' which hindered the growth of some hotel groups. Particularly in Europe, convincing family-run companies of the logic of a franchise or management contract was very difficult. In response to this cultural challenge, the case study organisation placed country managers into different country markets. These country managers were responsible for the identification of the franchise and management contract opportunities, and helping the Hotel Group Global to facilitate growth. Country managers, based in these host country environments, were considered to be the 'owners' of the expansion process within the company. They tended to be either local nationals or people who had lived long enough in the related country or region to know the local culture and the business context.

Moreover, in this case study organisation, the international expansion decision-making process at first sight seemed rational: decision makers followed a specific path and made the final decision based on the company's strategy, procedures and standards. Distinct stages and guidelines provided a framework for the decision-making process. This ordered process, however, was only one facet of organisational activity. Although there appeared to be an ordered process in this organisation, decisions were not simply the result of a logical step-by-step sequence of events. The process was more dynamic than this. Company strategy, procedures/standards and different people with conflicting perceptions and interpretations contributed to the expansion decision-making process and gave shape to the final decision.

Although country managers seemed to have an obvious role in assessing franchise and management contract projects confined to their geographical region, people higher up in the organisational hierarchy were often required to assess the relative merits of projects for the long-term success of the whole company. Power and authority also remained very centralised, in that everyone knew that those working at the corporate level could, and would, control and override decisions made by the country managers.

The implications of this tight control-oriented management structure were not promising. Such an approach not only limited the organisation's ability to react to the opportunities arising in the market, but also served to demotivate and frustrate the country managers. Although the centralised, tight decision-making approach aimed to preserve the system integrity and protect the brand reputation of Hotel Group Global, at the same time such a management approach resulted in isolating innovative, opportunity-seeking, entrepreneurial country managers from the mainstream of the organisation. It can therefore be concluded that organisations whose growth performance is highly dependent on having market-based organisational members in diverse host country environments need to structure differently and bring about a new way of thinking.

Case study questions:

1   What was the role of country managers in corporate entrepreneurship for Hotel Group Global?

2   How could country managers help the organisation grow in different country markets?

3   What factors created barriers to corporate entrepreneurship for the country managers?

4   How could Hotel Group Global break down these barriers to facilitate corporate entrepreneurship?

For details please see: Altinay, L. and Altinay, M. ((2004), The influence of organisational structure on entrepreneurial orientation and expansion performance, *International Journal of Contemporary Hospitality Management*, **16**(6), 334 – 344

6 Ethnic Minority Entrepreneurship

Anna Farmaki, University of Central Lancashire, Cyprus
Levent Altinay, Oxford Brookes University, UK

Introduction

The importance of small and medium-sized enterprises (SMEs) is widely rec-ognised. SMEs account for over 99% of businesses in OECD countries, 70% of employment and over half of value added (OECD, 2010). In many countries, ethnic minority owned SMEs are responsible for a considerable percentage of new business start-ups. For example, in the UK 6.3% of SMEs are ethnic minority led, contributing £25 billion to gross value added (Small Business Survey, 2010). Ethnic SMEs typically consist of two to fifty employees. They have a centralised decision-making structure whereby the members of a single ethnic family living in a host country own and manage the business (Basu and Altinay, 2002; Iyer and Shapiro, 1999) and possess limited financial, information and human resources (Altinay, 2008). Ethnic minority SMEs tend to dominate the hospitality and tour-ism industry, particularly the independent restaurant sector. The relative low entry barriers, limited skill requirements and the cultural business tradition of ethnic groups has led to an increase in the number of ethnic restaurants, takea-ways and cafes in developed countries (Basu and Altinay, 2002; Basu, 2004; Basu and Goswami, 1999).

Whilst ethnic minority SMEs are surrounded by the cultural environment of their community, relying heavily on co-ethnics for the sale of their products (Ram and Hillin, 1994), they tend to be influenced by economic, political and socio-cultural aspects of the host community (Barrett *et al.*, 2002). Ethnic minority SMEs face fierce competition not only from other ethnic minority businesses but also from mainstream businesses and brands. Major retailers, groceries and other service providers have adjusted their business strategies to target ethnic minority consumers, by selling ethnic products while attracting second generation immigrants whose needs and wants are more aligned with those of the host country.

The purpose of this chapter is to advance your knowledge on hospitality and tourism ethnic minority SMEs. Specifically, by the end of this chapter you should be able to:

- Explain the theories of ethnic minority entrepreneurship;

- Explain the immigrants' motives for self-employment;

- Evaluate how the networks of ethnic businesses influence their enterprises;

- Evaluate how the socio-cultural backgrounds of ethnic minority business owners influence their enterprises;

- Explain the strategic needs for ethnic minority businesses in order to remain competitive.

The chapter begins by presenting the theoretical background of ethnic entrepreneurship. The motives of immigrant entrepreneurship are discussed and then the relationship between ethnic networks and entrepreneurship is explored, by identifying related influential factors. Finally, the chapter considers competitive strategies that ethnic businesses can adopt to improve their performance and chances of survival.

Theories of ethnic entrepreneurship

The nature of ethnic entrepreneurship is at the centre of a long-standing debate, with theory demonstrating a strong economic-sociological influence. One stream of literature suggests that ethnic SMEs are often simultaneously founded, owned and managed by one or more ethnic minority entrepreneurs, and hence, manifest certain cultural traits which are associated with the entrepreneur's origin (Zhou, 2004). Ethos and culture are ethnic resources conducive to entrepreneurship (Werbner, 1990). Wilson and Portes (1980) proposed the *ethnic enclave theory* to discuss the interconnectedness of ethnic SMEs with a complex system of co-ethical social networks characterised by co-ethnicity, co-ethical social structures and location (Light and Karageorgis, 1994). However, as ethnic enclaves are evolving into multi-ethnic neighbourhoods and new businesses developing in affluent middle-class suburbs, with skilled and educated second generations of ethnic minorities transforming the ethnic SME landscape, this theory has begun to lose its relevancy.

Another school of thought argues that the role of ethnicity has been overstated and proposes that attention is paid to class-based relationships and the wider socio-economic context in which ethnic SMEs operate (Virdee, 2006; Deakins *et al.*, 2007). Ward (1987) suggested that ethnic entrepreneurship arises as a reaction to the structural disadvantage in the labour market, whereby structural barriers in the socio-economic context act as a driver for entrepreneurial activity. Reconciling these opposing viewpoints, Waldinger *et al.* (1990) conceptualised the *interactionism approach*, which proposes that ethnic entrepreneurship stems from the interaction of the opportunity structures in the environment with ethnic minority group characteristics. In parallel to these theories the *concept of embeddedness*, first formulated by Polanyi (1957), was proposed by Granovetter (1985) as relevant to ethnic entrepreneurship. The embeddedness approach synthesises the previously advanced notions of ethnic disadvantage, ethnic resources and opportunities and class resources. It argues that the nature, depth and extent of an individual's ties into the environment are configuring elements of businesses. Therefore, the concept advances understanding of how broader socio-economic factors promote or impede the entrepreneurial process (Karlsson and Dahlberg, 2003). Immigrant entrepreneurship depends on the interaction of socio-economic and ethno-social characteristics of the immigrant group in the opportunity structure. For example, unemployment pushes immigrants towards entrepreneurial activity in traditional sectors (retailing, restaurants and cafes) where informal production gives them a competitive advantage. Additionally, immigrant entrepreneurs tend to set up businesses within their neighbourhoods, where high concentration of their co-ethnic population exists, and which allows them to establish a co-ethnic network with easy access to information, capital and labour (Altinay, 2008).

What is generally agreed by scholars is that entrepreneurship requires means as well as motive. Motive for entrepreneurship is a dominant factor in ethnic entrepreneurship theory. Whilst immigrants tend to be over-represented in the self-employment sector, there is little consensus over the reasons for immigrants' propensity to self-employment. Motives for self-employment are discussed in the section below.

Motives for self-employment

Three sets of explanations for immigrant business entry are identified in the literature (Altinay and Altinay, 2006). The first set of explanations focuses on the disadvantage suffered by immigrants in the host country's labour market. Poor knowledge of the host country's language, lack of qualifications, lack of job market information and racial discrimination force immigrants into self-employment.

Nonetheless, the assertion that 'blocked upward mobility' in employment drives immigrants into a preferred self-employment option, opposed to unemployment, has failed to explain why some equally disadvantaged immigrant groups have higher rates of entrepreneurship than others. Similarly, cultural explanations of entrepreneurship are ignored by this set of explanations.

A second set of explanations centres on the role of ethnic resources, such as co-ethnic labour and capital, in stimulating immigrant business entry. Ethnic labour is generally regarded as cheaper, trustworthy and more hardworking, and start-up loans from family and community members may be available on favourable terms. These resources give ethnic minorities a competitive advantage. Ethnic opportunities may occur for immigrant entrepreneurs in ethnic markets that are abandoned, forgotten and underserved by the mainstream market. However, not all ethnic minorities have equal access to ethnic resources due to diverse cultural heritage and historical experience. For example, many Asian communities have a cultural tradition in business that enables them to access ethnic resources easily while reinforcing their powerful sense of identity. On the contrary, Afro-Caribbeans tend to demonstrate weak family and community ties, poor individual motivation and lack of personal resources as a result of a history of oppression.

6

A third set of explanations emphasises the role of class resources, such as ownership of private property, human capital embodied in knowledge and skills and finance for investment (Altinay and Altinay, 2008). Class resources coupled with ethnic resources are assumed to stimulate immigrant entrepreneurship. For example, Macedonian immigrants in Canada exhibited a dire economic situation due to a lack of class resources including skills, qualifications and financial capital. Such factors prevent immigrants from achieving immediate upward mobility, forcing them to occupy low-status positions. Additionally, migrants are more likely to enter self-employment as provisional employment encourages thrift and hard work in order to reach one's long-term goal of returning to the home country.

Ethnic networks and ethnic entrepreneurship

Ethnic networks consist of ethnic resources which interrelate with external opportunity structures and play a significant role in enabling immigrants to find their economic and social niches in the host society (Altinay and Altinay, 2006). These ethnic networks comprise family members and friends. The capital obtained from these networks is called co-ethnic capital; the labour recruited from these networks is co-ethnic labour; the information and advice sought from these networks is co-ethnic advice; the customer groups from these networks are co-ethnic customers.

Co-ethnic capital

Racial discrimination faced by ethnic minority enterprises limit their ability to raise funds from formal resources such as banks and to receive credit from suppliers. Inevitably, the business survival of ethnic SMEs depends greatly on access to cheap family capital and close community networks that may provide low-cost capital.

Co-ethnic labour

Co-ethnic labour enables ethnic SMEs to reduce employment costs, where family members may provide cheap labour support. The lack of qualifications of immigrant communities allow ethnic entrepreneurs privileged access to cheap co-ethnic labour. However nepotistic management tactics and decision-making may result from co-ethnic labour recruitment, leading to problems in the growth of the ethnic business.

Co-ethnic information

Information support is deemed an important element for the successful growth of a business. As ethnic minority entrepreneurs rely little on mainstream institutional information (banks, accountants, business advisors and support service providers), informal social networks become common. Strong ties with informal networks may provide competitive advantages to ethnic minority businesses.

Co-ethnic market

Ethnic minority businesses rely heavily on co-ethnic markets for selling their products, especially at the initial stages of the business. Transacting in a language that the business owner is familiar with significantly influences business growth. On the other hand, dependence on co-ethnic customers may constrain further business growth. Therefore, to enable the growth of an ethnic minority business, a strategic breakout into the mainstream market is necessary.

Business growth has also been inherently related to the socio-cultural background of ethnic entrepreneurs. Several factors influence the entrepreneurial process and may explain the promotion or impediment of business growth in ethnic SMEs and these are discussed in the following section.

Socio-cultural background and ethnic entrepreneurship

Education

Educational qualifications contribute to the growth of a business, as educated entrepreneurs may use their improved communication skills to seek external financial resources from banks and other financial institutions. On the contrary, lack of education may act as a barrier to business development, restricting market penetration; for example, intimidation by the loan application process or inability to utilise government subsidies and assistance restricts the development of managerial and technological manpower. An increased educational level positively influences the pursuit of entrepreneurial opportunities. For example, second generation Greek immigrants in Sydney expanded their family businesses successfully due to their educational qualifications, which allowed them to remain flexible and open to market opportunities. Similarly, Turkish entrepreneurs in London with higher educational attainment have responded to changing consumer needs better than those without educational qualifications, by synthesising market information and developing new products (Altinay, 2008).

A high level of education equips entrepreneurs with the communication skills, market intelligence and analytical ability required to develop appropriate strategies that positively influence business growth. Education can contribute to the fostering of good relationships with credit officers and boost the confidence of business owners, who are able to take 'calculated risks' following a business environmental audit. Also, educational attainment improves entrepreneurs' management skills by providing them with a strategic long-term vision and the ability to systematically monitor customer needs and market trends. These skills are considered important in terms of the outcome of strategic decisions associated with investment, the introduction of new products and the targeting of new market segments.

Language ability

The ability to communicate with others in the host country language is an important factor in entrepreneurship, as language ability influences social and economic integration and productivity. Strong language skills may increase the level of confidence of ethnic entrepreneurs when seeking capital from banks and other financial institutions. Knowledge of the host country language can help to meet expectations of existing and current customers and enables ethnic entrepreneurs to penetrate the mainstream market successfully. In addition, the ability to speak the host country's language reduces ethnic entrepreneurs' reliance on co-ethnic capital and information sources, allowing them to exploit mainstream business support agencies. Good language skills facilitate communication with customers, suppliers and other stakeholder groups and therefore positively contribute to the growth of the business. Language skills can also increase the likelihood of acceptance into the wider community, which education alone may fail to achieve.

Religion

Religion is an important element of society as it predisposes ethical structures, encouraging or discouraging certain behaviours. In terms of ethnic entrepreneurship, religion plays a significant role in influencing business growth. There is a widespread belief that in strongly religious countries business owners are less receptive to innovation and proactiveness (Altinay and Altinay, 2008). Fatalism is embedded in the religion of many cultures and tends to be associated with less willingness to try new technical and non-technical products and to take risk. For example, in Muslim countries people tend to believe they have little control over their destiny. Similarly, Islam religion encourages a conservative culture that leads to a risk-adverse attitude among Muslim business people. The Islamic concept of *hellal* (translated as 'accepted' by the religion) discourages retail and hospitality owners from selling alcohol and pork which are considered as *haram* (translated as 'not accepted' by the religion).

Other factors related to religion which influence entrepreneurship include the prohibition of payment of interest on bank loans. Pakistanis, for example, are less willing to integrate with western culture and consequently their businesses tend to underperform as compared to non-Muslim businesses. Evidently, the religion of the business owner constitutes a barrier to capital access from banks, as Muslim managers tend to rely on co-ethnic capital for entrepreneurial activity. On the other hand, religion can be a source of trust, confidence and loyalty between customers and entrepreneurs. Therefore, religion may offer a competitive advantage to ethnic enterprises by establishing an intra-cluster ethnic loyalty. Nonetheless, this ethnic loyalty may limit the business' penetration of the mainstream market.

Sojourning orientation

The socio-cultural ideal shared by many immigrants has led to their survival and prosperity in the host country, through long hours of work. Hard work is a value self-employed immigrants exhibit and is strongly associated with the approach of sojourning. Sojourning is associated with the willingness to suffer short-term deprivation in order to achieve the long-term objective of returning to the home country. As a result sojourners work long hours, send their savings back home and encourage thrift (Altinay and Altinay, 2006). Such cultural factors tend to positively influence business growth.

Previous experience

Previous experience equips ethnic entrepreneurs with knowledge and access to market information and business networks, therefore enabling them to identify market opportunities, improve managerial capability and diversify products and services. Acquired experience is a critical success factor in the ethnic enterprise's expansion overseas, as the business owner may capitalise on existing relationships with customers and suppliers. Moreover, previous experience may encourage the development of innovative strategies through feedback obtained from customers and suppliers as well as other stakeholders. Knowledge gained through prior experience equips entrepreneurs with the skills required for creating new capabilities and for handling new ventures. Business owners with past experience are more ready to exploit opportunities and generally have a positive attitude towards risk-taking and entrepreneurship (Altinay and Wang, 2011). For example, the previous business experience of some Turkish entrepreneurs in the UK enabled them to respond to market trends and enter new product segments by anticipating and reacting to market changes. Accumulated knowledge of customer needs and market trends enables informed decision-making as well as the confidence required to communicate and negotiate with suppliers, bank representatives and council authorities. Additionally, experience in the same line of business leads to improved management skills in the areas of budgeting, stock management and human resource management.

Besides the characteristics and backgrounds of ethnic minority firms and entrepreneurs, firm level strategies adopted affect the competitiveness and survival of these businesses. The following section of the chapter will discuss these strategies.

Competitive and survival strategies of ethnic businesses

Ethnic businesses are hindered in their ability to develop further if the entrepreneur does not respond to market conditions and fails to attract mainstream customers. Therefore, the growth of ethnic businesses is linked to the adoption of a strong market orientation. Considered as a form of strategic marketing, market orientation focuses on meeting customer needs and understanding the competitive environment by collecting and exploiting market intelligence. Consequently, a market orientation approach can lead to better business performance as a result of strong internal coordination and knowledge of customer needs and competitor tactics (Altinay, 2009).

The informal network established among ethnic entrepreneurs, who rely on co-ethnic communities for selling their products, shapes the marketing practices adopted in ethnic SMEs. Ethnic and cultural affinity in marketing transactions between ethnic entrepreneurs and co-ethnic customers is a major determinant of trust. Ethnic businesses may become a cultural exchange platform between ethnic entrepreneurs and mainstream customers, as ethnic entrepreneurs act as bicultural intermediaries. By responding to both ethnic and mainstream customers' needs, ethnic entrepreneurs develop innovative strategies which facilitate the identification of niche markets, the education of the mainstream market and the consumption of ethnic products by mainstream customers (Altinay and Altinay, 2008).

Nonetheless, different dimensions of market orientation may exist depending on several factors. For example the centralised structure of ethnic SMEs, whereby the business is managed by the owners, may lead to the creation of a close and informal relationship with customers that will enable the gathering of customer intelligence. Simultaneously an owner-led management style which fails to involve employees in the decision-making process, limits the ethnic business' ability to respond to market trends. Moreover, the lack of educational qualifications of ethnic entrepreneurs may lead to a simplistic, short-term market orientation. Nowadays, ethnic SMEs operate in an increasingly globalised environment which changes swiftly. The ability to identify the needs of both co-ethnic and mainstream customers and monitor the tactics of co-ethnic and mainstream competitors is a prerequisite for business success.

Ethnic enterprises operate in a strong socio-cultural environment where co-ethnic and mainstream customer needs and competitor tactics shape the market orientation of ethnic SMEs. Therefore, market orientation is the outcome of the interplay between changes in ethnic and mainstream business environments. As co-ethnic customers modernise and their needs evolve over time, and as mainstream competitors begin to target ethnic customers, ethnic SMEs are forced to break out of their ethnic enclaves and adopt a more competitive market orientation (Altinay, 2009). Ethnicity and ethnical identification are not static phenomena and whilst they can promote trust between ethnic entrepreneurs and co-ethnic customers at the initial stages of the business, they cannot be exploited for sustainable, long-term advantage. Therefore, a universal market orientation needs to be adopted by ethnic entrepreneurs, which should arise from the interplay between cultural embeddedness and the socio-economic environment of the host country.

Hospitality and tourism ethnic SMEs tend to adopt a market orientation which is largely influenced by the industry's characteristics. Ethnic enterprises operating in the catering sector face competition from both domestic and international competitors as well as supermarket chains selling fast food. The increasing competition in the hospitality industry entails that ethnic entrepreneurs require higher levels of market intelligence than before. Moreover, the hospitality sector has traditionally attracted entrepreneurs that have experience but limited educational qualifications. Consequently, the market orientation adopted by ethnic SMEs operating in the hospitality sector is positively or negatively impacted by industry-specific factors (Altinay, 2009).

It can be concluded that adaptation of marketing tools and techniques is required to suit the unique context and characteristics of each SME. At the initial stages of the business, ethnic SMEs may sell their products to co-ethnics if a competitive advantage is to be gained through the use of a common language when transacting or the exploitation of an informal co-ethnic network. Commitment shown to their respective ethnic communities can be a driver of business growth as customer expectations are met and relationships established. Relational marketing strategies, however, are generally inadequate in guaranteeing business success (Altinay and Altinay, 2008). Differentiated pricing, for instance, might have to be adopted to respond to price conscious ethnic customers. Similarly, innovative marketing practices are required to enable ethnic SMEs to grow by penetrating into the mainstream market. Relational marketing strategies that maximise the competitiveness and survival of ethnic SMEs are presented below.

Relationship development strategies of ethnic enterprises

☐ A family atmosphere, reinforced by small promotions, such as the offering of side products, and informal discussion with customers, is used by ethnic SMEs in attracting and retaining customers.

☐ Culturally-bound marketing stimuli are used to develop trust and relationships with ethnic and mainstream customers. Although co-ethnic customers see these stimuli as normal practice, mainstream customers perceive these as a sign of special treatment.

☐ Cultural ties and ethnic affinity promote credibility among ethnic customers and ethnic entrepreneurs by enhancing understanding and the identification of customer expectations. A sense of empathy among different ethnic customer groups is also a dominant factor in building relationships with ethnic customers.

☐ The sense of being 'local' is a factor that promotes pride and contributes to relationship development, as it reinforces mainstream customers' perception of ethnic entrepreneurs.

☐ The development of trust between ethnic entrepreneurs and ethnic and mainstream customers is influenced by the evolution of skills and competences acquired by ethnic SME owners. Whilst soft elements such as ethnicity are considered adequate for relationship building within the ethnic community, honesty and professionalism are required for the establishment of long-term relationships with the mainstream market. The quality of raw materials and a competent workforce are key ingredients to the development of relationships with mainstream customers.

☐ Common ethnic background, language and culture may act as antecedents of trust between ethnic SMEs and ethnic customers in the initial stages of relationship development. However, care in meeting unrealistic expectations from co-ethnic customers and managing the ethnic bond is needed to avoid the dissolution of relationships.

The following diagram summarises the key motives pushing ethnic minorities towards entrepreneurship, the socio-economic factors influencing entrepreneurial opportunities and access to ethnic networks, and a series of competitive strategies for improving performance.

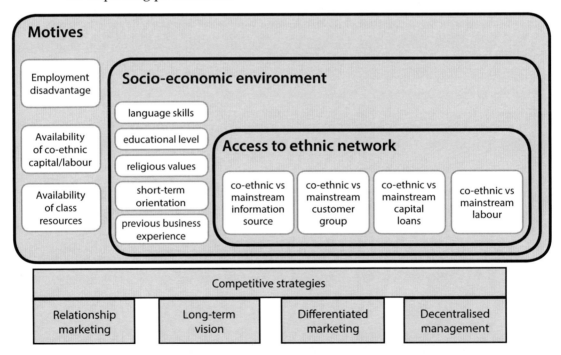

Figure 6.1: Key features in the study of entrepreneurship and ethnic minorities

Conclusion

This chapter explained the nature of ethnic entrepreneurship by presenting relevant theory and discussing the socio-cultural factors that influence ethnic SMEs. Cultural attributes of ethnic entrepreneurs, in the form of language skills, prior business experience and educational attainment, were identified as precursors of business survival and growth. In the initial stages of the business, reliance on informal ethnic networks is usual, as this reduces the cost of operation and overcomes communication obstacles in the transaction process. However, ethnic entrepreneurs need to embrace a new way of doing things if they are to remain competitive. Therefore, it is recommended that:

a) ethnic entrepreneurs assess their learning needs and attend relevant courses offered by business support units to improve their entrepreneurial orientation;

b) ethnic entrepreneurs move away from the traditional centralised management style and empower individuals who possess the appropriate educational background and experience;

c) succession of the ethnic SME by the second generation should place emphasis on educational qualifications and experience; and

d) government and community groups should offer training and short courses to help ethnic entrepreneurs capitalise on their socio-cultural strengths in order to gain a competitive advantage.

Additionally, owners of ethnic start-ups must pay attention to the extent of competition facing the business and the location in which it will operate, and should adopt creative and innovative ideas to differentiate from competition.

6

Questions

1 What is ethnic entrepreneurship and why is it important to study?

2 Which theories relate to ethnic entrepreneurship?

3 Why are ethnic minority groups inclined to become entrepreneurs?

4 How does the socio-cultural background of business owners influence their entrepreneurial orientation?

5 What strategies can strengthen the growth of ethnic minority enterprises?

Case study: The Kowalskis' restaurant

The Kowalski family moved to the UK several years ago from their native country, Poland. Pawel Kowalski was the first to move, followed by his wife Alina and their two young children. To support their family, Pawel and Alina Kowalski took up various jobs including waitressing, cleaning houses, washing cars and working in a factory. After working long hours for several years they managed to save up enough money to open up their own restaurant. Alina was a good cook and Pawel had previously owned a small mini market in his native country. Therefore, opening up a Polish restaurant in the UK seemed a reasonable idea. The couple's lack of education and employability skills had also impacted their decision to be self-employed, as in their previous jobs in the mainstream market they worked long hours and were underpaid. Entering the restaurant sector as entrepreneurs allowed them to exploit their know-how by doing something they were familiar with. Nonetheless, setting up the business proved to be challenging. Pawel and Alina could not speak English well and were unaware of the process of setting up a business in the UK. Compiling the necessary documentation took up much of their time. Equally, finding supplies from retail stores was not easy and so the family had to negotiate with Polish store owners over the prices of ingredients that were paramount in Polish cuisine. With the cost of the business start-up exceeding their original budget, Pawel and Alina decided to run the restaurant on their own, rather than hiring staff. However, over time it became obvious that balancing work life with family obligations was challenging. Pawel then decided to hire two Ukrainian waitresses but could not afford to pay them a high salary. After one month both waitresses left, with Pawel having to fill in for them until the financial situation of the business was improved. Despite the Kowalski's efforts to sustain their business the restaurant was eventually closed down. Whilst the couple worked hard to promote the restaurant in the neighbourhood, the business was not performing satisfactorily. One of the problems the business had to face was that of location. The Kowalskis decided to set up the restaurant in a neighbourhood where mostly British reside. As Polish cuisine was not well-known to the British, the Kowalskis found it difficult to appeal to the mainstream market. Similarly, the restaurant was not particularly successful with attracting the Polish community as Polish immigrants in the UK did not go out to restaurants to eat food that they could cook at home. If the Kowalskis had thought about such obstacles in advance their restaurant could have proven to be more successful.

1   What were the motives pushing the Kowalskis towards self-employment?
2   Which factors influenced the entrepreneurial opportunities available to the Kowalskis?
3   What led to the failure of their restaurant business?
4   What strategies could have been adopted to ensure the survival of the business?

References

Altinay, L. and Altinay, E. (2006) Determinants of ethnic minority entrepreneurial growth in the catering sector, *Service Industries Journal*, **26**(2), 203-221.

Altinay, L. and Altinay, E. (2008) Factors influencing business growth: The rise of Turkish entrepreneurship in the UK, *International Journal of Entrepreneurial Behaviour and Research*, **14**(1), 24-46.

Altinay, L. and Altinay, E. (2008) Marketing strategies of ethnic minority businesses in the UK, *Service Industries Journal*, **28**(8), 1183-97.

Altinay, L. (2008) The relationship between an entrepreneur's culture and the entrepreneurial behaviour of the firm. *Journal of Small Business and Enterprise Development*, **15**(1), 111-129.

Altinay, L. (2009) Market orientation of small ethnic minority-owned hospitality firms, *International Journal of Hospitality Management*, **29**(1), 148-156.

Altinay, L. and Wang, C. (2011) The influence of an entrepreneur's socio-cultural characteristics in the entrepreneurial orientation of a firm, *Journal of Small Business and Enterprise Development*, **18**(4), 673-694.

Barrett, J., Vallack, H., Jones, A. and Haq, G. (2002) *A material flow analysis and Ecological Footprint of York*. Stockholm: Stockholm Environment Institute.

Basu, A. and Goswami, A. (1999) Determinants of South Asian entrepreneurial growth in Britain: A multivariate analysis, *Small Business Economics*, **13**, 57-70.

Basu, A. and Altinay, E. (2002) The interaction between culture and entrepreneurship in London's immigrant business. *International Small Business Journal*, **20**(4), 371-394.

Basu, A. (2004) Entrepreneurial aspirations among family business owners: an analysis of ethnic business owners in the UK. *International Journal of Entrepreneurial Behaviour & Research*, **10**(1/2), 12-33.

Deakins, D., Ishaq, M., Smallbone, D., Whittam, G. and Wyper, J. (2007) Ethnic minority businesses in Scotland and the role of social capital. *International Small Business Journal*, **25**(3), 307-326.

Granovetter, M. (1985) Economic action and social structure: the problem of embeddedness. *American Journal of Sociology*, **91**, 481-510.

Iyer, G. R. and Shapiro, J. M. (1999) Ethnic entrepreneurial and marketing systems: implications for the global economy. *Journal of International Marketing*, 7(4)83-110.

Karlsson, C. and Dahlberg, R. (2003) Entrepreneurship, firm growth and regional development in the new economic geography: introduction. *Small Business Economics*, **21**(2), 73-76.

Light, I. and S. Karageorgis (1994) The ethnic economy, in N. Smelser and R. Swedberg (eds.) *Handbook of Economic Sociology*. New York: Russell Sage Foundation, pp. 646-671.

6

OECD (2010) OECD Studies on SMEs and Entrepreneurship: SMEs, Entrepreneurship and Innovation, OECD [accessed 25th September 2014] Available at: http://www.keepeek.com/Digital-Asset-Management/oecd/industry-and-services/smes-entrepreneurship-and-innovation_9789264080355-en#page1

Polanyi, K. (1957) The economy as instituted process, in Polanyi, K., Arensberg, C.M., Pearson, H.W. (Eds.), *Trade and Markets in the Early Empires.* Glencoe, IL: Free Press, pp. 243-270.

Ram, M. and Hillin, G. (1999) Achieving break-out: Developing mainstream ethnic minority businesses, *Small Business and Enterprises*, **1**, 15-21.

Small Business Survey (2010) Department of Business Innovation and Skills [accessed 25th September 2014] Available at: https://www.gov.uk/government/uploads/system/uploads/attachment_data/file/32228/11-p74-bis-small-business-survey-2010.pdf

Virdee, S. (2006), Race, employment and social change: a critique of current orthodoxies, *Ethnic and Racial Studies*, **29**(4), 605-28.

Waldinger, R., Ward, R., Aldrich, H. E. and Stanfield, J. H. (1990). *Ethnic entrepreneurs: Immigrant business in industrial societies*. University of Illinois at Urbana-Champaign's Academy for Entrepreneurial Leadership Historical Research Reference in Entrepreneurship.

Ward, R. (1987) Ethnic entrepreneurs in Britain and Europe, in Goffee, R. and Scase, R. (eds.) *Entrepreneurship in Europe*, London: Croom Helm, pp. 83-104

Werbner, P. (1990) Renewing an industrial past: British Pakistani entrepreneurship in Manchester. *Migration*, **8**, 7-41.

Wilson, K. L. and Portes, A. (1980) Immigrant enclaves: An analysis of the labor market experiences of Cubans in Miami. *American Journal of Sociology*, **86**(2) 295-319.

Zhou, M. (2004) Revisiting ethnic entrepreneurship: convergencies, controversies, and conceptual Advancements1. *International Migration Review*, **38**(3), 1040-1074.

7 Franchising and Entrepreneurship

Maureen Brookes, Oxford Brookes University, UK

Introduction

Within the marketing literature, franchising is described as a market entry mode, a channel of distribution, a vertical marketing system and a business format. What these different terms all reflect however, is a contractual agreement between two key stakeholders; a franchisor and a franchisee. One specific type of franchising, business format franchising, is a popular choice for hospitality and tourism firms seeking domestic and international expansion. Franchised firms now operate in over 160 countries worldwide (IFA, 2014) and play an important role in the growth of global entrepreneurship (Chirico *et al.*, 2011). Business format franchising is therefore recognised as a key opportunity for aspiring entrepreneurs (True *et al.*, 2003).

The purpose of this chapter is to develop your understanding of hospitality and tourism franchising from an entrepreneurial perspective. More specifically, by the end of this chapter you should be able to:

- Explain business format franchising and its growth within hospitality and tourism;
- Evaluate the potential benefits of business format franchising from different stakeholder and theoretical perspectives;
- Evaluate the role of franchisors and franchisees from an entrepreneurial perspective.

The chapter begins by defining business format franchising before examining its growth within hospitality and tourism. The potential benefits of franchising are then explained using popular franchise theories. Finally, the chapter considers the role of franchisors and franchisees as entrepreneurs, and franchising as an entrepreneurial partnership.

Business format franchising explained

In business format franchising, a franchisor develops a business concept which franchisees replicate and operate on the franchisor's behalf. The franchisor develops a brand name, a trade mark, a specific product and/or service, and a defined method for operating franchised units (Weaven and Frazer, 2003). The franchisor then sells the right to operate one or more units to franchisees for a contractually determined period of time. The franchisor normally provides the franchisee with initial training and detailed operating manuals, as well as ongoing operational, technical and marketing support. In return, the franchisee pays an upfront fee for the franchised unit and ongoing royalty fees based on a percentage of gross sales and advertising fees.

There are different variations of franchise contracts used within hospitality and tourism. While some franchisees operate as single-unit franchisees, others grow the number of units they operate sequentially over time to become multiple-unit franchisees (Grunhagen and Mittelstaidt, 2005). Some franchisors offer contracts which entitle the franchisee the rights to operate multiple franchised units (area franchise) and/or to grant these rights to third parties as sub-franchisors (master franchise) in a defined geographical territory (Brookes and Roper, 2011). These contracts often stipulate the number of units to be opened within a specified time frame. Text box 1 provides an overview and examples of the different types of franchising.

Text box 1: Types of franchising

Single Unit: a franchisee signs a contract to operate a single franchise unit. These agreements are used by franchise firms such as Pappa John's Pizza and Dairy Queen.

Multiple Unit: A franchisee signs one or more contracts to operate more than one franchise unit; units are frequently added sequentially over time. Subway franchisees frequently open subsequent units. Multi-unit franchise operators control 55% of all franchised units in the U.S.

Area Franchise (also called corporate): A franchisee signs a contract to develop and operate multiple franchised units over a defined geographical territory; development targets are frequently set by the franchisor. Yum Brands used this type of contract when entering China with the KFC franchise.

Master Franchise: A master franchisee signs a contract to operate multiple franchise units and/or sub-franchise units to other franchisees over a defined geographical territory; development targets are frequently set by the franchisor. Choice Hotels used these agreements when expanding into Europe.

The growth of franchising in hospitality and tourism

The development of the business format franchise model (as described above) is generally accredited to Ray Krok in the 1950s. Kroc recognised the ingenuity of the McDonald brothers fast-food formula for a limited menu and efficient customer service. He also identified a gap in the US market for restaurants that offered good service, value and cleanliness (mcdonalds.com, 2014). Realising the importance of maintaining quality through uniform standards of production, the business format franchise model was developed to expand McDonald's fast-food restaurants throughout the USA. This model grew rapidly in the fast-food sector as well as in quick-service restaurants, lodging and subsequently in travel and transportation, the cruise industry, campgrounds, event planning and other industrial sectors first in the USA and then internationally.

In Europe, franchising also became a popular business model. Today France, Germany and Spain boast the greatest number of franchise brands, although Belgium, Sweden and Poland have recently witnessed the largest franchise growth (EFF, 2011). In Australia, franchising began in the 1970s with the introduction of US fast-food chains like KFC and Pizza Hut and has continued to grow ever since. More recently franchising has grown rapidly in emerging markets such as Brazil, China and Turkey.

In many of these countries, hospitality and tourism franchises represent a significant proportion of the total franchise industry. In Brazil, hospitality and tourism represents approximately 27% of the franchise sector (Asgharian *et al.*, 2013). The food and beverage sector in China represents 35% of the industry (IFA, 2014) and nearly one-half of the top 100 restaurants are franchised. KFC is the leading QSR restaurant in China with over 3400 outlets in 700 cities (Herman, 2014). In Spain, the retail and restaurant sector represent 40% of the franchise industry (Polo-Redondo *et al.*, 2011) and in Saudi Arabia, 40% of the restaurant sector is franchised (Sadi and Henderson, 2011). In the USA, fast-food is the largest franchise sector and McDonalds, the largest franchisor (IFA, 2014). Hospitality and tourism franchise chains represent six of the top ten franchises in Entrepreneur's 2014 top 500 ranking and 38 of the top 100 in Franchise Direct (2014) global ranking. While most of these are food and beverage franchise chains, hotel groups such as Wyndham, InterContinental, Marriott, Hilton and Choice are also included. The on-going trend of separating hotel ownership from hotel management (Brookes and Roper, 2012) has helped to fuel franchise growth is this sector.

Business format franchising thus has its roots in hospitality and tourism and it remains a popular choice for many firms. The reasons for this popularity can be explained by the potential benefits it offers to the countries where it is established, as well as to franchisors and franchisees.

The potential benefits of franchising

National economic benefits

Some countries, such as China, are actively encouraging the development of franchising due to the economic benefits it yields (EFF, 2011). Franchising creates employment within the franchise chain and within the supply and distribution systems necessary for them to operate. It therefore contributes to tax revenues and to gross domestic product (GDP). It also encourages capital investment by the franchisee which serves to further stimulate economic growth. Within hospitality and tourism more specifically, it encourages the transfer of knowledge and innovation between countries (Hjalager, 2007) and can help contribute to local tourism development or regeneration by stimulating entrepreneurship and innovation (Mason and Duquette, 2008). It is obvious why many argue that franchising plays an important role in the creation of entrepreneurial wealth (Croonen and Brand, 2013). Through its growth, franchising contributes value to both national and global economies (Grunhagen *et al.*, 2012) as Text box 2 depicts.

Text box 2: Economic contributions of franchising

- ☐ In the USA, over 1500 franchisors operate 900,000 franchise units and employ 18 million people, generating over $2.1trillion and contributing 4.5 % of GDP (IFA, 2014).

- ☐ The Canadian franchise industry comprises 78,000 units, employs over 1 million people and contributes 10% of GDP (CFA, 2014).

- ☐ In Australia, franchising contributes 14% of GDP through 1100 franchisors with 71,400 units (Wright and Grace, 2011).

- ☐ The UK franchise industry employs 561,000 people in 39,000 outlets, has a turnover of £13.7bn, and contributes 1% of GDP (BFA, 2014).

- ☐ The Turkish franchise sector contributes US$ 35 million through 100 franchisors and 1500 franchisees (UFRAD, 2014).

- ☐ In China, experts forecast 800,000 franchised units employing over 10 million people by 2016 (Research in China, 2011).

Franchisor benefits

Franchising also offers potential benefits to franchisors. Entrepreneurial franchisors are able to grow their business through the resources of franchisees. A number of researchers explain the rationale for franchising from this perspective, using resource scarcity theory (Caves and Murphy, 1976; Norton, 1988).

Franchisees provide the financial capital to expand the franchisor's business by buying their franchised unit, enabling franchisors to expedite chain growth and gain market share. They also provide the human capital and local market knowledge required to operate franchised units (Brookes and Altinay, 2011). Access to franchisees' local market knowledge is particularly important in international franchising, where cultural and environmental differences may be great (Altinay and Wang, 2006). The more franchised units that are opened, the more brand awareness is developed and franchisors reap greater financial rewards through further unit sales, royalty fees and through realising economies of scale. Some resource scarcity theorists report that when franchisors mature and reach a financially stable position, they then buy back franchised units so that they become corporate-owned (Penard *et al.*, 2003), although there is little empirical evidence to support this ownership redirection theory.

Franchising also offers control benefits to franchisors, a key benefit that is a central tenet of agency theory. Agency theory, one of the most popular franchise theories (Perryman and Combs, 2012), explains the relationship between a principal (the franchisor) and an agent (the franchisee). As franchisees have invested in the business and make money through the profits realised, agency theorists (Brickley and Dark, 1987; Lafontaine, 1992; Castrogiovanni *et al.*, 2006) argue that franchisees have more incentive to act in the best interest of franchisors than managers of company-owned units (Grewel *et al.*, 2011). As the goals of franchisors and franchisees are aligned, franchisees are less likely to behave opportunistically and damage the franchisor brand (Kidwell *et al.*, 2007).

Franchisee benefits

Franchisees also benefit when joining a chain as they gain access to a recognised brand name, the knowledge required to operate their franchised unit, and ongoing operational and marketing support. Together these benefits mean that franchisees can open their units more quickly than if they were to establish an independent business, and they gain access to a ready-made customer base (Altinay *et al.*, 2013). As such, franchisees realise the benefit of becoming their own boss but with the support of the franchisor. Researchers investigating franchisees' motivation to join a chain identify that the ability to be your own boss is a key motivator (Knight, 1986; Stanworth and Kaufmann, 1996; Weaven and Frazer, 2006; Bennet *et al.*, 2010). Indeed franchising is often sold under the banner of 'working for yourself but not by yourself', a tagline developed by Ray Kroc to promote the original business format franchise (mcdonalds.com, 2014).

However, it is franchisees' desire for autonomy that often causes conflict in the franchise chain as it encourages franchisees to act independently. In addition, while franchisors reap financial benefits based on sales, franchisees realise financial gains through the profits generated in their units. Franchisees are tempted to respond to the demands of their customers or to free ride on the franchise brand name (Carney and Gedajlovic, 1991) or shirk their responsibilities (Brown *et al.*, 2014) in order to realise greater profits. These behaviours, which can damage the franchisor brand reputation, are well-recognised problems by agency theorists. However franchisors also act opportunistically at times (Weaven and Fraser, 2006) and these problems cause conflict between the franchise partners and impact on the realisation of franchise benefits.

Realising the benefits of franchising

In order for franchisors to realise the potential benefits identified above, they need to maintain control over franchisees and ensure they do not shirk or free ride. The franchise contract is important in achieving this control and franchise chains are often characterised by high degrees of centralisation and standardisation for control purposes (Cox and Mason, 2007). Franchisors also monitor units closely in order to maintain brand uniformity, protect the brand reputation and continue to grow their chain. Many franchisors maintain a mix of company-owned and franchised units for control purposes, a mix explained through the theory of plural distribution (Bradach, 1998; Brookes and Roper, 2012). Plural theorists argue that maintaining company-owned units enables franchisors to better understand market conditions and therefore maintain greater control over franchisees and protect brand name value (Lafontaine and Shaw, 2001). Many franchisors in the food and beverage sectors operate under this model today.

However, it is important to remember that franchisees are key stakeholders. Franchisees have local market knowledge that franchisors access as a key resource, particularly within international franchise agreements (Brookes, 2014). Franchisors must therefore determine an appropriate degree of centralisation (Windsperger, 2004) in order to use franchisees' knowledge effectively within their franchise chain. This argument suggests that both franchisors and franchisees have an entrepreneurial role to play in order to realise the potential benefits of franchising. The following section discusses these roles in further detail.

Franchising and entrepreneurship

This chapter has previously identified the importance of franchising to the growth of global entrepreneurship and the creation of entrepreneurial wealth (Croonen and Brand, 2013). True *et al.* (2003, p. 82) argue that the notion of entrepreneurship may even be the ontology (e.g. explain the existence) of franchising. In Chapter

1 you were introduced to the characteristics or traits of entrepreneurs. While researchers identify a wide range of entrepreneurial traits, there is consensus that entrepreneurs are autonomous, innovative and proactive risk-takers who demonstrate high levels of motivation (Baron, 2006). The importance of understanding entrepreneurship as a process (Gartner *et al.*, 2010) has also been identified in Chapter 2. As a process, entrepreneurship focuses on the activities and behaviours of entrepreneurs to identify, evaluate and pursue opportunities (Shane and Venkataram, 2000). In this section, the role of the franchisor and franchisee will be examined in relation to these traits and the entrepreneurial process.

Franchisors as entrepreneurs

Opportunity identification is a critical first step in the entrepreneurial process. Opportunities are 'those situations in which new goods, services, raw materials, and organizing methods can be introduced and sold for greater than their cost of production' (Shane and Venkataraman, 2000:220), although a profit is not guaranteed (Shane, 2012). Opportunities are alternatively argued to be discovered through changes in the business environment or created through entrepreneurs' interaction with the environment (Shane and Venkataraman, 2000). They are therefore considered the core ingredient of the entrepreneurial process required to generate economic value (Baron, 2006).

As explained earlier in the chapter, it is the franchisor who originally develops a business concept after identifying a new business opportunity. For example, Donna Hubbard, recognised that many women wanted to lose weight and get into shape, but disliked the atmosphere in traditional gyms. In 2003, she founded the UK's women-only Gymphobia franchise network, which now has over 40 locations and 200,000 women members. More recently, the founders of the Italian Motel K franchise, identified an opportunity for a new hotel brand which helped to meet the experiential needs of travellers.

At this stage of the process, franchisors are considered nascent entrepreneurs (Cessar, 2010). Although they have identified an opportunity, they still need to evaluate its commercial potential and determine whether, and how, to best exploit it. In business format franchising, franchisors must develop the brand name, trademark, and a method of operating the franchised units. Franchisors must also develop contracts which define the level of support provided to the franchisee and the control mechanisms that will be used. They must also develop codified manuals which document quality standards and operating procedures. A certain degree of proactivity, motivation and innovation is therefore required to turn the opportunity into a business reality.

In some countries in Europe, franchisors are also required by legislation to demonstrate the viability of the franchised units by operating them for a minimum time period. While this requirement may help franchisors to refine their concept and further test its viability, it also increases competitor risks for franchisors during this development process. Franchisors also face risks in attracting and recruiting suitable franchisees in order to exploit opportunities (Michel, 2003; Clarkin and Rosa, 2005). Franchisors therefore demonstrate a range of entrepreneurial traits throughout the entrepreneurial process of opportunity identification, evaluation and exploitation. It is not surprising therefore that there is consensus within the literature that franchisors are entrepreneurs (Ketchen *et al.*, 2011).

Franchisees as entrepreneurs

There is less agreement in the literature, however, as to whether franchisees are entrepreneurs. Some researchers who argue franchisees are not entrepreneurial, do so according to the nature of the franchise contract. This chapter has previously identified that franchisors try to minimise their risks, ensure brand uniformity and protect brand reputation by issuing contracts which require a high level of standardisation and codification (Hoy, 2008). These researchers argue therefore that any entrepreneurial activity by the franchisee is prohibited, or at least constrained (True *et al.*, 2003) by these contracts.

Franchisees have even been declared the 'antithesis of entrepreneurs' (Clarkin and Rosa, 2005:305) and there is another body of research which has examined franchisee traits relative to those of independent entrepreneurs to support this argument. This research stream reveals that compared to independent entrepreneurs, franchisees exhibit less motivation, self-reliance, (Knight, 1984), initiation and autonomy (Withane, 1991). Studies also suggest franchisees possess lower quality skills (Williams, 1999) or have less confidence in their skills and abilities (Sardy and Alon, 2007). Franchisees report joining franchise chains in order to reduce the risks generally associated with new business start-ups (Brookes and Altinay, 2011). From an entrepreneurial process perspective, Seawright *et al.* (2011) advise that franchisees lack expertise in opportunity recognition and in the evaluation of new ventures.

In contrast, other studies reveal that franchisees have similar motivations for autonomy as independent entrepreneurs (Davies *et al.*, 2011), as suggested earlier in this chapter. Many franchisees have been self-employed prior to joining a franchise chain (Watson and Johnson, 2010). They also seek fulfilment of entrepreneurial goals, particularly if they grow their number of franchised units sequentially (Grunhagen and Mittelstaidt, 2005). Other research identifies franchisees face a variety of risks when joining franchise chains. These risks relate to the realisation of profit from their investment (Kaufmann and Dant, 1999), receiving the necessary support from franchisors (Clarkin and Rosa, 2005) and franchisor failure (Michael and Combs, 2008). Risks of franchisor failure are greater when franchisors pursue goals of chain growth over recruitment of suitable franchisees (Holmberg and Morgan, 2004) and in uncertain (Grewel *et al.*, 2011) and international markets (Chen, 2010).

Franchisees are also frequently reported to be the source of innovation in franchise chains (Grewel *et al.*, 2011). This chapter has previously identified that franchisees have greater insight into local market demands. Franchisees use their local market knowledge to make adaptations to the franchisor's products or services (Gillis *et al.*, 2011) in order to meet that demand and realise greater unit profits. Brookes *et al.* (2015) also identify that franchisees make adaptations as a result of the franchisor's failure to innovate. Text box 3 identifies some of the well-known innovations of franchisees. Franchisees have also been shown to pursue first-mover advantages. In a different study by Brookes *et al.*, (2012), franchisees identified opportunities and then joined a franchise chain in order to exploit the opportunities quickly and before competitors entered the market.

Text box 3: Franchisee innovations

In the McDonalds franchise, the Big Mac, Filet-o-Fish and Egg McMuffin are all menu items created by innovative franchisees. The Big Mac, developed in 1960, became one of the chain's best-selling menu items when it was adopted by the franchisor, accounting for 19% of all sales (Mcdonalds.com, 2014).

In Hardees, a franchisee invented the breakfast biscuit which helped to increase breakfast sales to 30% of revenue across the chain.

In Pizza Hut, a franchisee developed the innovation for achieving equal distribution of pepperoni on pizzas.

In the UK, a franchisee of Esquires Coffee Houses was responsible for the introduction of open mic and comedy nights which have been replicated across the chain.

In Brazil, it was a franchisee that developed the Gringo sandwich for the Giraffas franchise, which became the 3rd best-selling sandwich on the menu.

Given the disparity in the research findings presented above, opinions as to whether franchisees are entrepreneurs therefore remain divided (Hoy, 2008). However, as there is empirical evidence to suggest that franchisees do indeed possess many of the same entrepreneurial traits as franchisors, identify opportunities, and have a role to play in exploiting those opportunities, a number of researchers argue that franchisees represent a distinct type of entrepreneur (Ketchen *et al.*, 2011).

Franchising as an entrepreneurial partnership

Recognising the potential entrepreneurial contributions of both franchisors and franchisees, some researchers argue that franchising creates an entrepreneurial partnership (Davies *et al.*, 2011; Grewel *et al.*, 2011) or unique entrepreneurial structure (Meek *et al.*, 2011). Although empirical studies are limited, some researchers have used the concept of entrepreneurial orientation (EO) to examine franchising from this entrepreneurial perspective. EO describes how a firm operates (Lumpkin and Dess, 1996) and comprises three dimensions; risk-taking, proactiveness and innovativeness (Wales *et al.*, 2013). At the firm level, risk-taking reflects the firm's willingness to support projects where the outcome is uncertain; proactivity, are actions undertaken relative to competitors; and innovativeness is the search for new solutions to the challenges faced (Dada and Watson, 2013).

Although contractual requirements for standardisation could limit EO within franchise chains, Maritz and Nieman (2006) found evidence of EO with multiple-unit franchisees in their South African study. Dada and Watson (2013) also found evidence of EO in their study of UK franchise chains. Moreover, they identified that franchisor support and contract clauses were antecedents of EO and found a positive relationship between EO and chain performance. The researchers advise that franchisors should develop flexible strategies which encourage EO within their chains to improve performance.

The need for franchise chains to innovate to remain competitive is well recognised. However, finding the appropriate level of flexibility to allow franchisees to use their entrepreneurial skills remains a challenge. Although franchisees are often the source of new knowledge or innovation, Kalnins and Mayer (2004) argue that franchisors must first filter this knowledge of local market idiosyncrasies and codify it before it can be effectively transferred and used effectively across the chain. This process also enables franchisors to test the viability of innovations across multiple markets and through codification, maintain greater uniformity across the chain. Bradach (1998) argues that the plural mix of company-owned and franchised units is best suited for this process.

Whatever types of business format franchising used, making use of franchisees' entrepreneurial talent is nonetheless important to chain performance. Davies *et al.* (2009) argue that franchisees have more belief in their entrepreneurial ability the longer they spend in their chain. Franchisees unable to use their entrepreneurial skills may lose their commitment to the franchisor. The challenge therefore is to balance franchisees' entrepreneurial ambitions with system compliance.

Conclusion

This chapter set out to explain the concept of business format franchising and demonstrate its growth within hospitality and tourism. The popularity of business format franchising was explained through the potential benefits it offers to national economies, franchisors and franchisees. These benefits can be explained through the popular theoretical explanations of franchising including resource scarcity, agency and plural form theories. It is important that the entrepreneurial contributions of both franchisors and franchisees are recognised in order to realise the potential benefits. Treating franchising as an entrepreneurial partnership so that the entrepreneurial skills of franchisees are used to increase the entrepreneurial orientation of the franchise chain can help to improve the performance of the franchise chain. Making the most of franchisees' entrepreneurial skills and ambitions is particularly important, given the growing competition within hospitality and tourism in both developed and emerging markets. The key challenge, however, is determining how to harness these skills in a way that encourages innovation within the chain to remain competitive, but at the same time protects the franchise's brand uniformity and reputation.

Questions

1 What are the distinct characteristics of business format franchising?
2 Compare and contrast the benefits of franchising from the franchisor and franchisee perspective.
3 Why are franchisors generally considered to be entrepreneurs?
4 How can franchisees contribute to a franchise network as entrepreneurs?

Case study: Little Sheep

Little Sheep is a restaurant chain that specialises in Mongolian hot pot. The parent company, Little Sheep Group, was founded in Inner Mongolia, China in 1999 as a private company. The restaurants specialise in serving hot pot, a traditional Inner Mongolian dish served in metal pots. Each hot pot is filled with hot aromatic broth and a variety of other fresh ingredients. The popularity of these hot pots was such that the chain grew rapidly throughout mainland China, Hong Kong and Macau via a plural model of ownership and franchising.

When entertaining Indonesian business clients on a trip to Shanghai, an entrepreneur was introduced to the Little Sheep brand. His clients insisted on waiting over an hour for a table at the restaurant, despite being the type of people who do not like waiting. Recognising the popularity of the Little Sheep brand in China, the growing Sino-Indonesia trade, and the size of the Chinese population in Indonesia, this entrepreneur spotted an opportunity and approached the franchisor.

Once the franchise contract was signed, the franchisee set about finding an ideal location for the first Little Sheep restaurant in Jakarta. This franchisee also had to determine how to source ingredients, particularly meat for the hot pots. In due course, a 120-seat, Little Sheep restaurant opened, but it was positioned more 'high end' than the brand in China. The franchisee had to recoup the higher cost of the meat imported from Australia and New Zealand and considered that customers would be willing to pay a higher price for the brand in Indonesia. The franchisee was correct in this assumption and the restaurant attracted people from all across Jakarta, many who became regular customers. To meet the demand from customers, a second, 140-seat restaurant was opened in another central location.

This second restaurant proved to be a success as well, so this entrepreneurial franchisee approached the franchisor again, but this time with a view to expanding the number of franchised units he operated via a master franchise agreement. The franchisee also recognised that while the upmarket restaurant concept was popular with the Chinese population, many other local people could not afford the restaurant's prices. Recognising potential demand from this sizable market, the franchisee set about developing a smaller restaurant concept. The new concept comprised an 80-seat restaurant, which required less operating space and in secondary cities in Indonesia where rents would be cheaper. In addition, menus were adapted so that set menu packages were included at a more affordable price. While the original restaurants charged around US$15.00 per head, the newer, adapted Little Sheep restaurants were able to charge around US$ 8.00 per head by using cheaper ingredients. The growth of these newer branded Little Sheep restaurants was financed through sub-franchised agreements.

Since that time, the Little Sheep restaurant chain continued to grow. It was awarded the most popular hot pot restaurant award by the Chinese Restaurant Association in 2007. It was listed on the Hong Kong Stock Exchange in 2008 and realised 2% of the dining out receipts in China in 2010. Today, Little Sheep has over 300 restaurants and has expanded further afield to the US, Canada, the UK, Japan and South Korea. In 2011, the company was acquired by Yum Brands Inc, the US fast-food franchise conglomerate for $587 million.

Case study questions

1   Explain how the franchisee demonstrated entrepreneurial characteristics during the development of the original Little Sheep Restaurant in Jakarta.

2   Identify the characteristics that make the relationship between the franchisor and franchisee an entrepreneurial partnership.

References

Asgharian, E., Dadfar, H. and Brege. S. (2013) Entrepreneurial process in franchised outlets, *Journal of WEI Business and Economic,* **2** (1), 59-104.

Altinay, L. And Wang, C. (2006) The role of prior knowledge in international franchise partner recruitment, *International Journal of Service Industry Management,* **17** (5), 430-443.

Altinay, L, Brookes, M. and Aktas, G. (2013) Selecting franchise partners: Franchisee perspectives, processes and criteria, *Tourism Management,* **37**, 176-185.

Baron, R. (2006) Opportunity recognition as pattern recognition: How entrepreneurs "connect the dots" to identify new business opportunities, *Academy of Management Perspectives,* **20** (1), 104-119.

Bennet, S., Frazer, L. and Weaven, S. (2010) What prospective franchisees are seeking, *Journal of Marketing Channels,* **17** (1), 69-87.

Bradach, J. (1998) *Franchise Organisations,* Boston: Harvard Business School Press.

Brickley, J. and Dark, F. (1987) The choice of organizational form: The case of franchising, *Journal of Financial Economics,* **18**(2), 401-420.

British Franchise Association (BFA) (2014) Franchise Industry Research: Natwest BFA Franchise Survey, Retrieved on 16 May, 2015 from http:www.thebfa.org/about-franchising/franchising-industry-research/

Brookes, M. and Roper, A. (2011) International master franchise agreements: An investigation of control from operational, relational and evolutionary perspectives, *European Journal of Marketing,* **45 (**7/8), 1253-1276.

Brookes, M. and Roper, A. (2012) Realising plural form benefits in international plural chains, *Tourism Management,* **33** (3), 580-591.

Brookes, M.and Altinay, L. (2011) Franchise partner selection: Perspectives of franchisors and franchisees, *Journal of Services Marketing,* **25** (5), 336-348.

Brookes, M. (2014). The dynamics and evolution of knowledge transfer in international master franchise agreements, *International Journal of Hospitality Management,* **36,** 52-62.

Brookes, M., Altinay, L. and Aktas, G. (2015) Opportunistic behaviour in hospitality franchise agreements, *International Journal of Hospitality Management,* **46**, 120-129.

Brookes, M., Altinay, L. and Yeung, R. (2012) Opportunity identification and evaluation in franchisee business start up. EuroCHRIE Conference, Lausanne, Switzerland, 25-27th October.

Brown, J., Krishen, A. and Dev, C. (2014) The role of ownership in managing interfirm opportunism: A dyadic study, *Journal of Marketing Channels,* **21** (1), 31-42.

Canadian Franchise Association (CFA) (2014) Retrieved on 15 May, 2015 from http://www.cfa.ca/

7

Carney, M. And Gedajlovic, E. (1991) Vertical integration in franchise systems: Agency theory and resource explanations, *Strategic Management Journal*, **12 (**8**)**, 607-629.

Castrogiovanni G., Combs, J. and Justis, R. (2006) Shifting imperatives: an integrative view of resource scarcity and agency reasons for franchising, *Entrepreneurship, Theory &Practice*, **30** (1), 23-40.

Caves, R. and Murphy, W. (1976) Franchising: Firms, Markets, and Intangible Assets, *Southern Economic Journal*, **42**(4), 572-586.

Cessar, G. (2007) Money, money, money? A longitudinal investigation of entrepreneurial career reasons, growth preferences and achieved growth, *Entrepreneurship & Regional Development*, **19** (1), 89-107.

Chen, H. (2010) The explanations of Agency Theory on international multi-unit franchising in the Taiwanese marketplace, *International Journal of Organizational Innovation*, **3**(1), 53-71.

Chirico, F., Ireland, R. and Sirmon, D. (2011) Franchising and the family firm: Creating unique sources of advantage through "familiness", *Entrepreneurship Theory and Practice*, **35** (3), 483-501.

Clarkin, J. and Rosa, P. (2005), Entrepreneurial teams within franchise firms, *International Small Business Journal*, **23** (3), 303-334.

Combs, J. and Ketchen, D. (2003) Why do firms use franchising as an entrepreneurial strategy? A meta-analysis, *Journal of Management*, **29** (3), 443-465.

Cox, J. And Mason, C. (2007) Standardisation versus adaptation: Geographical pressures to deviate from franchise formats, *The Service Industries Journal*, **27** (8), 1053-1072.

Croonen, E. and Brand, M. (2013) Antecedents of franchisee responses to franchisor-initiated strategic change, *International Small Business Journal*, **33**, DOI: 10.11.1177/0266242613499805.

Dada, O. and Watson, A. (2013) The effect of entrepreneurial orientation on the franchise relationship, *International Small Business Journal*, **31**(8), 955-977.

Davies, M., Lassar, W., Manolis, C., Prince, M. and Winsor, R. (2011) A model of trust and compliance in franchise relationships, *Journal of Business Venturing*, **26** (3), 321-340.

EFF (2011) Franchising: A vector for economic growth in Europe, Retrieved on 15th August 2015 from http://www.eff-franchise.com/spip.php?rubrique9

Franchise Direct (2014) Top 11 global franchises, Retrieved on 18th September 2015 from http://www.franchisedirect.com/top100globalfranchises/

Gartner, W., Carter, N. and Reynolds, P. (2010) Entrepreneurial behavior: Firm organizing processes, in Z. Acs & D. Audretsch (Eds.), *International handbook series on entrepreneurship*, Springer, New York: Springer, pp. 99–127.

Gillis. W., McEwen, E., Crook, T. and Michael, S. (2011) Using tournaments to reduce agency problems: The case of franchising, *Entrepreneurship Theory and Practice*, **35** (3), 427-447.

Grewel, D., Iyer, R., Javalgi, R. and Radulovich, L. (2011) Franchise partnership and international expansion: A conceptual framework and research propositions, *Entrepreneurship Theory and Practice*, **35 (**3), 533-557

Grunhagen, M., Dant, R. and Zhu, M. (2012) Consumer Perspectives on American Franchise Offerings: Variety Seeking Behaviour in China, *Journal of Small Business Management*, **50**(4), 596-620.

Grunhagen, M. and Mittelstaedt, R. (2005), Entrepreneurs or investors: Do multi-unit franchisees have different philosophical orientations?, *Journal of Small Business Management*, **43 (**3), 207-225.

Herman, M. (2014) China is hot on franchising, Retrieved 15 September from www.franchiseKnowHow.com

Hjalager, A. (2007) Stages in the economic globalization of tourism, *Annals of Tourism Research*, **34** (2), 437-457.

Holmberg, S. and Morgan, K. (2004) Retail Marketing Channel Franchise Failure A Strategic Management Perspective and Longitudinal Analysis, *Journal of Marketing Channels*, **11**(2-3), 55-76.

Hoy, F. (2008) Organizational learning at the marketing/entrepreneurship interface, *Journal of Small Business Management*, **46** (1), 152-158.

IFA (2014) International franchising. Retrieved 15th March, 2014 from www.franchise.org/

Kalnins, A. and Mayer, K. (2004) Franchising, Ownership and Experience: A Study of Pizza Restaurant Survival, *Management Science* **50**(12), 1716-1728.

Kaufmann, P. and Dant, R. (1999) Franchising and the domain of entrepreneurship research, *Journal of Business Venturing*, **14** (1), 5-16.

Ketchen,D., Combs, J. and Short, J. (2011) Is franchising entrepreneurship? Yes, no and maybe so, *Entrepreneurship Theory and Practice*, **35** (3), 583-593.

Kidwell, R., Nygaard, A. and Silkoset, R. (2007) Antecedents and effects of free riding in the franchisor-franchisee relationship, *Journal of Business Venturing*, **22** (4), 522-544.

Knight, R. (1986) Franchising from the franchisor's and franchisee's points of view, *Journal of Small Business Management*, **24** (3), 1-15.

Lafontaine, F. (1992) Agency theory and franchising Some empirical results, *Rand Journal of Economics*, **23** (2), 263-283.

LaFontaine, F. and Shaw, K. (2001) Targeting managerial control: Evidence from franchising, *Rand Journal of Economics*, **36** (1), 131-150.

Mason, S, and Douquette, H. (2008) Exploring the relationship between local hockey franchises and tourism development, *Tourism Management*, **29** (6), 1157-1165.

7

Maritz, A. and Nieman, G. (2006). Entrepreneurial orientation in a franchised home entertainment system, *SAJEMS*, **1**, 1-15.

McDonalds.com (2014) Our story, Retrieved on 15th September, 2014 from http://www.mcdonalds.com/us/en/our_story.html

Michael, S. (2003) First mover advantage through franchising, *Journal of Business Venturing*, **18** (1), 61-80.

Meek, W., Davos-Sramek, B., Baucus, M. and Germain, R. (2011) Commitment in franchising: The role of collaborative communication and a franchisee's propensity to leave, *Entrepreneurship Theory & Practice*, **35** (3), 559-581.

Michael, S. and Combs, J. (2008) Entrepreneurial failure: The case of franchisees, *Journal of Small Business Management*, **46** (1), 73-90.

Norton, S. (1988) An empirical look at franchising as an organizational form, *The Journal of Business*, **16** (2), 197-21.

Penard, T., Raynaud, E. and Saussier, S. (2003) Dual distribution and royalty rates in franchised chains: An empirical analysis using French data, *Journal of Marketing Channels*, **10** (3/4), 5-31.

Perryman, A. and Combs, J. (2012) Who should own it? An agency-based explanation for multi-outlet ownership and co-location in plural form franchising, *Strategic Management Journal*, **33** (4), 368-386.

Polo-Redondo, Y., Bordonaba-Juste, V. and Palacios, L. (2011) Determinants of firm size in the franchise distribution system, *European Journal of Marketing*, **45** (1/2), 170-190.

Research in China (2014) Retrieved on May 16 2015 from http://www.researchinchina.com/Htmls/Category6.html

Sadi, M. and. Henderson, J. (2011) Franchising and small medium-sized enterprises (SMEs) in industrializing economies: A Saudi Arabian perspective, *Journal of Management Development*, **30** (4), 402 – 412

Sardy, M. and Alon, I. (2007) Exploring the differences between franchisee entrepreneurs and nascent entrepreneurs, *International Entrepreneurship Management Journal*, **3** (4), 403-418.

Seawright, K., Smith, I., Mitchell, R. and McClendon, R. (2011) Exploring entrepreneurial cognition in franchisees: A knowledge-structure approach, *Entrepreneurship Theory & Practice*, **37** (2), 201-227.

Shane, S. and Venkataraman, S. (2000), The promise of entrepreneurship as a field of research, *Academy of Management Review*, **25** (1), 217-226.

Shane, S. (2012) Reflections on the 2010 AMR Decade Award: Delivering on the promise of entrepreneurship as a field of research, *Academy of Management Review*, **37** (1), 10-20.

Stanworth, J. and Kaufmann, P. (1996) Similarities and differences in UK and US franchise research data: Towards a dynamic model of franchisee motivation, *International Small Business Journal*, **14 (**3), 57-70.

True, S., Pelton, L. and Strutton, D. (2003) The lost frontier in entrepreneurship: aggregation, saturation and decimation of the franchising channel, *Journal of Marketing Channels*, **11** (1), 79-89.

UFRAD (2014). *National Franchise Association.* Retreived 15th May, 2014 from http:www. franchisedunyasi.com/English/index.php

Wales, W., Gupta, V. and Mousa, F. (2013) Empirical research on entrepreneurial orientation: An assessment and suggestions, *International Small Business Journal*, **31**(4), 357-383.

Watson, A. and Johnson, R. (2010) Managing the franchisor-franchisee relationship: A relational marketing perspective, *Journal of Marketing Channels*, **17 (**1), 51-68.

Weaven, S. and Frazer, L. (2003) Predicting multiple unit franchising: A franchisor and franchisee perspective, *Journal of Marketing Channels*, **10** (3/4), 53-81.

Weavin, S. and Frazer, L. (2006) Investment incentives for single and multiple unit franchisees, *Qualitative Market Research: An International Journal*, **9** (3), 225-242.

Williams, D. (1999) Why do entrepreneurs become franchisees? An empirical analysis of organizational choice, *Journal of Business Venturing*, **14** (1), 103-124.

Windsperger, J. (2004) Centralization of franchising networks: evidence from the Austrian franchise sector, *Journal of Business Research,* **57** (12), 1361-1369.

Withane, S. (1991) Franchising and franchisee behaviour: An examination of opinions, personal characteristics, and motives of Canadian franchisee entrepreneurs, *Journal of Small Business Management*, **29 (**1), 22-29.

Wright, O. and Grace, A. (2011) Trust and commitment within franchise systems: an Australian and New Zealand perspective, *Asia Pacific Journal of Marketing & Logistics*, **23**(4), 486-500.

7

8 Social Franchising

E. Hachemi Aliouche, Udo Schlentrich,
Rosenberg International Franchise Center,
University of New Hampshire, USA

Introduction

Poverty and its corollary of hunger, malnutrition, lack of education, infant mortality, poor health, etc. are still endemic in much of the world. Though much progress has been made in the fight against extreme poverty since the United Nations adopted in 2000 the Millennium Development Goals – that range from halving extreme poverty to halting the spread of HIV/AIDS and providing universal primary education – many social, economic and environmental challenges remain (United Nations, 2015). It is now increasingly recognised that the traditional methods of addressing these challenges, such as government programmes, international foreign aid, charities, etc., are not sufficient to combat durably these daunting challenges. Nor can the profit-maximising private sector alone provide inclusive and sustainable solutions for the problems of billions of impoverished and vulnerable human beings (Schwab Foundation for Social Entrepreneurship, 2013). A new approach combining social mission (such as fighting poverty) with market-based solutions is emerging. This approach is commonly referred to as *social entrepreneurship*. Because of the massive magnitude of the social, economic and environmental problems impacting billions of people worldwide, scale is a key consideration for a meaningful and lasting impact. *Social franchising* – the application of franchising to social entrepreneurship – provides a potentially effective model to multiply the impact of social enterprises to match the magnitude of these challenges.

The main objective of this chapter is to present social franchising and to show how it can help tackle intractable social, economic, and environmental problems. By the end of this chapter, you should be able to:

- Explain social entrepreneurship and why it is a promising approach to address difficult social challenges faced by billions of people worldwide;

- Appreciate the importance of franchising as a business model for entrepreneurial firms and individual entrepreneurs to expand their businesses and create value;

- Understand the promise of franchising as a potentially effective method of magnifying the impacts of social entrepreneurship;

- Identify some key issues facing social franchising that need to be addressed in order for this fledgling field to fulfill its promise.

First, we discuss the emerging field of social entrepreneurship. Then we present the franchise business model – and its record of value creation. Finally, we focus on social franchising – an emerging field combining social entrepreneurship and franchising – and its promise to help address the vast social, economic and environmental challenges still afflicting much of the world population.

Social entrepreneurship

Billions of human beings all over the world are not able to live decent and fulfilling lives because of extreme poverty and other social, economic, and environmental problems. It is estimated that over two billion people barely survive on less than $2 per day (London and Hart, 2011). Lack of economic opportunities, hunger, lack of education, child mortality, lack of health care, spread of HIV/ AIDS, malaria and other diseases, and environmental degradation continue to be endemic in many parts of the world, particularly in the developing world (United Nations, 2013). Even in the relatively prosperous countries of Europe and North America millions of people are affected by poverty, homelessness, hunger, mental illness, drug abuse, and other problems. A number of institutions, including non-governmental organisations (NGOs), government agencies, private charities, and international organisations such as UNICEF and FAO have been engaged for decades in a struggle to alleviate these problems with varying degrees of success. These organisations have had some commendable successes in reducing extreme poverty and helping improve people's lives in many parts of the world. For example, the United Nations estimates that the global poverty rate fell by half between 1990 and 2010, moving 700 million people out of extreme poverty over this period. However, much remains to be done. For example, 1.2 billion people worldwide still live in conditions of extreme poverty (United Nations, 2015).

8

As laudable as the efforts and the achievements of these aid organisations have been, an unfortunate consequence has been that many of their beneficiaries have become overly dependent on them for their everyday sustenance. Another concern is the long-term sustainability of these efforts as most of the providers (NGOs, charities, etc.) depend themselves on the generosity of donors for their financial survival. A common aspect for almost all of the aid institutions is that they are not-for-profit organisations that are dependent on public and/or private donations for their activities. More recently, an entrepreneurial approach to tackling social problems has been gaining ground. This new approach, generally referred to as social entrepreneurship, essentially applies market-based principles to solving social problems. The success of many social enterprises in helping poor people become more self-reliant, creating sustainable incomes, providing sustainable access to food, and affordable basic health care and education for people who had none, makes this approach a promising one in the struggle against social problems worldwide. This approach can also be applied to economic and environmental problems, which in many cases are related to social issues.

What is social entrepreneurship?

The social entrepreneurship literature is relatively young. Short *et al.* (2009) report that only 152 journal articles on social entrepreneurship have been published since 1991, of which 40% were in management journals. As can be expected of any emerging field, a multitude of definitions for 'social entrepreneurship' have been proposed. Dacin *et al.* (2010) discussed 37 definitions and identified four key elements, including characteristics of the entrepreneurs; operating sector, processes and resources; mission; and outcomes (Spencer, 2013). More definitions have appeared more recently. For Gidron and Hasenfeld (2012:2):

> "social enterprises are organizations that are driven by a social mission and apply market-based strategies to achieve a social or environmental purpose."

The Schwab Foundation for Social Entrepreneurship defines social entrepreneurship as:

> "the application of innovative, practical and sustainable approaches to benefit society in general, with an emphasis on those who are marginalized and/or poor."

Among other things, it involves the application of business methods and practices to produce a direct social and/or environmental impact; and it pursues financial value creation as a secondary objective, not an end in itself (Schwab Foundation for Social Entrepreneurship, 2013). Most of the proposed definitions have two elements in common: use of market-based principles and pursuit of a social mission.

The simplest definition that captures the essence of social entrepreneurship can thus be stated as:

"the application of market-based principles to solving social and environmental problems".

In recent years, a number of social enterprises have been launched around the world. These enterprises are called different names in different contexts: "market-based solutions to poverty, inclusive businesses, impact enterprises, social enterprises, or enterprises serving the Bottom of the Pyramid (BoP)" (Harvey *et al.*, 2014). These enterprises use market-based principles to address the basic needs of the poor and the underprivileged, such as providing employment and decent incomes, affordable access to goods and services, drinking water, power, and low cost healthcare and educational services.

Social entrepreneurship has recently found its way into the hospitality industry. An example of a social enterprise in the restaurant industry is Jamie Oliver's Fifteen. Its founder, Jamie Oliver, wanted to "use the magic of food to give unemployed young people a chance to have a better future" (jamieoliver.com, 2015). Jamie Oliver was thus naturally attracted by the social enterprise model and in 2002, he opened Jamie Oliver's Fifteen in London and hired 15 young apprentices. Using the same social enterprise model with its Apprenticeship Programme at its core, he has since opened two other restaurants, one in Amsterdam in 2004, and the other in Cornwall in 2006.

Jamie Oliver inspired another individual halfway across the world in Singapore – Se Teo, a high school dropout who got addicted to heroin, spent more than a decade in and out of prison and drug rehabilitation centers. After kicking his drug habit, Se Teo transformed himself into a social entrepreneur with a mission to rehabilitate delinquents and help them back into society. After a one-month internship at Jamie Oliver's Fifteen in London in 2006, Se Teo learned how to run both a kitchen and a social enterprise. A year later, he founded Eighteen Chefs, a restaurant chain located in Singapore that provides jobs and decent, sustainable incomes to ex-criminals and troubled youths. Se Teo's simple message, "You don't have to identify as a gangster, you can be a chef", inspired many former criminals. Now, his five restaurants employ about 140 people, nearly half of whom are ex-offenders. In 2012, he received Singapore's President's Challenge Social Enterprise Award, and in 2013, the Emerging Enterprise Award (BBC, 2015).

There are a large number of social enterprises operating in the developing world. As one can imagine, these are focused for the most part on the most basic and most urgent needs of the population there such as healthcare (e.g. Naya Jeevan in Pakistan, Aravind in India, Projecto Cies in Brazil); education (e.g. PlanetRead in India, Lumni in Peru); employment (e.g. Friends International in Cambodia,

Education for Employment in the Middle East, Hapinoy in the Philippines); urban development (e.g. Cinepop/Hormiga in Mexico, Waste Concern in Bangladesh); and rural development (e.g. SELCO in India, Proximity Designs in Myanmar, HSSI in the Philippines) (Schwab Foundation for Social Entrepreneurship, 2013).

To date, there have not been many social enterprises in the hospitality sector reported in developing countries. But given the evolution of social entrepreneurship in the hospitality industry in the more economically-developed countries as well as in many sectors of a number of developing countries, one can expect that it is only a matter of time before social entrepreneurship makes significant inroads into the hospitality industries of developing countries. One area where it has started to have an impact is tourism. Community-Based Tourism Initiatives (COBATI) is an example of a social enterprise focused on tourism. Founded by Uganda-born single mother Maria Baryamujura, COBATI's mission is to combat poverty and urban migration through the development of community-based tourism where rural households use their rural cultures and livelihoods to create alternative tourist attractions and experiences and provide income-generating services to the tourism industry in Uganda (Ashoka 2015).

A number of organisations have been actively promoting social entrepreneurship all over the world. These include Ashoka, the Skoll Foundation, the Omidyar Network, the Schwab Foundation for Social Entrepreneurship, Athgo, New Profit Inc., National Social Entrepreneurship Forum, Echoing Green, and the Global Social Benefit Institute, among others. A social entrepreneur who has helped promote social entrepreneurship and has had a major impact on a large number of people is Muhammad Yunus, the founder and manager of social enterprise Grameen Bank and the father of microcredit. The microfinance revolution Muhammad Yunus helped launch has allowed millions of poor people in global rural communities access small loans that significantly improved their living conditions. Yunus was awarded the Nobel Peace Prize in 2006.

As social entrepreneurship gains momentum, questions are being raised about the impact and sustainability of many social enterprises. Given the vast magnitude of the social problems that still plague billions of people all over the world, scaling a successful approach to match the magnitude of the problems is an urgent necessity. Over the last several decades, franchising has proven to be a very potent method of multiplying business operations. Applying the principles of franchising to grow and multiply successful social enterprises – *social franchising* – may provide the necessary scale to make a substantial and lasting impact in the struggle to resolve intractable global social challenges.

Franchising

The basic concept of franchising can be traced all the way back to the Middle Ages in Europe when a monarch – or a local authority – (the *'franchisor'*) offered certain persons (the *'franchisees'*) the right to collect taxes, maintain civil order, etc. in exchange for a given portion of the tax revenues collected. The earliest examples of franchise-inspired distribution systems in the United States were used by the McCormick Harvesting Machine Company and the Singer Sewing Machine Company in the 1850s (Judd and Justis, 2008). The modern form of franchising took off in earnest starting in the 1950s in the United States with the launch of several firms that are dominant franchisors today (McDonald's, KFC, International House of Pancakes, etc.). It is generally agreed that the first person in the hospitality industry to use the franchise model is Howard Johnson. Starting in the 1940s, he expanded his original ice cream business first into the Red Roof coffee shops and then further into motor lodges (Aliouche *et al.*, 2012).

Today, two major categories of franchising can be distinguished: product distribution franchising and business format franchising. The International Franchise Association (IFA) characterises product distribution franchising as a supplier-dealer relationship whereby the owner of a branded product or service (the franchisor) licenses its trademark and logo to an independent business (the franchisee – who could be an individual or a group of people) and allows them to sell its products or services. Soft drinks (Coca-Cola, etc.), automobiles (Ford Motor Company, etc.), and gasoline distribution (ExxonMobil, etc.) commonly use product distribution franchising (IFA, 2015).

Business format franchising, on the other hand, involves not only the use of the franchisor's product, service and trademark, but also all the information necessary to operate the business itself, such as the marketing plan and operation manuals. In exchange, franchisees pay franchise fees and ongoing royalty fees to the franchisor. Business format franchising is now the most common form of franchising, accounting for almost twenty times as many establishments as product distribution franchising (788,285 business format establishments vs. 39,853 product distribution establishments in 2007 in the United States) and providing more than five times as many jobs (IFA, 2011).

Business format franchising is the preferred format of franchising in the hospitality industry (Aliouche *et al.*, 2012). Data provided by Smith Travel Research (STR) indicate that out of 30,440 hotel chain properties in the USA, 85.8% are franchised. Worldwide, out of 59,185 hotel chain properties, 62.7% are franchised (STR, 2014). Quick-service restaurants accounted for more establishments, jobs, output, and value-added than any other single line of business among business format franchises. The quick service restaurant sector alone generates 25% of the economic output of the franchising sector (IFA, 2011).

A fledgling entrepreneurial business can grow by building its own establishments or by franchising. Two theoretical frameworks – resource scarcity theory and agency theory – have been used by franchising scholars to explain the motivation of business firms to franchise rather than expand through company-owned units. Resource scarcity theory postulates that franchising provides a solution to the capital, managerial and informational constraints faced by expanding business firms (Oxenfeldt and Kelly, 1968; Caves and Murphy, 1976; Norton, 1988; Carney and Gedajlovic, 1991; Shane 1996). Franchising allows the growing firm to gain access to scarce capital (the franchisee's capital) in a cost-effective way. For example, it would have cost Kentucky Fried Chicken (KFC) $450 million to establish its first 2,700 stores – a sum that was not available to KFC in the early stages of its expansion (Tikoo, 1996). Franchising allowed KFC to grow fast to the point where it is now the world's most popular chicken restaurant chain with over 18,000 outlets in 115 countries and territories around the world (KFC, 2015). Franchising also provides an efficient way to obtain the dedicated managerial expertise needed to grow the business. Because franchisees invest a significant amount of their assets and time into their units and because they have direct claims to the residual profits of their units, they have strong incentives to maximise revenues and profits, thereby generating value for the franchisor. Additionally, franchisees can provide valuable local market knowledge for a firm as it expands into new markets (Minkler, 1990).

Agency theory asserts that franchising helps mitigate the agency problems that exist whenever the owner of a business (the principal) delegates management responsibilities to an individual or an organisation (the agent) (Jensen and Meckling, 1976; Eisenhardt, 1989). Franchising helps align the interests of both the franchisor (the principal) and the franchisee (the agent) as both benefit from a successful franchise system. Franchising thus reduces shirking and opportunistic behavior by the agent that may damage the brand (Rubin, 1978; Brickley and Dark, 1987; Sen, 2001; Castrogiovanni *et al.*, 2006; Ehrmann and Spranger, 2006).

More recently, a new thesis has gained acceptance among a number of franchising scholars. The plural form thesis asserts that a hybrid system composed of a mix of company-owned and franchised units, i.e., 'plural form', is the optimal choice for businesses as it allows them to reap the benefits of both a pure company-owned structure and a pure franchised structure (Baker and Dant, 2007; Bradach and Eccles, 1989; Lafontaine and Kaufmann, 1994; Dant and Kaufmann, 2003; Dant *et al.*, 2011).

For business concept owners (the franchisors), then, the franchise business model provides compelling benefits as a vehicle for growing a business: access to lower-cost capital, motivated managerial talent, valuable local knowledge, and mitigation of agency problems.

Individuals with aspirations to start their own venture may choose to start an independent business or join an established franchise brand. Buying into a franchise system provides many valuable benefits to a budding entrepreneur: possibility to use an established brand; joining a proven business concept; franchisor-provided technical and managerial support and assistance in critical areas such as site selection, facility design and layout, inventory purchasing and control, equipment purchasing or leasing; training; quality control standards; marketing support; etc. Furthermore, a franchisee may be able to obtain better financing terms with the assistance of the franchisor. Franchising allows a budding entrepreneur "to go into business for yourself, but not by yourself" (Besthel, 2001). As entrepreneurship is inherently risky, franchising allows a prospective entrepreneur to mitigate some of the risk. However, it is not for every entrepreneur, as being part of a franchise system requires the sacrifice of some independence. Franchising would not be an appropriate choice for a fiercely independent entrepreneur.

Given the intrinsic benefits of franchising, it is to be expected that franchised businesses create more financial value than non-franchised businesses in the same sector, as shown by Aliouche and Schlentrich (2009) for the US restaurant sector and Aliouche et al. (2012) for different business sectors. Franchising has been a successful business model to grow individual businesses as well as the overall economy. The IFA estimates that in 2007 the franchising sector accounted directly or indirectly for 17.4 million US jobs (11.8% of the US total), $2.1 trillion of total US output (9.0% of the US total), and $1.2 trillion of Gross Domestic Product (9.7% of US GDP) (IFA, 2011). By 2007, franchised businesses operated 828,138 establishments in the United States. IHS Economics projects employment in the US franchise sector to grow faster than in the rest of the economy in 2015 as it did in the previous four years. It also projects that the growth of the GDP of the US franchise sector to exceed that of the US economy in 2015 (IHS Economics, 2015). Franchising is one of the fastest growing US exports. In a 2006 survey of US franchise firms, 79% reported plans to open new units outside the United States in the following three years, a 44% increase since 1996 (Schlentrich and Aliouche, 2006). Franchising is now expanding even faster globally than in the USA (Grunhagen, 2010). Franchising is now pervasive in most hospitality business sectors. Given the significant economic successes of the franchise business model, franchising is increasingly seen as a potentially effective method of scaling the impacts of social entrepreneurship. This has led to a growing interest in social franchising – the application of the franchise model to social entrepreneurship.

Social franchising

As social franchising is just emerging as a potentially powerful model, its theoretical foundations have yet to be adequately developed. At this early stage of its emergence, it appears that neither the dominant franchise theories (agency theory, resource scarcity theory) nor other alternative theories of franchising, such as institutional theory and social capital theory, are able to fully explain this new phenomenon (Tracey and Jarvis, 2007; Volery and Hackl, 2010; Spencer, 2013; Litalien, 2013;). Not surprisingly there is no agreed upon definition of social franchising as of yet (Montagu, 2002; Piggot, 2004; Tracey and Jarvis, 2007; Hackl, 2009; Zafeiropoulou and Koufopoulos, 2012; Spencer, 2013).

A number of definitions have been proposed in recent years. For Temple (2011:3):

> "social franchising is simply the application of commercial franchising methods and concepts to achieve socially beneficial ends."

For Hackl (2009:4), social franchising is the:

> "application of traditional franchise principles to social sector."

Some types of enterprises have also been defined as social franchises. *Microfranchising* is defined as:

> "a business model that, although adopting many of the business practices employed in mainstream commercial franchising, involves businesses that are affordable enough to be owned and operated by people living at the base of the economic pyramid" (Spencer, 2013:10).

Tandem franchising has been characterised as:

> "a funding and mentoring programme for franchisees from previously disadvantaged backgrounds… [that is] focused on creating an alternative funding mechanism that enables transfer of ownership over time, in tandem with achieving skills transfer through a mentoring programme" (du Toit, 2007:1).

From these proposed definitions and others, three elements appear to be fundamental in social franchising: first, it incorporates elements of commercial franchising; second, a social purpose is inherent; and third, the element of scale (and replication) is important. A simple definition that captures the essence of social franchising is that it is:

> "franchising with a social purpose" (Spencer, 2013).

Social franchising has many common features with commercial franchising. These include (Temple, 2011):

- A proven, scalable business model with defined systems and processes documented in an operating manual. This manual, often referred to as the 'bible' of the franchise system, covers the essential administrative, legal, and functional aspects of the franchise system.

- A trademark, owned by the franchisor and licensed to the franchisees for the term of the franchise relationship. The use of trademarks is a cornerstone in the franchise relationship.

- The delivery of a standardised product and/or service.

- A set of support services provided by the franchisor to the franchisees. These services may include training, quality control, advertising and marketing.

- Payment of fees by the franchisees to the franchisor. These fees may include one-time franchise fees, ongoing royalty fees, and advertising fees.

These elements are usually documented in a legally-binding franchise agreement that details the rights and responsibilities of the franchisor and the franchisees, as well as the length of the franchise agreement, geographical territory of exclusivity, fee structure, brand usage, intellectual property ownership, etc.

Social franchising, however, differs greatly from commercial franchising in some key aspects. The first obvious difference is the underlying mission of the organisation. Whereas a commercial franchise's primary goal is to generate financial returns for its owners, social franchising may have a "double bottom line": generate positive social benefits for its beneficiaries (social bottom line – generally the primary objective) and a financial bottom line (profits). This different mission may determine the types of concepts and end-users (beneficiaries vs. customers) that social franchises may target (Volery and Hackl, 2010). In social franchising, most franchisees may be social enterprises instead of individual entrepreneurs as in commercial franchising. Most participants in social franchising are more concerned with social goals than with making profits (Volery and Hackl, 2010).

These differences have practical implications for social franchises. Because of their social mission, social franchisors may be less stringent in their enforcement of quality standards, and in their recruitment and management of franchisees and employees. Though delivery of a standardised product and/or service is important in both forms of franchising, it is less so in social franchising as flexibility and adaptation to local needs in order to increase social impact are more important than brand promotion and repeat purchases. Also, because social franchisees generally do not have much capital at risk (as compared to commercial franchisees), one of the key benefits of franchising (i.e., mitigated agency problems) to the franchisor may be missing in social franchising. However, since the motivation of the social franchisee is generally providing social impact, agency problems may

8

not be a significant issue. Also, a social franchisee may not be in a position to pay the various franchise fees that are required of a commercial franchisee. It can then be expected that fees and payments to the social franchisor would be much lower than to a commercial franchisor. Furthermore, due to the nature of their mission, social franchisors are much less likely to rely on legal remedies to enforce the franchise agreement clauses.

A number of social franchises have been launched across the world. In the more economically developed countries of Europe and North America, the major motivation for social franchising is the scaling of social enterprises and the creation of employment for disadvantaged people (European Social Franchising Network, 2015). In Europe, 56 social franchises and aspiring social franchises across 12 countries were identified in 2011. The UK had the largest number with 30. Germany came next with six. It is estimated that the social franchise sector in Europe employed at least 13,000 people and had a turnover of €400 million in 2011. The average European social franchise system had 21 social franchisees. Some of the European social franchise systems had attained a significant size. Komosie's De Kringwinkel recycling shops and refurbishment business (Belgium) employed 3,861 people and Cap Markt supermarkets (Germany) employed 1,200. The growth of the social franchise systems in Europe has been accelerating. For example, whereas German social franchisor CAP Markts opened one franchise per year in 1999 and 2000, it opened 11 in 2010, growing its employees from 9 in 1999 to 1,133 in 2010 (652 of whom had disabilities). The vast majority of European social franchise systems are recent, with 80% of them having been established over the ten years prior to the ESFN study.

An example of a European social franchise system in the hospitality and tourism sector is LE MAT. Based on the successful experience of Hotel Tritone in Trieste (Italy), LE MAT developed in 2004 the concept of a social franchise network in the hospitality and tourism sectors, providing high quality accommodations while creating job opportunities for individuals who have difficulties finding employment – generally individuals with disabilities, mental illness, or drug addiction. Though the LE MAT model has historically been based on small size hotels (30-rooms) located in major cities, close to transportation facilities, it is now also aiming at creating a network of inns, hotels and B&Bs in rural areas. A crucial characteristic of the LE MAT franchise system is that its facilities must be completely accessible and usable by people with disabilities and that its management includes people with experiences of exclusion, disabilities, and discrimination. LE MAT has now ten franchised properties ('Special Places') in Italy, owned and operated by worker-owned cooperatives. Starting in Italy, LE MAT has now expanded to Sweden and is targeting other European countries as well (LE MAT, 2015).

A common instance of social franchising in the hospitality sector, especially in the USA, is when a hospitality franchise company partners with mission–driven non-profit organisations as franchisees. An example is the Ben & Jerry's PartnerShop Program. Ben & Jerry's, the ice cream maker and franchisor founded by two college dropouts in Vermont (USA) in 1978 offers PartnerShop scoop shop franchises that are independently-owned and operated by community-based non-profit organisations. Ben & Jerry waives the standard franchise fees and delivers additional support services to help these organisations succeed. The Ben & Jerry PartnerShop Program's main mission is to provide job and entrepreneurial training and opportunities to young people who may be faced with barriers to employment (Ben & Jerry, 2015). A number of other hospitality franchisors have teamed up with mission-driven franchisees, including Auntie Anne's, Popeye's, Maggie Moo's, Ponderosa, Dunkin Donuts, Nathan's, Pizza Hut and Taco Bell) (CWV and IFA, 2004).

In developing countries, social franchises have focused mainly on providing basic services to impoverished communities. An example of such a social franchise system is the one created by the HealthStore Foundation, a Minnesota-based non-profit corporation founded in 1997 by Scott Hillstrom and Eva Ombaka (HealthStore Foundation, 2015). Its mission is to provide access to essential drugs, basic healthcare, and prevention services to marginalised populations in the developing world using business models that maintain high standards, are geometrically scalable, and achieve economies of scale. In 2000, The Healthstore Foundation launched the Child and Family Wellness Shops network (CFW), a branded business format franchise system of micro-pharmacies and clinics in Kenya. The CFW outlets target the most common killer diseases including malaria, respiratory infections and dysentery. They also provide education and prevention services. The CFW network has grown to 65 locations (17 drug outlets and 48 basic medical clinics) and now treats an average of 40,000 people per month in Kenya. It has served over four million patients since its inception. The HealthStore Foundation plans to grow the CFW franchise system to reach over one million patients per year in Kenya, and to expand to Rwanda.

Another successful example of a social franchise in a developing country is the Hapinoy network in the Philippines. Launched in 2007, Hapinoy's (i.e., Happy Filipino) mission is:

> "sustainably uplifting the lives of those at the base of pyramid by empowering Nanays [Filipino mothers] to become more effective micro-entrepreneurs with the goal of eventually harnessing the store network to provide communities access to high impact products" (Hapinoy, 2015).

Based on a network of sari-sari stores (small neighborhood convenience stores), the Hapinoy Sari-Sari Store Program supports the Nanays by providing them with extensive business training, access to capital through microfinancing, and assistance with new business development. The objective is to provide sustainable incomes for Filipino mothers and families and to supply socially-needed products and services to impoverished communities, including affordable access to mobile technology, financial services, nutritious food and over-the-counter medicine. By 2015, Hapinoy had trained more than 3,000 Nanays to own and operate sari-sari stores using the Hapinoy franchise system.

Conclusion

This chapter first presented social entrepreneurship, its potential to help address intractable social challenges still faced by billions of people worldwide, and the need for scale in order for it to make a significant and lasting impact. The franchise model was then summarised, along with its record for business growth and value creation in the commercial arena. This chapter supports the notion that marrying franchising to social entrepreneurship – i.e., social franchising – may be a potentially effective method to scale the impact of social entrepreneurship.

Though social franchising is just emerging, its potential to address on a large scale the tough social challenges still afflicting most of humanity is promising. However, a number of key issues need to be addressed before it can fulfill its full potential. Some of these key issues include:

- The inclusion of a social mission alters significantly some of the features of franchising as was discussed above. Extant theories of franchising do not fully explain social franchising, so more appropriate theoretical foundations need to be developed to explain the emergence of this novel form of franchising.

- Social franchise ventures can take a number of forms, with varying degrees of the three essential elements identified earlier (social mission, franchise model, scale), as is apparent from the very distinct examples presented above. An important issue then is the determination of the optimal form for particular contexts (social need addressed, geographic location, institutional environment, business sector, etc.) and participants (non-profit organisations, for-profit businesses, international agencies, etc.).

- There are a large number of parameters for each of the three essential elements of social franchising. An important issue is the determination of which particular parameters are key success drivers and which ones are of secondary importance.

- Social entrepreneurship and social enterprises can take a variety of forms, from non-profit charitable organisations dependent on philanthropic donations to for-profit businesses with a social mission. An important issue then is how can a social franchise system be designed with enough flexibility to deal with vastly different forms of social enterprises as potential franchisees?

- Another key issue is the need to measure the impact of social franchising initiatives. To attract more franchisees, more beneficiaries, and more funding, it is essential that the social impacts of the social franchising initiatives be evaluated and it is ascertained that they do indeed create social value.

Questions

1 Compare and contrast the differences between business format franchising and social franchising.

2 How can franchising be used to improve social conditions or inequalities?

3 Identify the characteristics of Jamie Oliver's Fifteen restaurant concept that makes it a social enterprise.

4 Explain the concept of tandem franchising using a hospitality our tourism enterprise to illustrate your answer.

5 What are the current challenges facing social franchise organisations?

6 What is the approach used by Ben & Jerry's PartnerShops to support social franchising?

8

References

Aliouche, E.H., Kaen, F.R., and Schlentrich, U. (2012) The market performance of franchise stock portfolios, *International Journal of Contemporary Hospitality Management*, **24**(5), 791-809.

Aliouche, E.H. and Schlentrich, U. (2009) Does franchising create value? An analysis of the financial performance of the US Public restaurant franchisors, *International Journal of Hospitality and Tourism Administration*, **10**(2), 93-108.

Ashoka (2015) Maria Baryamujura, retrieved on 15 February 2015 from http://eastafrica. ashoka.org/fellow/maria-baryamujura.

Baker, B.L. and Dant, R.P. (2007) Stable plural forms in franchise systems: An examination of the evolution of ownership redirection research, *Working Paper* presented at 2007 EMNet Conference, Rotterdam.

Besthel, B. (2001) *An Introduction to Franchising*, IFA Educational Foundation and the Pepsi Foundation: Washington, DC. 2001.

Ben & Jerry (2015) Ben & Jerry's PartnerShop Program, retrieved on 14 February 2015 from http://www.benjerry.com/values/how-we-do-business/partnershops.

BBC (2015) Former convict cooks up social change with restaurant chain, retrieved on 15 February 2015 from http://www.bbc.com/news/business-30077649.

Bradach, J.L. and Eccles, R.G. (1989) Price, authority and trust: From ideal types to plural forms, *Annual Review of Sociology*, **15**, 97-118.

Brickley, J. Dark, F. (1987) The choice of organizational form: The case of franchising, *Journal of Financial Economics*, **18**, 401–420.

Caves, R. and Murphy, W. (1976) Franchising: Firms, markets and intangible assets, *Southern Economic Journal*, **42**, 572–586.

Carney, M. and Gedajlovic, E. (1991) Vertical integration in franchise systems: Agency theory and resources explanations, *Strategic Management Journal*, **12,** 607–629.

Castrogiovanni, G.J., Combs, J.G. and Justis, R.T. (2006) Shifting imperatives: An integrative view of resource scarcity and agency reasons for franchising, *Entrepreneurship Theory and Practice*, **30** (1), 23-40.

CWV and IFA (2004) Nonprofit-owned franchises: a strategic business approach (March 2004), Retrieved on 20 February 2015 from http://www.franchise.org/sites/default/files/ek-pdfs/html_page/nonprofit_owned_1.pdf.

HealthStore Foundation (2015) About the Healthstore Foundation, retrieved on 15 February 2015 from http://www.cfwshops.org/overview.html.

Dacin M.T., Dacin P.A. and Matear M. (2010) Social entrepreneurship: Why we don't need a new theory and how we move forward from here, *Academy of Management Perspectives*, **24**(3), 37-57.

Dant, R.P. and Kaufmann, P.J. (2003) Structural and strategic dynamics in franchising, *Journal of Retailing*, **79**, 63–75.

Dant, R.P., Grunhagen, M. and Windsperger, J. (2011) Franchising research frontiers for the twenty-first century, *Journal of Retailing*, **87** (3), 253-268.

du Toit A. (2007) The financing and mentoring of emerging franchisees through tandem franchising, *3rd International Conference on Economics and Management of Networks*, June 2007, Rotterdam

Eisenhardt, K. (1989) Agency theory: An assessment and a review, *Academy of Management Review*, 14, 57–74.

Ehrmann, T., and Spranger, G. (2006) Why do franchisors combine franchises and company-owned units?, Working paper presented at the 20th Annual Conference of the International Society of Franchising, Palm Springs, CA.

European Social Franchising Network (2015), Social franchising in Europe 2011, Retrieved on 22 February 2015 from http://www.lemat.it/en/the-brand/le-mat-europe.

Grunhagen M. (2010) Effects of US-based franchising in the developing world: A Middle-Eastern consumer perspective, *Journal of Consumer Behavior*, **9** (1), 1-17.

Gidron B. and Hasenfeld Y. (2012) Introduction in Gidron B. and Hasenfeld Y. (eds.) *Social Enterprises: An Organizational Perspective*. Hampshire, UK: Palgrave Macmillan.

Hackl, V. (2009) Social franchising – scaling social impact, Retrieved on 21 February 2015 from http://www.slideshare.net/schokocookie/social-franchising.

Hapinoy (2015) The Hapinoy Sari-Sari Store program, retrieved on 16 February 2015 from http://hapinoy.com/about/the-hapinoy-sari-sari-store-program.

IHS Economics (2015) Franchise business economic outlook for 2015, retrieved on 10 February 2015 from http://emarket.franchise.org/FranchiseBizOutlook2015.pdf.

International Franchise Association (2011) Economic impact of franchised businesses, Vol. 3, retrieved on 10 February 2015 from http://www.franchise.org/sites/default/files/ek-pdfs/html_page/EconomicImpact11_5.pdf.

Jensen, M.C., and Meckling, W.H. (1976) Theory of the firm, managerial behavior, agency costs, and ownership structure, *Journal of Financial Economics*, *October*, 305–360.

Judd, R.J. and Justis, M.C. (2008) *Franchising* (4th ed.). Mason, OH: Thompson Custom Publishing.

KFC (2015) Kentucky Fried Chicken, retrieved on 19 February 2015 from http://www.kfc.com/about/.

Koh, H., Hedge, N. and Karamchandani, A. (2014) Beyond the pioneer: Getting inclusive industries to scale, retrieved on 16 February 2015 from http://www.beyondthepioneer.org/wp-content/themes/monitor/Beyond-the-Pioneer-Report.pdf.

Jamie Oliver (2015) About Fifteen, retrieved on 16 February 2015 from http://www.jamieoliver.com/the-fifteen-apprentice-programme/about/story.

Lafontaine, F. and Kaufmann, P. (1994) The evolution of ownership patterns in franchise systems, *Journal of Retailing*, **70** (2), 97-113.

Litalien, B. (2013) 'Social franchising: A new paradigm for a global challenge', *27th Annual International Society of Franchising Conference*, Zhuhai, China, March 12-16, 2013.

London, T. and Hart, S.L. (2011) *Next Generation Business Strategies for the Base of the Pyramid*, Upper Saddle River: Pearson Education.

Minkler, L.P. (1990) An empirical analysis of a firm's decision to franchise. *Economic Letters*, **34,** 77–82.

Montagu D. (2002) Franchising of health services in developing countries, *Health Policy and Planning*, **17**(2), 121-30.

Norton, S. (1988) An empirical look at franchising as an organizational form, *Journal of Business*, **61,** 197–218.

Oxenfeldt, A.R. and Kelly, A.O. (1968) Will successful systems ultimately become wholly-owned chains? *Journal of Retailing*, **44** (49), 69–83.

8

Piggot, C. (2004) Up, up, and away. The possibilities of social franchising, *Social Enterprise*, **3**, 8-10.

Rubin, P. (1978) The theory of the firm and the structure of the franchise contract, *Journal of Law and Economics*, **21**, 223–233.

Schlentrich, U. and Aliouche, E.H. (2006) Rosenberg center study confirms global franchise growth, *Franchise World*, August, 63–65.

Schwab Foundation for Social Entrepreneurship (2013) Breaking the binary: Policy guide to scaling social innovation, April 2013.

Sen, K.C. (2001) Information asymmetry and the franchising decision, *Journal of Marketing Channels*, **8** (1/2), 91–109.

Shane, S.A. (1996) Hybrid organizational arrangements and their implications for firm growth and survival: A study of new franchisors, *Academy of Management Journal*, **39**, 216–234.

Short J.C., Moss, T.W. and Lumpkin, G.T. (2009) Research in social enterpreneurship: Past contributions and future opportunities, *Strategic Entrepreneurship Journal*, **3**, 161-94.

Spencer, E.C. (2013) Deriving meaning for 'social franchising' from commercial franchising and social enterprise. *27th Annual International Society of Franchising Conference*, Zhuhai, China, March 12-16, 2013.

STR (2014) Hotel industry foundations, October, www.strglobal.com.

Temple, N. (2011) The social franchising manual, Social Enterprise Coalition. Retrieved on 20 February 2015. Available at http://www.socialenterprise.org.uk/uploads/files/2011/11/social_franchising_manual.pdf.

Tikoo, S. (1996) Assessing the franchise option. *Business Horizons*, May-June, 78–82.

Tracey, P. and Jarvis, O. (2007) Toward a theory of social venture franchising. *Entrepreneurship Theory & Practice*, **31**(5), 667-685.

United Nations (2013) Millennium Development Goals Report, retrieved on 10 February 2015 from http://www.un.org/millenniumgoals/pdf/report-2013/mdg-report-2013-english.pdf.

United Nations (2015) Millennial Development Goals and Beyond 2015, retrieved on 10 February 2015 from http://www.un.org/millenniumgoals/poverty.shtml.

Volery, T. and Hackl, V. (2010) The promise of social franchising as a model to achieve social goals, in *The Handbook of Research on Social Entrepreneurship*. Fayolle, A. and Matley, H. (Eds.) Cheltenham, UK: Edward Elgar.

Zafeiropoulou, F. and Koufopoulos, D. (2012) The influence of relational embeddedness on the formation and performance of social franchising: An explorative qualitative analysis of four social franchises active in the UK from a social network theory perspective. 26th *Annual International Society of Franchising Conference*, Fort Lauderdale, FL, May 17-19, 2012.

Theme 3: The Growth of Entrepreneurship

Within this final theme of the textbook, we examine the growth of entrepreneurship. Specifically, the chapters in this section identify the requirements for entrepreneurial growth and the challenges faced by different stakeholders within the hospitality and tourism industry. Throughout this text, the importance of entrepreneurship to the economic prosperity of nations has been identified and many national governments undertake concerted efforts to encourage entrepreneurial behaviour and thus economic growth. Nonetheless, entrepreneurs still face a number of challenges when starting out and trying to grow their business. Research also suggests that many entrepreneurial businesses fail within their first year. These failure rates vary from country to country, with some reports placing failure rates for small–to-medium sized enterprises (SMEs) as high as 76% in South Africa and 70% in Nigeria within their first three years of operation. In the UK, 50% of new business ventures are reported to fail within 5 years and 53% in New Zealand within the first three years of operation. Understanding how entrepreneurs can overcome challenges to succeed and make it through the early, difficult years, or what has been termed the 'valley of death' (Li, 2008) is therefore important for economic growth.

Chapter 9, examines one key challenge for entrepreneurs and that is their access to capital. This chapter examines entrepreneurship within the context of SMEs and the 'equity gap' these entrepreneurial organisations face relative to larger firms. It is well recognised that SMEs are often considered risky by financial lending institutions and that loans are made on the basis of assets, rather than projected growth (Li, 2008). These constraints may create a situation of under-capitalisation which in turn, may lead to a higher risk of failure for SMEs as a result of credit constraints. This chapter examines the characteristics of SMEs, relative to larger firms, which underpin these risks, before exploring different measures implemented in the European Union to support SMEs and nurture their growth. It also examines the relatively new concept of crowdfunding to support new entrepreneurial SME enterprises. Crowdfunding is becoming a popular way for entrepreneurs to raise capital funds from individuals seeking to invest their funds in different ventures. For example, US firm iCrowdHotels Inc. allows entrepreneurs to raise funds for hotel development and individuals to invest in hotel portfolios online and to track their progress. The concept of crowdfunding is explained within the chapter with examples provided of SMEs who have closed their equity gap through this fundraising medium. Other government-driven initiatives to support SME development and growth are also explored.

Chapter 10 investigates a different capital requirement of entrepreneurs – that of social capital. The importance of social capital in facilitating access to persons important to the success of entrepreneurial ventures has been identified by entrepreneur researchers (Baron and Markman, 2003). This chapter, however, considers the importance of social capital within the tourism industry. Recognising that many enterprises within the tourism industry are small and resource constrained, the author argues the importance of social capital and its physical, human and knowledge assets for economic growth through tourism. An argument is also presented of the need for public-private partnerships to provide this social capital within developing economies. The way that public and private organisations can work collaboratively is demonstrated through a case study of Kenya and the collaboration between the government and a private organisation, Adventure Alternative. Through tourism development, Adventure Alternative provides social and economic support to the communities in which it operates.

The concept of social capital is also explored in Chapter 11, but this time in relation to entrepreneurial networking processes. The importance of social networks has been identified in Theme 1 and the theoretical perspectives of entrepreneurship in relation to ethnic minority entrepreneurship in Chapter 6. Research has shown that successful entrepreneurs have large networks of professional and social acquaintances (Kontinen and Ojala, 2011). In Chapter 11, however, the critical role of social networks in the start-up and continued development of tourism enterprises is examined. More specifically, the author explores how different network elements support tourism entrepreneurs. Key arguments are illustrated using a variety of international tourism entrepreneur examples that demonstrate the value of networking to support entrepreneurial growth. The chapter concludes with an Italian case study that demonstrates how networking processes and the local environment can facilitate the development of tourism destinations.

The final chapter of this textbook, examines how hospitality and tourism entrepreneurs can face and overcome the challenges of natural disasters. Unfortunately, most of us are familiar with what seems to be a growing number of natural disasters that impact upon many tourism destinations. In this chapter, the author identifies and explains the different impacts that such disasters have on tourism destinations and the tourism enterprises that operate within these destinations. The author also explains how tourism destinations and individual entrepreneurs can prepare for disastrous events. A range of recovery strategies to help small tourism businesses to overcome or mitigate the impact of disasters is also identified. Practical approaches to disaster recovery are illustrated through a case study of Gippsland in Australia.

Dr Maureen Brookes, Oxford Brookes University, UK

References

Baron, R. and Markman, G. (2003) Beyond social capital: the role of entrepreneurs; social competence in their financial success. *Journal of Business Venturing*, **18**, 41-60.

Kontinen, T., and A. Ojala (2011) International opportunity recognition among small and medium sized family firms, *Journal of Small Business Management*, **49**(3), 490-514.

Li, L. (2008) A review of entrepreneurship published in the hospitality and tourism management journals, *Tourism Management*, **29**, 1013-1022.

9 Nurturing Small and Medium-Sized Enterprises in Europe

Mark Camilleri, University of Malta

Introduction

Tourism is one of the world's major industries, responsible for economic growth, foreign exchange earnings, employment opportunities and regional balances in individual countries and across regions. This industry generates over 5% of the European Union (EU) gross domestic product and has strong linkages with other economic sectors. In fact, tourism triggers infrastructural developments that are related to the industry, such as airports, seaports, parks, roads and rails. Within the EU alone, the tourism sector consists of about 1.8 million businesses. Most of these tourism businesses are small and medium-sized enterprises (SMEs) and together employ 5.2% of the total European workforce; that translates to approximately 9.7 million jobs, with a significant proportion of young people (EU, 2010). This chapter considers relevant academic literature that differentiates SMEs from their larger counterparts. It maintains that small businesses are often constrained by their size and limited resources. Arguably, the accessibility to finance is one of the most critical factors for the SMEs' inception and growth. These entities are often viewed by financial institutions as relatively risky when compared to enterprises from other industries. Therefore, this chapter contends that tourism SMEs may easily find themselves in an equity gap where it may prove very difficult to raise capital for further investment. Consequently, national governments and other regulatory stakeholders are increasingly stepping in to support micro and small enterprises in many contexts. In this light, the European Union (EU) has reaffirmed its commitment for SMEs. As a matter of fact, the EU has drafted the Small Business Act in 2008 and refined it again in 2011. The EU's commitment is quite evident from their frequent calls for research and training schemes in the subject areas of SMEs and tourism; where grants are frequently issued under the Marie Curie and Cordis FP7 programmes. Therefore, this chapter identifies specific policies and initiatives that are aimed at fostering a climate for job creation and competitiveness for SMEs in Europe. By the end of the chapter you should be able to:

■ Define SMEs in the European Union context;

■ Distinguish the differences between small and medium-sized enterprises and large firms;

■ Learn about the European Union measures that support the financing needs of SMEs;

■ Be knowledgeable of crowdfunding as an alternative form of financing.

SMEs in tourism

The European Union has set its own criteria for SMEs, as illustrated in Figure 9.1.

Company category	Employees	Turnover (€)	Balance Sheet (€)
Medium	< 250	≤ € 50 m	≤ € 43 m
Small	< 50	≤ € 10 m	≤ € 10 m
Micro	< 10	≤ € 2 m	≤ € 2 m

Figure 9.1: EU Definition of Small and Medium-sized Enterprises. (Source: EU, 2003/361/EC; EU, 2015a)

These ceilings apply to the figures that represent individual firms. According to the above criteria, most businesses in Europe can be classified as SMEs as over 99% of enterprises employ fewer than 250 individuals (EU, 2015a). The terminology of what constitutes small or medium-sized organisations in tourism may vary in the literature (Storey, 1994; IC, 2011). For instance, in Canada small enterprises are defined as companies that have 99 employees or fewer, whereas the medium-sized enterprises are defined as those that have between 100 and 499 employees. The size of the enterprise is usually measured in terms of their staff count, sales turnover and/or profitability. Generally, SMEs may be regarded at sectorial level. Where in some industries the firms may be considered small, in others they are simply not recognised as SMEs.

There are many parameters which have often been used in the past to identify SMEs. In past academic literature, many authors have used multi-dimensional concepts of SMEs. For example, Storey (1994) maintained that there are issues about uncertainty, evolution and growth, entrepreneurial leadership and informality which are important differentiating factors. However, the broad parameters which often categorise SMEs may not always be derived from the size perspective. Arguably, an organisation employing five people and another employing 100 can both be classified as SMEs. Yet, both companies can behave significantly differently in their approaches and practices. The small and medium-sized firm may not always be a 'smaller' version of the larger firm. The numerous theories relating to SMEs must consider all the distinctive variables which distinguish them from their larger counterparts. The most common and easiest criterion to define SMEs and to differentiate them from the larger firms is by using different thresholds, as illustrated in Figure 9.1 above.

Characteristics of tourism SMEs

SMEs have a desire for independence, freedom from intervention and bureaucracy. Smaller businesses tend to exhibit less formal structures as they have looser control systems, less documentation on transactions and fewer procedural hurdles (Morris *et al.*, 2002). It may appear that there is better communication in such firms since the owner or manager is closer to the workforce. Therefore, the owner-manager of the smaller firm may be better placed to lead the organisation and to make the best decisions in the interest of all employees (Storey, 1994). For these reasons, SMEs may offer interesting work prospects as there can be closer social relationships between management and employees. This informal style of management may also translate to better communications with other stakeholders.

Moreover, SMEs can offer more varied duties and responsibilities, as employees may participate in different kinds of work in a stable workplace. The familiar environment is usually characterised by infrequent industrial disputes. The absence of trade unionism is particularly conspicuous among smaller businesses. An empirical study among small and medium-sized Chinese firms revealed that there are relatively fewer SMEs experiencing unionisation (Zheng et al., 2009). In SMEs there may be fewer strikes since the collective element needed for strike action is absent and the potential conflict may be expressed through more individualistic means of protest such as absenteeism and labour turnover (Carraher, 2011). Some of the characteristics of SMEs as opposed to their larger counterparts are laid out in Figure 9.2.

Strategic orientation	SMEs	Large firms
Consolidated	Independence	Group
		Joint ventures
		Alliances
	Internally financed	Externally financed
	Cash limited	
	Multi-tasking	Diversified
	Flexibility	Rigidity
	Economies of scope	Economies of scale
	Owner-management	External management

Strategic orientation	SMEs	Large firms
Emerging	Competitiveness-keeper	Competitiveness-maker
	Informality	Formalised
	Invisible to the media	Visible to media and NGOs
	Largely local	National
		Multinational
		Global
	Relational	Transactional
	Personal Relationship	Structured relationship
	Trust	Branded
	Openness	

Figure 9.2: Characteristics of Different Firms. (Source: Russo and Perrini, 2010)

On the other hand, some empirical studies have demonstrated that tourism SMEs can offer poorer economic rewards, employment terms and physical working conditions, and a lower level of job security when compared to larger enterprises (Davidson *et al.*, 2006). Other findings reveal that the quality of the job environment is much poorer within smaller firms than it is within larger businesses (Nadiri and Tanova, 2010). Moreover, it may appear that SME owner-managers often "lack the necessary skills, expertise or resources to function efficiently and effectively" (Ritchie and Crouch, 2003:141). As firms grow, they start employing more individuals to act as managers or supervisors (Kusluvan *et al.*, 2010). Within large organisations, there is a clear distinction between ownership and management, as described in agency theory (Ramon Rodrigues, 2002). Moreover, the employees of the bigger enterprises often enjoy superior employment packages and better perquisites than those employees working in small businesses. Small firms frequently lack the required resources; comprising both the financial capital and human competencies (Altinay *et al.*, 2013). The very size of small businesses often creates a special condition, which is referred to as `resource poverty'. This factor distinguishes SMEs from the larger corporations (Morrison and Teixeira, 2004; Getz and Carlsen, 2005).

Financing of SMEs

Small firms tend to find themselves in an equity gap, where sometimes it can prove quite hard to acquire capital finance for further investment. Although banks are key providers of finance for many enterprises through the provision of loans; unsecured bank finance is very limited. Therefore, the SMEs' growth into viable investment opportunities may be severely restricted. Cashflow-based lending is relatively rare and growing businesses rarely have unused security at their disposal. Tourism SMEs are very reliant on personal savings to finance their business (IC, 2011). The main source of financing during the start-up phase is usually through personal savings, with more SMEs in tourism industries using this source (EU, 2014). SMEs in tourism industries are significantly more likely to make use of lease financing and significantly less likely to use retained earnings (IC, 2011). Moreover, SMEs in tourism industries are almost twice as likely as SMEs in non-tourism industries to use informal financing (loans from friends and family) to finance their ongoing operations (IC, 2011). This issue could be an indication that tourism SMEs may encounter more difficulty in obtaining credit from financial institutions than SMEs in non-tourism industries. As a result they will inevitably need to turn to alternative means of financing their business (i.e., either through personal savings and/or informal financing).

Despite the changing debt market, one of the main reasons why small businesses fail to acquire debt finance is due to their inability to provide adequate and sufficient collateral. Even small businesses with high growth potential can experience difficulties in raising relatively modest amounts of risk capital. Moreover, certain external forces and potential threats in the business environment can impact harder on the small businesses than on the larger corporations. Changes in government regulations, tax laws, labour legislation and interest rates may potentially affect a greater percentage of expenses for the smaller businesses than they do for their larger counterparts.

Throughout the years, the EU has dedicated several funds to help enterprises. Recently, the EU's Enterprise and Industry Division has reiterated the importance of improving access to finance for SMEs. On the 2nd May 2013, the European Commission/European Investment Bank (EIB) joint report maintained that their support for SMEs has reached €13 billion in 2012. In addition, the Commission funded guarantees that have helped 220,000 small businesses across Europe as it mobilised loans that were worth more than €13 billion. This interesting development led to numerous funding schemes as well as to the new generation of financial instruments that support SMEs' financing needs. In addition to these financial resources that were made available to SMEs, there was a €10 billion injection in the European Investment Bank's (EIB) capital. Moreover, the EU Commission has also launched a new single online portal on all financial instruments (for SMEs) as well as an information guide to promote SMEs' stock listings. It has committed itself to boost its support for SMEs through various financing programmes, as illustrated in Figure 9.3.

EU programme for the Competitiveness of Enterprises and Small and Medium-sized Enterprises (COSME)	Guarantees for loans up to EUR 150 000 to small and medium-sized enterprises.
Competitiveness and Innovation Framework Programme (CIP)	Supports innovation activities (including eco-innovation).
InnovFin Programme (Horizon 2020)	Loans and guarantees to innovative businesses. Financing of research & development projects. Equity (early and start-up phase).
The SME instrument	Funding and coaching support to innovative SMEs.
Creative Europe	Loans to small and medium-sized enterprises in the cultural and creative sectors.
Programme for Employment and Social Innovation (EaSI)	Microloans up to EUR 25,000 to micro-enterprises and vulnerable persons who wish to set up or develop a micro-company. Equity up to EUR 500,000 to social enterprises.

Figure 9.3: EU Measures that support SMEs. (Adapted from EU, 2015b; Welcome Europe, 2014)

Evidently, Europe is responding to the contentious issues facing SMEs by providing a mix of flexible, financial instruments under programmes such as the Competitiveness and Innovation Framework Programme (CIP), Progress Microfinance, the Risk Sharing Instrument (FP7), EIB loans and Structural Funds. For example, the EU allocated a budget of €2.3bn specifically to bolster the Competitiveness of Enterprises and Small and Medium-sized Enterprises

(COSME) for the period between 2014 to 2020. This initiative has been designed to support European SMEs in four key areas: developing entrepreneurship; helping SMEs access finance; supporting SMEs who wish to internationalise their business; and reducing the legislative and regulatory burden on SMEs. Almost 220,000 SMEs have benefited from the Commission's Competitiveness and Innovation Framework Programme (CIP) as it helped them through the provision of collateral for their loans. EU (2013a) envisaged that for every euro that was dedicated to loan guarantees, it has in turn stimulated €30 in bank loans. CIP has helped to mobilise over €13 billion of loans and €2.3 billion of venture capital for SMEs across Europe (EU, 2014). An example of a project that has been co-funded by the Eco-Innovation initiative under the auspices of the EU's CIP is featured below.

Text box 1: A CIP-funded project

MOVE-IT was supported by the EU's CIP funding. This project was made up of various organisations, namely; Stockholm Environment Institute from Tallinn (Estonia), KATE (Germany), Eco-Counseling Enterprise (Belgium), Groupe One (Belgium), TIME Foundation (Bulgaria), Aeoliki Ltd (Cyprus) and Menschels Vitalresort (Germany) (EU, 2015c).

MOVE-IT developed and tested eco-innovative coaching and learning models that helped many tourism SMEs to acquire an Eco-Management Audit Scheme (EMAS) certification and Eco-labels. It provided service packages for its clients, "by linking cultural, economic, ecological and social aspects" (EU, 2015c).

Some of the outcomes of MOVE-IT included the provision of coaching on environmental sustainability; vocational training for regional development agents and consultants; an online platform for communication, e-learning and coaching at European level (that was available in six languages); the preparation of cluster management guides that explained how to make an excellent tourist destination in terms of local governance and environmental performance; and the development of web-based tools and green software that facilitated integrated management systems.

The European Commission launched a consultation programme (between the 3rd October to 31st December 2013) to explore the costs and benefits of 'crowdfunding' as an alternative form of finance (EU, 2013b). Contributions were sought from competent authorities, crowdfunding platforms, entrepreneurs and individuals who launched crowdfunding campaigns. This new form of financing entails the collection of funds through small contributions from many parties in order to raise capital for a particular project or venture. This latter source of financing has the potential to bridge the equity gap many start-ups face. It is hoped that this recent initiative stimulates entrepreneurship amid different regulatory, supervisory, fiscal and social structures of the European Union. Apparently, the EU is delving through extant national legal frameworks to understand better how businesses can raise their capital through such open forms of financing. Whilst some crowdfunding campaigns are local in nature, there may be others who are already benefiting from easier access to financing within the single European market. In a similar vein, the United States' Securities and Exchange Commission (SEC) is also considering crowdfunding. Crowdfunding was incorporated in Jumpstart Our Business Startups Act (Stemler, 2014). It is very likely that the proposal for crowdfunding will bring a major shift in how small U.S. companies can raise their money in the private securities market.

Alternative sources of finance which are already secured via the internet include monetary contributions in exchange for rewards, product pre-ordering, lending and/or investment. Arguably, these plans can be successful only if the regulatory costs are kept as low as possible. Otherwise, small enterprises may not be intrigued by such financing propositions. From the outset, it may appear that crowdfunding is still not so popular among tourism SMEs. However, there are start-ups that have taken advantage of such financing programmes. A case in point is Outski Inc., as this innovative start-up is still raising its capital requirements through public fundraising (see Text box 2). Probably one of the main causes of concern about crowdfunding will be the reporting requirements for small companies to file their annual financial statements. The most experienced entrepreneurs and their intermediaries will have no difficulty in meeting crowdfunding rules and regulations, but first-time entrepreneurs may require further support. At present, the smaller businesses earning revenues (and profits) below a certain threshold are not legally obliged to provide audited financial statements. Moreover, small enterprises may not always hold historical financials. This means that financial services authorities will find it quite daunting to determine how small companies are truthful and fair in their financial reporting. According to the US proposals, the businesses that opt for crowdfunding as a source of financing will have to audit their annual accounts (Stemler, 2013). In a similar vein, the European enterprises would have to meet certain regulations to acquire this new source of finance. It is hoped that facilitative, soft-law measures on crowdfunding will lead to fruitful legislative and regulatory actions across many contexts. Through crowdfunding, more capital will be unlocked for start-ups, investments and projects. This additional capital finance will also help to spur the economic growth of SMEs.

Text box 2: Crowdfunding for etourism

Outski Inc., an information communications technology (ICT) enterprise that is based in Tucson, Arizona, has already raised more than $629,000 of its seed financing requirements through crowdfunding (Crowdfunder, 2015). This start-up enables its users to plan and save for their future vacations by setting aside a portion of the employees' pay-cheques for their future vacations. Therefore, Outski offers B2B solutions that are related to employee incentives and benefit packages with an integrated vacation savings account.

Employees can search and book flights and hotels through Outski's site. There is also a social element to this site, where vacation plans can be shared with family and friends. Outski's site (or app) allows people to discuss vacation ideas and share links and reviews. What differentiates Outski from other travel sites is that its users can set up savings accounts and plan for their future trips. They can also add funds to their account through their own credit and/or savings accounts or through PayPal. Users can send and request money from each other and have the ability to withdraw funds at any time. Their money is accessible through an Outski Visa or Discover Travel Savings Card, which has a PIN and works like any other debit or credit card.

Outski has partnered with 14 different companies and all of those companies are integrated into its website. Most of the partnerships deal with financial elements of the site, but there are also companies like Expedia and Amazon. In 2014, the company launched its beta web product with over 1,000 users and has also developed an iOS app for iphones.

Conclusion

No longer are smaller businesses considered as reactive and peripheral forces in terms of innovation, employment and productivity. This chapter has provided a definition of SMEs in the European context. It discussed how these enterprises possess certain characteristics that set them apart from big businesses. SMEs are often constrained by their organisational size and their limited, scarce resources. Very often these entities may find themselves in an equity gap as they may find it difficult to access finance to start up or grow their business. This chapter has featured some relevant EU practitioner-oriented policies and instruments that are helping European SMEs to raise capital for further investment. It is hoped that this chapter informs readers on how small and medium-sized enterprises can access finance through EU institutions. Indeed, the wider European political initiatives that bring economic growth, jobs and competitiveness may not be realised without the contribution of all SMEs, including those in the tourism sector.

9

Questions

1   What is the difference between a micro, small and medium-sized enterprise in Europe?

2   What are the key characteristics of SMEs that differentiate them from larger enterprises?

3   Explain the term 'equity gap'.

4   Identify the key challenges faced by start-up SMEs.

5   Explain how crowdfunding can help SMEs to overcome start-up challenges.

References

Altinay, L, Brookes, M. and Aktas, G. (2013) Selecting franchise partners: Franchisee perspectives, processes and criteria, *Tourism Management*, **37**, 176-185.

Carraher, S. M. (2011) Turnover prediction using attitudes towards benefits, pay, and pay satisfaction among employees and entrepreneurs in Estonia, Latvia, and Lithuania, *Baltic Journal of Management*, **6**(1), 25-52.

Crowdfunder (2015) Travel and Tourism. Retrieved on 18th January from https://www.crowdfunder.com/crowdfunding/travel-and-tourism.

Davidson, M., Guilding, C. and Timo, N. (2006) Employment, flexibility and labour market practices of domestic and MNC chain luxury hotels in Australia: Where has accountability gone?, *International Journal of Hospitality Management*, **25**(2), 193-210.

EU (2003) Structure, performance and competitiveness of European tourism and its enterprises. Retrieved on 18th January 2015 from http://ec.europa.eu/enterprise/sectors/tourism/files/studies/structure_performance_competitiveness/pwc_en.pdf.

EU (2003/361/EC) SME definition. Retrieved on 18th January 2015 from http://eurlex.europa.eu/LexUriServ/LexUriServ.do?uri=OJ:L:2003:124:0036:0041:EN:PDF.

EU (2010) Communication from the Commission to the European Parliament, the Council, the European Economic and Social Committee and the Committee of the Regions - Europe, the world's No 1 tourist destination – a new political framework for tourism in Europe. Retrieved on 18th December 2014 from http://eur-lex.europa.eu/legal-content/EN/TXT/?uri=CELEX:52010DC0352.

EU (2013a) European Commission Enterprise and Industry: Improving access to finance for SMEs: key to economic recovery- IP/13/387. Retrieved on 18th January 2015 from http://europa.eu/rapid/press-release_IP-13-387_en.htm.

EU (2013b) European Commission Enterprise and Industry: Public consultation: Crowdfunding in Europe? Exploring the added value of potential EU action.

Retrieved on 18th January 2015 from http://ec.europa.eu/internal_market/finances/crowdfunding/.

EU (2014) CIP success stories (on Youtube). Retrieved on 12th January from http://ec.europa.eu/cip/successstories/index_en.htm.

EU (2015a) What is an SME? Retrieved on 13th February, 2015 from http://ec.europa.eu/enterprise/policies/sme/facts-figures-analysis/sme-definition/index_en.htm.

EU (2015b) Access to Finance. Retrieved on 12th January 2015 from http://europa.eu/youreurope/business/funding-grants/access-to-finance/index_en.htm.

EU (2015c) Environmental Compliance Assistance Programme for SMEs: Small, clean and competitive. Retrieved on 28th January 2015 from http://ec.europa.eu/environment/sme/cases/moveit_en.htm.

Getz, D. and Carlsen, J. (2005) Family business in tourism: state of the art, *Annals of Tourism Research*, **32**(1), 237-258.

Hall, C.M. (ed.) (2007) *Pro-poor Tourism*. Clevedon, New Zealand: Channel View.

IC (2011) Industry Canada: Financing profiles: Small and medium-sized enterprises in tourism industries. Retrieved on 10th January 2015 from https://www.ic.gc.ca/eic/site/061.nsf/eng/02245.html.

Kusluvan, S., Kusluvan, Z., Ilhan, I., and Buyruk, L. (2010) The human dimension a review of human resources management issues in the tourism and hospitality industry, *Cornell Hospitality Quarterly*, **51**(2), 171-214.

Morris, M. H., Schindehutte, M., Walton, J., and Allen, J. (2002) The ethical context of entrepreneurship: Proposing and testing a developmental framework, *Journal of Business Ethics*, **40**(4), 331-361.

Morrison, A. and Teixeira, R. (2004) Small business performance: a tourism sector focus, *Journal of Small Business and Enterprise Development*, **11**(2), 166-173.

Nadiri, H. and Tanova, C. (2010) An investigation of the role of justice in turnover intentions, job satisfaction, and organizational citizenship behavior in hospitality industry, *International Journal of Hospitality Management*, **29**(1), 33-41.

Ramón Rodríguez, A. (2002) Determining factors in entry choice for international expansion. The case of the Spanish hotel industry, *Tourism Management*, **23**(6), 597-607.

Ritchie, J. B. and Crouch, G. I. (2003) *The Competitive Destination: A Sustainable Tourism Perspective*, Cabi Publishers, Wallingford, UK.

Russo, A. and Perrini, F. (2010) Investigating stakeholder theory and social capital: CSR in large firms and SMEs, *Journal of Business Ethics*, **91**(2), 207-221.

Stemler, A.R. (2013) The JOBS Act and crowdfunding: Harnessing the power—and money—of the masses, *Business Horizons*, **56**(3), 271-275.

Storey, D.J. (1994) *Understanding the Small Business Sector*, Routledge, London.

9

Welcome Europe (2014) European Funds for the tourism sector, Retrieved on the 6th January 2015 fromhttp://www.welcomeurope.com/fact-of-the-day/european-funds-tourism-sector-211+111.html.

Zheng, C., O'Neill, G., and Morrison, M. (2009) Enhancing Chinese SME performance through innovative HR practices, *Personnel Review*, **38**(2), 175-194.

10 Tourism Entrepreneurship and Social Capital

Victoria Waligo, Middlesex University, UK

Introduction

Given that the tourism sector is dominated by small firms, tourism development is increasingly linked to the entrepreneurial behaviour of tourism businesses. Tourism entrepreneurship has made significant contributions to tourism destinations through the range of products and services offered in the accommodation, transportation, visitor attraction, travel organising and entertainment sectors. The potential of tourism as an engine for economic and social development underscores the importance of access to various forms of capital for small tourism enterprises, particularly in developing countries (UNWTO, 2011). One type of capital that is important is social capital – one that enables the acquisition of other capital assets to achieve economic development and good governance (Putnam, 1993; Larsen *et al.*, 2004). Tourism entrepreneurship presents opportunities for bottom-up approaches to tourism development since tourism relies on local conditions, e.g. the physical infrastructure and the labour market (Ateljevic, 2009). However, social capital accumulation is fundamental to achieving socio-economic goals.

This chapter examines the relationship between tourism entrepreneurship and social capital in recognition of 'new' forms of tourism and entrepreneurship. By the end of the chapter you should be able to:

- Understand key trends in tourism entrepreneurship;
- Appreciate the contribution of social capital to tourism entrepreneurship;

- Consider investment in social capital and adaptation to local contexts as logical processes of tourism entrepreneurship in developing/remote destinations.

The chapter begins with a review of tourism entrepreneurship and the role of social capital before the nexus between the two concepts is discussed. The chapter then describes a case study of tourism entrepreneurship in Kenya, East Africa before drawing conclusions.

Tourism entrepreneurship: key trends

Entrepreneurship symbolises value creation with a potential change to the status quo in the market – an innovative process which Schumpeter (1934) referred to as creative destruction (Smilor, 1997). Early tourism entrepreneurship is evidenced in initiatives such as Thomas Cook, the UK international travel company founded in 1841, and Southwest Airlines, the US low-cost airline set up in 1949, in their attempts to circumvent social and market failures. At the destination level, entrepreneurship underpins policy objectives for tourism development in many regions of the world (Ateljevic and Page, 2009). Previously, the lack of responsibility for tourism developments and the absence of national policies resulted in adhoc strategies (Page and Thorn, 1997). Tourism development then transformed from *boosterism* (promoting tourism growth) to *sustainable*, with priorities changing from growth targets to strategic planning (Hall, 2000). These days, value creation can focus on social value creation, economic value creation or a combination of both (Meyskens *et al.*, 2010). Likewise, the primary market impact can be for-profit or purely focussed on social impact depending on the mission (Neck *et al.*, 2009). The difference lies in the relative priority given to social or economic goals.

There is a move towards social entrepreneurship in tourism, e.g. by using eco-tourism as a tool for poverty alleviation in developing countries such as Malaysia (UNWTO Knowledge Network, 2015). Social entrepreneurship draws its identity from both the social and entrepreneurship sectors and social enterprises are hybrid organisations that possess characteristics of both commercial and non-profit ventures (Certo and Miller, 2008; Miller and Wesley, 2010). The mission of social enterprises is to create social value for the public good, unlike commercial enterprises which aim to gain private profit (Austin *et al.*, 2006). However, a number of constraints have been identified with tourism entrepreneurship including limited access to finance, low skills and high operational costs such that private-public sector cooperation is necessary (Ateljevic, 2009) especially in developing countries where the private sector is inexperienced and government support is deficient. As such, social enterprises tend to address unmet social needs due to market and government failures (Dufays and Huybrechts, 2014). Furthermore, entrepreneurship is socially situated and the result of social interactions between the initiators and other stakeholders (Jack and Anderson, 2002). Therefore, tourism entrepreneurship can be influenced by the characteristics of the communities where it occurs (Tucker, 2010) and can generate different social impacts (Hall *et al.*, 2012).

The role of social capital

The capacity to exploit entrepreneurial opportunity in tourism depends on a range of capital resources (e.g. see Bennet *et al.*, 2012) and there is controversy over which type is most important. However, social capital increases the likelihood of achieving socio-economic goals (Lin, 1999). Historically rooted in the fields of economics and sociology, the concept of capital represents a market asset (Casson, and Della Giusta, 2007). Hanifan (1916:130), defined social capital as:

> "those tangible substances [that] count for most in the daily lives of people: namely goodwill, fellowship, sympathy, and social intercourse among the individuals and families that make up a social unit . . . the community as a whole will benefit by the cooperation of all its parts, while the individual will find in his associations the advantages of the help, the sympathy, and the fellowship of his neighbors" (McGehee *et al.*, 2010:487).

Social capital is a specific type of resource that is embedded in the relations between an individual and other entities and with the capacity to facilitate productive activity (Coleman, 1988). Social capital comprises physical, human and knowledge assets necessary for economic growth (Audretsch and Keilbach, 2004) but also encompasses cooperation, norms, trust and networks (Park *et al.*, 2012). Although controversy exists in the conceptualisation of social capital (e.g. Granovetter, 1985; Burt, 1992), social capital concerns the different network structures that facilitate or hinder access to social resources and the nature of the social resources embedded in the network (Seibert *et al.*, 2001). The impact of different networks on entrepreneurial initiatives is varied and dependent on the actors' objectives and effectiveness of the networks (Westlund and Bolton, 2003).

Entrepreneurship is perceived as a social process involving social networks with the capacity to identify and/or support business opportunities. For example during the process of firm creation, nascent entrepreneurs interact with key stakeholders in order to gain legitimacy (Williams Middleton, 2013) since social capital is embedded within a particular setting (Zhao *et al.*, 2011). In the context of tourism, the relationships or ties that constitute social capital are so important that if stakeholders are consulted and involved, developmental initiatives are more likely to succeed (Waligo *et al.*, 2013) and conflict management improved

10

(Park *et al.*, 2012). It is therefore not surprising that research into the significance of social capital for tourism development is gaining momentum (e.g. Macbeth *et al.*, 2004; Jones, 2005; Jeong, 2008; Mbaiwa, 2011; Lee, 2013).

Tourism entrepreneurship and social capital

The entrepreneurial process involves gathering resources through processes such as networking in order to achieve the adopted missions (Chell, 2007). More importantly, opportunity creation or discovery draws from the social context through actions such as acquiring local knowledge, credibility and resources using networks and relationships developed within them (Guclu *et al.*, 2002). Social capital as a mechanism for facilitating social interaction and personal commitment is important for economic growth and may inhibit entrepreneurship (Audretsch and Keilbach, 2004). Different networks, including but not limited to partnerships with government and other institutions, facilitate the creation, development and growth of social ventures (Haugh, 2007). These social enterprises provide opportunities associated with large constituents, a social purpose, long-term social change, an understanding of stakeholders and commitment that exceeds traditional entrepreneurial boundaries (Murphy and Coombes, 2009). Nonetheless, although the United Nations Development Programme (2014) emphasised collective action for progress towards addressing global challenges, social relations in tourism entrepreneurship have not been paid much attention (Park *et al.*, 2012) and neither has the role of social capital in determining residents' responses to tourism development (Park *et al.*, 2015).

Public-private partnerships

With the need for community/public participation in tourism planning and development (Murphy, 1985; Haywood, 1988), tourism entrepreneurship requires public-private sector collaboration. As Brent (1993:379) observed, "the desire of peoples all over the world to recapture control of the political processes which affect their daily lives" is one of the most significant factors for destination development. Hence, public-private partnerships embedded in social capital are crucial for tourism entrepreneurship. For example, the role of the public sector towards tourism entrepreneurship is highlighted in Article 9 of the Global Code of Ethics for Tourism which calls for the rights of workers and entrepreneurs in the tourism industry to be guaranteed. Therefore, shared goals, collective responsibilities and effective leadership are necessary (Waligo *et al.*, 2014).

In developing economies and emerging tourist destinations, the success of tourism entrepreneurship is a function of stakeholder communication, community capacity and a supportive entrepreneurial climate (Moscardo, 2008; Hingtgen *et al.*, 2015; Tolkach and King, 2015). Similarly, in rural destinations of developed economies, tourism development relies on stakeholder collaboration rather than the destination management organisation (Waligo *et al.*, 2013; Komppula, 2014). In these contexts, governments need to support the private sector by providing the funding, infrastructure and institutions necessary for tourism development. Nevertheless, public-private partnerships are particularly essential in developing economies because 90% of tourism enterprise is small businesses and profit is the driving force (Thomas *et al.*, 2011). Consequently, the on-going rhetoric and attempts to implement sustainable tourism are dependent on the provision of incentives, the conviction of stakeholders and guidance from the public sector.

Case study: Tourism entrepreneurship and social capital: lessons from Kenya, East Africa

The predominant feature of African countries is their struggle for economic independence. For example, while sub-Saharan Africa is one of the world's fastest growing regions in the world, household investments in preventive health products, such as insecticide-treated mosquito nets are hindered by financial constraints in countries like Kenya (World Bank, 2015). With the abundance of natural tourism attractions, the United Nations World Tourism Organisation (UNWTO, 2014) promotes the development of responsible, sustainable and universally accessible tourism, in developing countries such as those in Africa. This form of tourism tends to limit the threats posed by uncontrolled tourism development while recognising the huge contribution of the tourism sector towards foreign exchange earnings, local employment and regional development. Alongside these developments, is the concept of the 'new tourist' (Krippendorf, 1986) who is more informed and seeks newer tourism activities, thereby providing opportunities for tourism entrepreneurship.

Located in East Africa, Kenya offers sandy beaches, snow-capped mountains, rich cultural heritage and abundant wildlife such as the 'big five' (lion, leopard, rhino, elephant, buffalo), positioning Kenya as a premier tourist destination focusing on eco, cultural, sports and conference tourism (www.tourism.go.ke)

The Secretary General of UNWTO described Kenya as "a true tourism success story and a long-term tourism leader, not only in Africa but globally" with the ability to bounce back after the terrorist attacks (UNWTO, 2015). Kenya was raised to a lower middle-income country, the ninth largest in Africa in 2012 (World Bank, 2015) and its long-term plan (Vision 2030) includes a strategy to expand the contribution of the tourism sector (Kenya Tourism Development Corporation, 2015).

10

Adventure Alternative: The Responsible Adventure Travel Company

Adventure Alternative (AA) is an independent tour operator in Kenya, operating alongside and investing in Moving Mountains (MM), its associated charity through which aid is provided for the relief of poverty and inequality in local communities. AA was initiated by Gavin Bates in 1991 and its wide remit of products, including mountain climbs and treks, safaris in East Africa, Gap trips, specialist expeditions, visiting rainforests and volunteering opportunities, reflects Kenya's tourism potential and vision. The business model of AA aims to achieve sustainable tourism using local staff and suppliers, equitable salaries, and ensuring real benefits for the communities where tourism is promoted. The idea is to secure social, economic and environmental value from tourism entrepreneurship, 'more like a social enterprise' for which tourism is thought to be well suited (Adventure Alternative, 2015).

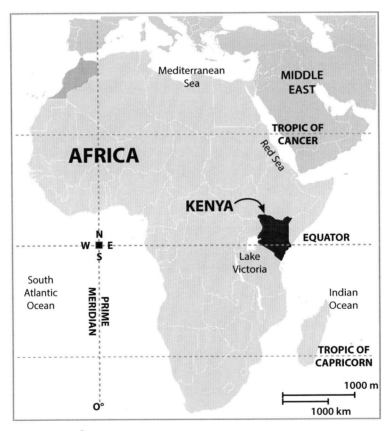

Figure 10.1: Location of Kenya

AA demonstrates the relationship between tourism entrepreneurship and social capital through its collaboration with stakeholders and the communities of people where they operate. Empirical evidence collected in 2012-13 revealed that the enterprise has reached communities at grass-root level in various parts of the country through programmes such as the Ulamba Children's Home, Embu Rescue Centre for Street Children, Ushirika Clinic HIV

Testing Programme & Community Health Team, Black Cat Football & Sports, Family and Social Welfare Support and employment of locals nationwide. AA was established on a strong ethos towards tackling social injustice, whilst being a viable profitable business (Adventure Alternative, 2012). This tourism social entrepreneurship orientation arose from the extensive experiences of the founder in the slums of Nairobi, the mountains of Nepal and the rainforests of Borneo as he explained:

> "one of the biggest things in life that drives me is social injustice … I couldn't and I still can't reconcile the fact that it boils down to exploitation of essentially uneducated illiterate people."

Since entrepreneurship is a logical process of developing opportunity (Corner & Ho, 2010) and social capital is a necessity, a range of relationships are pursued from both the private and public sectors as the company director described:

> "We work with the schools, we also work with the clinics and hospitals, we work with churches and people from the parish, then there are orphanages and children's homes. As a company we are registered with KATO [Kenya Association of Tour Operators] so we are under their umbrella…also we get the licences from the Kenyan Ministry of Tourism…and also as an NGO we are registered with the National NGO council…we are also members of the Children's Right umbrella."

In addition to the local context, resources are drawn from external people and/or entities.

> "The biggest source of funding is clients coming for holidays, also we have people like the medical students and people on a gap year; from the money they pay to come out to Kenya some of the profit goes to the kids at the orphanage, the salaries, the school fees for the kids, and the parents and kids who are sick, because we have a number of people with HIV."

Consequently, various networks are targeted for their potential contribution to the socio-economic mission thereby building a resource portfolio of social, financial, political and human capital through the interactions that occur. Notably, adapting to the local context is underscored for social capital accumulation as the founder asserted:

> I thought to myself, if I am going to run a business in this part of the world, then the least I can do is understand the people…I never ever went down the road of believing that I knew everything about their lives, I can't…born in England I cannot really in my guts understand what it is like to be born into that environment."

Local context adaptation helps avoid potential conflict from socio-cultural disparities that exist between the entrepreneur and other parties. Without this understanding, individuals are neither motivated to accept nor participate in the entrepreneurial mission, even if it is for their benefit. Hence, it is important to build a network of relationships – the social capital.

10

Case study questions

1   Evaluate the significance of investing in social capital for the survival of Adventure Alternative.

2   Critically analyse the role of the Kenyan government in the promotion of new forms of tourism entrepreneurship and the enhancement of social capital accumulation for tourism development.

Conclusion

The purpose of this chapter was to examine the relationship between tourism entrepreneurship and social capital. Tourism entrepreneurship is largely recognised for its economic contribution to job creation and regional development. However, in order to realise tourism entrepreneurial opportunities, particularly in developing/remote destinations, social capital accumulation is necessary. This entails creating, maintaining and/or extending various relationships on which the required resource portfolio depends. In the case of tourism social entrepreneurship, which tends to focus on long-term change, collaboration needs to be sustained. Social capital is embedded in the degree of collaboration and diversity of those involved in shaping the outcome of tourism entrepreneurship in a destination. Tourism entrepreneurship is a logical process involving an investment in social capital and adaptation to the local context. However, social competence and networking capability are essential (Chell, 2013).

The negative social impacts of tourism development tend to cast a shadow on the relationship between tourism entrepreneurship and social capital especially in developing destinations where host-guest relationships can be tense. However, the emergence of new forms of tourism such as 'responsible', 'inclusive', or 'sustainable' and indeed the growth of new forms of entrepreneurship including 'social', 'eco' and 'sustainable' provide a basis for considering the nexus between tourism entrepreneurship and social capital. Nonetheless, some questions need to be considered. In the meantime, there are clearly lessons to be learned from organisations such as Adventures Alternative.

Questions

1 How will the 'new' tourism entrepreneurship affect communities in developing economies in the long-term?

2 What is the influence of different networks on entrepreneurial initiatives and how can it be managed effectively?

3 In the future, will social capital drive the agendas of tourism entrepreneurship?

References

Adventure Alternative (2012) A Model of Sustainable Tourism. Retrieved from: http://www.adventurealternative.com/pages/our_business_model. Accessed 10/06/2012

Adventure Alternative (2015) About us. Retrieved from: https://www.adventurealternative.com/about_us/ Accessed 28/04/2015

Ateljevic, J. (2009) Tourism entrepreneurship and regional development: example from New Zealand. *International Journal of Entrepreneurial Behavior & Research*, **15**(3), 282-308.

Ateljevic, J. and Page, S. J. (Eds.) (2009) *Tourism and Entrepreneurship*, Routledge.

Audretsch, D. B. and Keilbach, M. (2004) Does entrepreneurship capital matter? *Entrepreneurship Theory and Practice*, **28**(5), 419-429.

Austin, J., Stevenson, H. and Wei-Skillern, J. (2006) Social and commercial entrepreneurship: same, different, or both? *Entrepreneurship theory and practice*, **30**(1), 1-22.

Bennett, N., Lemelin, R. H., Koster, R. and Budke, I. (2012) A capital assets framework for appraising and building capacity for tourism development in aboriginal protected area gateway communities. *Tourism Management*, **33**(4), 752-766.

Burt, R.S. (1992) *Structural Holes*. Cambridge: Cambridge University Press.

Casson, M., and Della Giusta, M. (2007) Entrepreneurship and social capital Analysing the impact of social networks on entrepreneurial activity from a rational action perspective. *International Small Business Journal*, **25**(3), 220-244.

Certo, T. and Miller, T., (2008) Social entrepreneurship: key issues and concepts. *Business Horizons*, **51**, 267-271.

Chell, E. (2007) Social enterprise and entrepreneurship: towards a convergent theory of the entrepreneurial process, *International Small Business Journal* **25**, 5.

Chell, E. (2013) Review of skill and the entrepreneurial process. *International Journal of Entrepreneurial Behavior and Research*, **19**(1), 6-31.

Coleman, J. S. (1988) Social capital in the creation of human capital. *American Journal of Sociology*, S95-S120.

10

Corner, P. D. and Ho, M. (2010) How opportunities develop in social entrepreneurship. *Entrepreneurship Theory and Practice*, **34**(4), 635-659.

Dufays, F. and Huybrechts, B. (2014) Connecting the dots for social value: A review on social networks and social entrepreneurship. *Journal of Social Entrepreneurship*, **5**(2), 214-237

Granovetter, M.S. (1985) Economic action and social structure, *American Journal of Sociology*, **91**(3), 481-510.

Guclu, A., Dees, J. G. and Anderson, B. B. (2002) The process of social entrepreneurship: Creating opportunities worthy of serious pursuit. *Center for the advancement of Social Entrepreneurship*, 1-15.

Hall, C.M. (2000) *Tourism Planning: Policies, Processes and Relationships*, Harlow: Prentice Hall

Hall, J., Matos, S., Sheehan, L. and Silvestre, B. (2012) Entrepreneurship and innovation at the base of the pyramid: a recipe for inclusive growth or social exclusion? *Journal of Management Studies*, **49**(4), 785-812.

Hanifan, L. J. (1916) The rural school community center. *Annals of the American Academy of Political and Social Science*, **67**, 130-138.

Haugh, H. (2007) Community-led social venture creation. *Entrepreneurship Theory and Practice*, **31**(2), 161-182.

Haywood, K. M. (1988) Responsible and responsive tourism planning in the community. *Tourism management*, **9**(2), 105-118.

Hingtgen, N., Kline, C., Fernandes, L. and McGehee, N. G. (2015) Cuba in transition: Tourism industry perceptions of entrepreneurial change. *Tourism Management*, **50**, 184-193.

Jack, S. L. and Anderson, A. R. (2002) The effects of embeddedness on the entrepreneurial process. *Journal of Business Venturing*, **17**(5), 467-487

Jeong, S. (2008) *Assessing social capital and community involvement: Social network analysis for the sustainable Amish community tourism development*. ProQuest

Jones, S. (2005) Community-based ecotourism: The significance of social capital. *Annals of Tourism Research*, **32**(2), 303–324.

Kenya Tourism Development Corporation (2015) Kenya's Vision 2030. Retrieved from: http://www.ktdc.co.ke/about-us Accessed 24.04.15

Komppula, R. (2014) The role of individual entrepreneurs in the development of competitiveness for a rural tourism destination–A case study. *Tourism Management*, **40**, 361-371.

Krippendorf, J. (1986) The new tourist—turning point for leisure and travel. *Tourism Management*, **7**(2), 131-135.

Larsen, L., S. Harlan, B. Bollin, E. Hackett, D. Hope, A. Kirby, A. Nelson, T. Rex and S.

Wolf (2004) Bonding and bridging: Understanding the relationship between social capital and civic action. *Journal of Planning Education and Research*, **24**: 64-77.

Lee, B. C. (2013) The impact of social capital on tourism technology adoption for destination marketing. *Current Issues in Tourism*, **13**(3), 149-165.

Lin, N. (1999) Social networks and status attainment. *Annual review of sociology*, 467-487.

Macbeth, J., Carson, D. and Northcote, J. (2004) Social capital, tourism and regional development: SPSS as a basis for innovation and sustainability. *Current Issues in Tourism*, **7**(6), 502–522.

Mbaiwa, J. (2011) The effects of tourism development on the sustainable utilisation of natural resources in the Okavango Delta, Botswana. *Current Issues in Tourism*, **14**(3), 251–273.

McGehee, N. G., Lee, S., O'Bannon, T. L. and Perdue, R. R. (2010) Tourism-related social capital and its relationship with other forms of capital: An exploratory study. *Journal of Travel Research*, **49**(4), 486-500.

Meyskens, M., Carsrud, A. L. and Cardozo, R. N. (2010) The symbiosis of entities in the social engagement network: The role of social ventures. *Entrepreneurship and Regional Development*, **22**(5), 425-455.

Miller, T.L and Wesley, C.L. (2010) Assessing mission and resources for social change: An organizational identity perspective on social venture capitalists' decision criteria. *Entrepreneurship Theory and Practice: Special Issue: Social Entrepreneurship* **34**(4), 705-733

Moscardo, G. (Ed.) (2008) *Building Community Capacity for Tourism Development*. Cabi.

Murphy, P.E. (1985) *Tourism: A Community Approach*. London: Methuen.

Murphy, P.J. and Coombes, S.M. (2009) A model of social entrepreneurial discovery. *Journal of Business Ethics* **87**(3) 325-336.

Neck, H., Brush, C. and Allen, E. (2009) The landscape of social entrepreneurship. *Business Horizons*, **52**,13-19.

Page, S.J. and Thorn, K.J. (1997) Towards sustainable tourism planning in NewZealand: Public sector planning response, *Journal of Sustainable Tourism*, **5**(1) 59-77.

Park, D. B., Lee, K. W., Choi, H. S. and Yoon, Y. (2012) Factors influencing social capital in rural tourism communities in South Korea. *Tourism Management*, **33**(6), 1511-1520.

Park, D., Nunkoo, R. and Yoon, Y. (2015) Rural residents' attitudes to tourism and the moderating effects of social capital, *Tourism Geographies: An International Journal of Tourism Space, Place and Environment*, **17**(1), 112-133.

Putnam, R. D. (1993) The prosperous community - social capital and public life. *The American Prospect*, **13**, 35-42.

Schumpeter, J. (1934) *The Theory of Economic Development. An inquiry into Profits, Capital, Credit, Interest, and the Business Cycle*, Cambridge: Harvard University Press.

10

Seibert, S. E., Kraimer, M. L. and Liden, R. C. (2001) A social capital theory of career success. *Academy of Management Journal*, **44**(2), 219-237.

Smilor, R. W. (1997) Entrepreneurship: Reflections on a subversive activity. *Journal of Business Venturing*, **12**(5), 341-346.

Thomas, R., Shaw, G. and Page, S. J. (2011) Understanding small firms in tourism: A perspective on research trends and challenges, *Tourism Management*, **32**(5), 963-976.

Tolkach, D. and King, B. (2015) Strengthening community-based tourism in a new resource-based island nation: Why and how?, *Tourism Management*, **48**, 386-398.

Tucker, H. (2010) Peasant-entrepreneurs: A longitudinal ethnography. *Annals of Tourism Research*, **37**(4), 927-946

United Nations Development Programme (2014) *Human Development Report: Sustaining Human Progress: Reducing Vulnerabilities and Building Resilience* UNDP: New York

UNWTO (2011) *World Tourism Organization and Banesto Foundation collaborate on sustainable tourism projects for poverty elimination in Africa*. Retrieved from: http://media.unwto. org/press-release/2011-09-21/world-tourism-organization-and-banesto-foundation-collaborate-sustainable-t. Accessed 01/04/2015

UNWTO (2014) *UNWTO Annual Report 2013*, UNWTO, Madrid

UNWTO (2015) UNWTO expresses its full support for Kenyan tourism. Retrieved from: http://media.unwto.org/press-release/2015-04-29/unwto-expresses-its-full-support-kenyan-tourism Accessed 30/04/2015

UNWTO Knowledge Network (2015) From Charity to Social Entrepreneurship, Borneo Ecotourism Solutions and Technologies Society. Retrieved from: http://know.unwto. org/content/charity-social-entrepreneurship-borneo-ecotourism-solutions-and-technologies-society Accessed 01/04/2015

Waligo, V. M., Clarke, J. and Hawkins, R. (2013) Implementing sustainable tourism: A multi-stakeholder involvement management framework. *Tourism Management*, **36**, 342-353.

Waligo, V. M., Clarke, J. and Hawkins, R. (2014) The 'Leadership–Stakeholder Involvement Capacity'nexus in stakeholder management. *Journal of Business Research*, **67**(7), 1342-1352.

Westlund, H. and Bolton, R. (2003) Local social capital and entrepreneurship.*Small Business Economics*, **21**(2), 77-113.

Williams Middleton, K. L. (2013) Becoming entrepreneurial: gaining legitimacy in the nascent phase. *International Journal of Entrepreneurial Behavior and Research*, **19**(4), 404-424.

Zhao, W., Ritchie, J. B. and Echtner, C. M. (2011) Social capital and tourism entrepreneurship. *Annals of Tourism Research*, **38**(4), 1570-1593.

11 Entrepreneurship and Networking Processes

Antonella Capriello, Universita del Piemonte Orientale, Italy

Introduction

A network is generally defined in the entrepreneurship literature as a specific type of relationship linking a defined set of people, objects or events (Nelson, 1988; Szarka, 1990). Paché (1990) defines networks in the context of organised systems as long-lasting exchange relationships between two or more companies that focus on the mutual interests of their members.

In the hospitality and tourism industry, networks are instrumental in sharing information and resources, in building knowledge-sharing alliances and in obtaining economies of scale and scope. Networking processes are therefore considered as key opportunities for small business entrepreneurs to overcome resource-constrained conditions in tourist destinations. The importance of networking processes is widely recognised in destination development planning, not only in tourism and hospitality for start-ups, but also subsequently in view of the multifaceted nature of tourism products. The complex coordination of tourism products thus engenders extensive collaborative relationships in the industry. Network relationships are particularly important for the tourism sector where groups of organisations cluster together to form a destination context (Pavlovich, 2003). Networks also achieve social and environmental objectives in accordance with the growing importance of EU funds for development projects and programmes (Long, 1996) and cross-sector initiatives that bring together different stakeholders in sustainable development initiatives (Selin, 1999). Networks increasingly facilitate the ongoing development, preservation and nurturing of culture as a resource for rural tourism (MacDonald and Jollife, 2003).

The purpose of this chapter is to develop an understanding of networking processes from an entrepreneurial perspective. More specifically, by the end of this chapter you should be able to:

■ Explain social networks and social capital in relation to entrepreneurial networking processes;

■ Describe the elements of a network from a theoretical perspective;

■ Discuss the links between local environments and networking processes.

The chapter begins by defining social networks and social capital before examining the fundamental elements of a network. Thereafter, the nature of ties is discussed, to identify the implications for business development. Finally, the local environment, cluster and networking processes are examined with a focus on destination development implications.

Entrepreneurship, social networks and social capital

Entrepreneurship

The concept of 'entrepreneurship' is associated with networks of continuing social relations whereby business implementation in an intense web of relationships is supported or constrained by links between entrepreneurs, resources and opportunities. Developing a new business idea requires different contacts and resources, as social relations affect the structure of decision-making processes (Starr and MacMillan, 1990; Reynolds, 1991; Larson and Starr, 1993; Borch, 1994; Hansen, 1995;) and are instrumental in obtaining advice and the salient resources to launch a new business (Granovetter, 1985, 1992).

Social networks

Social networks are defined by a set of actors (individuals or organisations) and a set of links between the actors (Brass, 1984). Social networks are not fixed structures; they represent the social context of businesses and can be activated according to different needs (Granovetter, 1985; Burt, 1992). Social network members can contact and organise themselves and thereby increase the opportunities they make available to entrepreneurs (Burt, 1992).

Family members and friends can play an essential part in analysing the nature of networks and thus entrepreneurs frequently involve their family members in their business networks to obtain help and support (Rosenblatt *et al.*, 1985). Birley (1985), Zimmer and Aldrich (1987) and Hara and Kanai (1994) find that a pre-existing web of relationships, in particular among friends and family, are resource providers in the new venture process.

In addition, the relationships between entrepreneurs and other actors provide resources that are important to establishing a business (Johannisson, 1988; Larson, 1991). More specifically, entrepreneurs require information, capital, skills and labour to start business activities. Although they hold some of the resources themselves, these are often complemented through accessing those of their contacts (Aldrich and Zimmer, 1986; Cooper *et al.*, 1995; Hansen, 1995). For example, entrepreneurs may have the ideas, knowledge and competencies to run the business but also require additional key factors to achieve their goals (Teece, 1987). They thus obtain support, knowledge and access to distribution channels through their social relationships.

Entrepreneurs are also linked to other people and organisations that interact and these contacts can increase the availability of resources that sustain a new firm (Hansen, 1995). These contacts are often informal work and non-work connections and the relations may extend across professional networks and to former colleagues.

Network reliance is not limited to the start-up stage, as entrepreneurs continue to rely on networks for business information, advice and problem-solving, with some relationships supplying multiple resources (Johannisson *et al.*, 1994).

Social capital

When the relationships of entrepreneurs contribute to their entrepreneurial goals, these social relations become their social capital (Burt, 1992). Social capital consists of the relationships that enable the achievement of successful outcomes and are a key component of entrepreneurial networks (Burt, 1992). Gabbay and Leenders (1999) define social capital as the set of tangible or virtual resources that accrue to actors through their social structure, and facilitate the attainment of their goals. In the entrepreneurship network literature, the following network elements emerge as critical to theoretical and empirical research:

1 The content that is exchanged between actors;

2 Trust and network governance;

3 The nature of the ties;

4 The network structure created by the intersecting relationships between actors.

These four elements are discussed in the following sections.

11

Network content

Network content can be explained in relation to the following key factors that also underline the benefits of networking processes for tourism and hospitality entrepreneurs.

Transaction costs

Networks have a role in lowering transaction costs and exploiting external economies of scale and scope in various activities (Tremblay, 2000). This objective can be achieved by pooling and spreading risk, and developing access to complementary resources (Kumar and van Dissel, 1996). From a transaction cost theoretical perspective (Williamson, 1985, 1999), networks allow members to benefit from the advantages of vertical integration.

Information and advice

A key benefit of networks in the entrepreneurial process is the access they provide to information and advice. Ties to professional service organisations, for example, are a means of tapping into key competencies and market information (Freeman, 1999).

Entrepreneurs consistently use networks to obtain ideas and gather information to identify entrepreneurial opportunities (Birley, 1985; Smeltzer *et al.*, 1991). Ties with distributors, suppliers, competitors or customer organisations can be important conduits of information and know-how (Brown and Butler, 1995).

Innovation and knowledge sharing

Sharing ideas among network members leads to greater understanding of the business challenges and to more innovative approaches to strategy formulation and implementation (Camagni, 1991; Roberts and Bradley, 1991; Roome, 2001). Consequently, learning-based innovative collaborative networks are essential to increasing firm capabilities (Kogut, 2000). Networks enable firms to increase their competencies by granting them access to innovative resources and knowledge. Network members can develop new activities, joint research projects and marketing programs, and thereby gain a competitive advantage without increasing their firm's infrastructure (Bocquet *et al.*, 2006). Text box 1 explores these potential advantages of networking processes.

Text box 1: Potential advantages of networking

In the UK, the National Farm Attractions Network (NFAN) is a cooperative group established in 1996 to assist farm and rural enterprises in their diversification into the tourism industry. The network represents members' interests offering guidance and information from nominated advisors across the UK. It provides support in different areas: legal and insurance, marketing, promotion and publicity, planning legislation and business rates, accountancy and taxation, health and safety, grant aid and animal welfare. The effectiveness of this network is related to information dissemination, exchanging ideas and learning opportunities. As an incentive to encourage high-quality farm-based attractions, the NFAN introduced the Farm Attraction Awards in 2002. The awards are based on different categories in relation to annual visitor numbers and provide an opportunity for the farm attraction industry to showcase their 'best in class' attractions.

Reputation signals

Relationships can also have a reputational or signalling content (Deeds *et al.*, 1997; Stuart *et al.*, 1999). Given the uncertain and dynamic conditions of entrepreneurial activities, consumers are likely to seek information that helps the decision-making process. Entrepreneurs seek to reduce this perceived risk by associating with, or obtaining explicit certification from, well-regarded individuals and organisations. These links help create positive customer perceptions and positively influence the entrepreneur's market reputation.

Collaborative networks and sustainable development

With a focus on sustainable development, collaborative networks are also instrumental in coordinating tourism policies and related planning actions (Lane, 1994). This networking helps small firms with few resources become part of the decision-making process, especially those that cannot pursue sustainable development in isolation. Text box 2 focuses on the role of a network in a reputation-building process and in sharing sustainable development best practices.

11

Text box 2: The role of a network in reputation building

Terranostra is an Italian agritourism network that aims to establish an alliance between farm producers and consumers. Network membership is related to the idea of signalling an eco-friendly and sustainable hospitality service provision and convenient tour packages to the tourism marketplace. Being a network member is a reputation signal as the accreditation and quality certification of supplied farm products is coherent with the principle of sustainability together with discovering the origin and culture related to local farm productions.

Trust and network governance

Trust

Trust between partners is a critical element for achieving higher quality resource exchanges (Larson, 1991; Lorenzoni and Lipparini, 1999). Trust also affects the depth and wealth of exchange relations, particularly in terms of information exchange (Saxenian, 1991; Lorenzoni and Lipparini, 1999). Saxena (2005) provides an examination of the importance of trust in developing organisational links that underpin tourism development in the Peak District.

Mutual trust as a governance mechanism is based on confidence in the other partner's reliability to fulfil their obligations in an exchange (Pruitt, 1981). Trust allows both parties to assume that each partner will take actions that are predictable and mutually acceptable (Powell, 1990; Uzzi, 1997; Das and Teng, 1998). Text box 3 illustrates how trust influences cohesion and involvement in networks.

Text box 3: The importance of trust in networks

Sussex Top Attractions was established in 1983 as a marketing network for small visitor attractions in Sussex, UK. This recognised institution represents over fifty major visitor attractions in the region. Network cohesion is based on trust among entrepreneurs, which is instrumental to identifying the network's marketing goals. In addition to formal meetings, information is disseminated via newsletters. Email contacts are fundamental to nurturing network involvement and ensure participant commitment.

Network governance

Network governance is based on social mechanisms such as power and influence (Brass, 1984; Thorelli, 1986; Krackhardt, 1990) rather than legal enforcement. Using a sample of UK cooperative tourism marketing associations, Palmer (2002) demonstrates that a formal governance style significantly influences effectiveness, membership commitment and diversity. This research shows the importance of stretching firm boundaries to achieve benefits from networking processes.

These social mechanisms of network governance can create advantages with respect to coordination through market or bureaucratic mechanisms (Thorelli, 1986; Jarillo, 1988; Starr and Macmillan, 1990; Lipparini and Lorenzoni, 1993; Jones *et al.*, 1997). Subsequently, this operating condition reduces transaction costs – for example, monitoring and renegotiating the exchange in response to environmental changes – particularly in highly complex business environments facing resource constraints (Jones *et al.*, 1997).

The nature of ties

Network literature traditionally distinguishes between strong and weak ties.

Strong ties

Strong ties relate to close friends and family members and are frequently based on long-term relationships where a high level of trust plays a key role (Krackhardt, 1990). These ties are more conducive to transferring accurate information and tacit knowledge (Inkpen and Tsang, 2005) and are based on shared values and a common vision, which are important for the destination to efficiently manage potential rejuvenation processes. Strong ties enable entrepreneurs to deal with uncertain and changing business environments. In relation to the hotel industry, Ingram and Roberts (2000) underline the importance of friendship as a strong tie to obtain information in a dynamic and competitive environment.

Weak ties

Weak ties frequently refer to acquaintances (Granovetter, 1973) and to a diverse group of people with whom one has some business connections. Weak ties tend to be formed by people who work in different contexts and are therefore instrumental in accessing different sources of information, resources and opportunities through ties that lie outside their immediate web of relationships. Weak ties connect different network cores, facilitate the information flow between these, and are often referred to as 'bridging ties' (Jenssen and Greve, 2002). From this perspective, entrepreneurs activate their weak ties for at least two purposes: to gain access to business information and to attract customers. Weak ties disseminate knowledge among individuals, including information and data on new business locations, potential markets for goods and services, sources of capital or potential investors, innovations and standard business practices.

Weak ties are frequently deemed to lead to a more varied set of information and resources than strong ties (Bloodgood *et al.*, 1995) and consequently enhance the entrepreneurs' ability to exploit emerging opportunities and innovation processes. Capriello and Rotherham (2008) demonstrate the importance of weak ties for farm visitor attractions in a rural area of Sussex, UK. Weak ties are instrumental in rejuvenating mature farm tourism products. Text box 4 illustrates how strong and weak ties are used during business development.

11

> ## Text box 4: The value of ties in business development
>
> Il Mulino della Villa (The Villa Mill) is a family-farm tourism enterprise located in a rural area of Piedmont, Italy and was founded by three brothers in 2006. The old mill has been elegantly renovated while preserving its original structure, creating a rustic, warm and cosy environment perfect for family or business dinners. The role of strong ties with family members was fundamental not only in the start-up stage, to obtain human and financial capital, but in the progressive development of hospitality and tourism products, such as the innovative service provision in the restaurant and local tours. In accordance with Terranostra's principle, the company has integrated farm production with sales and distribution activities; the restaurant offers seasonal menus and local products. To achieve and explore new markets, initial weak ties with TV channels were progressively developed by adopting farm life values as a message to market the firm. Weak ties with the local tourism board and local tour operators were strengthened and were fundamental to acquiring new competencies to offer tour packages.

Network structure

The network structure is defined as the pattern of ties between actors. The different position of entrepreneurs within a network structure is a key element, with important consequences on resource flows and firm outcomes.

Network measure

A variety of measures drawn from the network analysis literature are used to identify patterns in the social structure that can then be used to characterise the different positions of entrepreneurs or their ventures in the network. Network size is a fundamental indicator that measures the degree of integration in a network of individual units and defines the number of direct links between a focal actor and other actors. An analysis of network size measures the extent to which resources can be accessed by the entrepreneur (Aldrich and Reese, 1993; Hansen, 1995).

Scott *et al.* (2008) discuss density and centrality since these overall measures of network cohesion indicate the extent to which all members interact with all other members. Density is measured by the extent to which an actor's contacts are interconnected. The denser the entrepreneur's direct network of contacts, the less likely it will be that new resources enter and the more likely it will be that resources simply circulate within the group. Centrality explicitly includes the ability to access (or control) resources through indirect and direct links. Degree of centrality indicates the ability of actors to reach other actors in their network through intermediaries (Scott *et al.*, 2008).

Structural holes

In analysing the network structure, the absence of a direct relationship between two firms (called partner firms) can be identified, but these two firms may have a third firm (called focal firm) in common and are therefore indirectly linked to each other. This condition constitutes a structural hole (Burt, 1992:18). With regard to its position, the focal firm has more discretion in its actions, since the two partner firms cannot coordinate actions against the focal firm. The condition of being a focal firm enables identifying and exploiting opportunities by occupying a bridging position in a network (Burt, 1992). Subsequently, firm competitiveness depends on occupying structural holes due to the likelihood that firms in a bridging position will receive new and strategically important information sooner than others in the network.

Broker role

The broker role is a central position in networks resulting from network actors' attempts to minimise their transactions costs (Haythornthwaite, 1996). This position links actors with complementary interests by transferring information between those not directly connected to each other to facilitate the activities of entrepreneurs. Voluntary associations, trade associations, public agencies and other social units increase the likelihood of entrepreneurs connecting with each other. Text box 5 illustrates the broker role in relation to hospitality and tourism sectors.

Text box 5: The role of the broker

Associazione Startup Turismo (Tourism Startup Association) is a network of Italian start-up entrepreneurs offering digital solutions to the tourism and culture sectors. This broker aims to promote new solutions and transfer knowledge in order to support the growth of emerging innovative firms in Italy. Its role is enhancing the visibility of network members by organising trade fairs, workshops and events. The brokerage activity is intended to facilitate entrepreneur networking processes by combining different digital offers in the hospitality and tourism sectors.

11

The implications of networking on business development require the analysis of the role of the local environment in networking processes. In this environment, entrepreneurs generally pursue and exploit emerging opportunities to propose innovative tourism and hospitality products.

Local environment, networking and clusters

The local environment (including its culture, knowledge base and business attitude) often appears to be a success factor for new forms of entrepreneurship (Camagni, 1991). In this environment, local networks are a fundamental asset of clusters known as 'industrial districts' (Piore and Sabel, 1984; Scott, 1988; Scott and Storper, 1989; Pyke *et al.*, 1990; Harrison, 1992). Marshall (1964) introduced the concept of 'industrial districts' with enormous economic growth potential and the strong dynamics of industrial concentration where firms interact and thus obtain external economies of scale.

The term 'cluster' refers to a localised network of specialised organisations and includes close local relationships between firms on different levels in the industrial chain. According to Porter (1990), high positive externalities are generated in a cluster due to commonalities of geography and industry (Novelli *et al.*, 2006). Entrepreneurs embedded in a cluster can compete globally by cooperating locally through networks.

Entrepreneur cluster interdependence refers to value chain links through common technologies, inputs, customers, infrastructure and distribution channels (Van den Berg *et al.*, 2001). Based on close working relationships and reducing transaction costs, the complex web of local networks produce complementarities in industries and market niches, and between different sectors (Hopkins, 2001) fostering creativity and innovation to generate new services and products beyond firm boundaries.

Lazonick (1992) emphasises networking processes not only between the same type of organisations but also between organisations and firms operating in different industrial sectors. This aspect is fundamental for hospitality business entrepreneurs who need to establish a complex system of connections and inter-relationships resulting from complementary tourism and hospitality products (for example, accommodation, entertainment and catering facilities) that co-exist with the infrastructure provision in tourism clusters (Pavlovich, 2003).

Conclusion

This chapter sets out to explain the concept of networks and demonstrate their key role for entrepreneurs operating in the hospitality and tourism sectors. Networks and networking processes are analysed in relation to their content and their implications on the relationships of entrepreneurs. Trust between partners is a critical element of network governance since this relational tie affects the depth and wealth of exchange relations, particularly with respect to the quality of resource flows. Furthermore, the different positions of actors in a network structure has significant implications on resource flows and entrepreneurial outcomes. Entrepreneurs consistently use networks to obtain ideas and knowledge and gather information to identify entrepreneurial opportunities and achieve cost savings. Networking processes are particularly important given the growing competition in developed and emerging markets in the hospitality and tourism sectors. The key challenge for future hospitality and tourism managers is to disseminate network-based approaches to exploit the potentials of social capital for local sustainable development.

Case study: The District of Langhe, Roero and Monferrato, Italy

The District of Langhe, Roero and Monferrato is a wine-growing region in South Piedmont, Italy. This breathtaking landscape listed in the 2014 UNESCO World Heritage List, is characterised by rolling hills and vineyards and featured in the writings of Italian authors Cesare Pavese and Beppe Fenoglio. In the last two decades, the progressive creation of local networks of farm producers and the emerging hospitality sector have supported diversification from the agriculture to the tourism sector. Public actors have played a key role in establishing these local strategic alliances while public policies have addressed investments in new generations of entrepreneurs with innovative education programs and formative activities to nurture and maintain this human capital in the area. The Piedmont Region, European funds and local banks have funded this development process.

Two factors have significantly affected the growth of this tourist district: in the 1950s-60s, the local population remained in this rural area as they had the opportunity to work for the multinational company Ferrero in Alba and cultivate their own fields in their spare time. The second element was the restructuring of agricultural production processes and consequently achieving an outstanding capacity in the production of high quality wine and resource exploitation through innovative marketing activities.

The enhanced quality and visibility in international markets have induced the producers to become active network members in local entrepreneurial associations. These associations aim to improve the overall image of local producers through product certificates. The Export Association now includes over 60 wine producers and is a significant network with outstanding producers in equal positions. The three most important producers of the Barolo and Barbaresco Consortium produce only 8 percent of the 66 million bottles that constitutes the annual production of the overall network of members. Local producers also cultivate their own web of relationships to boost their brand reputation at the international level.

11

Festivals and cultural initiatives have contributed to the growing international reputation of this cluster, in cooperation with key institutions (the Pavese Foundation, Fondazione Culturale 'Emanuele di Mirafiore'). Gastronomic events have also played a key role involving local farmers; each year for around six weeks Alba is transformed and becomes the world market for truffles.

This area is becoming a popular location for holiday homes. International tourists visit the 'wine trail' through the typical local wineries (Dolcetto d'Alba, Barbera d'Alba and Nebbiolo d'Alba). The Barolo trail and the best Langa wines involve 18 municipalities, wine producers, accommodation providers, wine boutiques and cellars. Additional visitor attractions are the Literary Landscapes, the Wine Museum, the Eco-Museum 'Rocche' and 'Terrazzamenti'. The network members provide a high level of service. The 'Strada del Barolo e grandi vini di Langa' brand aims to ensure the service quality standard and is consistent with the principles of sustainable development in the area.

The social capital in this district is based on a complex web of relationships and is linked to the local history. Alba, one of the district towns, has had a strong reputation since the Middle Ages. During the Second World War, the partisans established the Republic of Alba. On 18 February 2015, a strong sense of community cohesion was shown worldwide during the funeral of Michele Ferrero, the founder of the aforementioned multinational company that also produces Nutella.

Innovation and creativity are fundamental in this district. The Slow Food Movement was born in Bra and the Gastronomy University in Italy was established in Pollenzo (a town in this district). In addition, the entrepreneurial concept of Eataly was created as an innovative approach to promoting agricultural and gastronomic products as well as the culture of this region.

Questions

1 Describe the features of the local environment in the District of Langhe, Roero and Monferrato.

2 Identify the networking processes undertaken by local entrepreneurs.

3 Analyse the role of cultural history in creating social capital.

References

Aldrich, H. and Zimmer, C. (1986) Entrepreneurship through social networks, in D. Sexton and R. Smiler (eds.), *The Art and Science of Entrepreneurship*, Cambridge, MA: Ballinger, pp. 3-23.

Aldrich, H. and Reese, P.R. (1993) Does networking pay off? A panel study of entrepreneurs in the research triangle, in N.S. Churchill, et al. (eds.), *Frontiers of Entrepreneurship Research*, pp. 325-339.

Birley, S. (1985) The role of networks in the entrepreneurial process, *Journal of Business Venturing*, **1**(1), 107-117.

Bloodgood, J.M., Sapienza, J., and Carsrud, A.L. (1995) The dynamics of new business startups: Person, context and process, in J.A. Katz, and S. Brockhaus, (eds.), *Advances in Entrepreneurship, Firm Emergence and Growth*, Vol. 2, Connecticut: JAI Press, pp. 123-144.

Bocquet, R., Cattellin, M., Thevenard-Puthod, C., Scaraffiotti, J., and Gentet, W. (2006), The inter-firm networks in the mountain tourism industry: between transactions and competence, *Druid Summer Conference*, 18-20 June.

Borch, O.J. (1994) The process of relational contracting: developing trust-based strategic alliances among small business enterprises, in P. Shrivastava, A. Huff and J. Dutton (eds.), *Advances in Strategic Management*, 10B, Greenwich, Conn.: JAI Press, pp. 113-135.

Brass, D.J. (1984) Being in the right place: a structural analysis of individual influence in an organization, *Administration Science Quarterly*, **29**(4), 518-539.

Brown, B. and Butler, J.E. (1995) Competitors as allies: a study of entrepreneurial networks in the U.S. wine industry, *Journal of Small Business Management*, **33** (3), 57-66.

Burt, R.S. (1992) *Structural Holes: The Social Structure of Competition*, Cambridge, MA: Harvard University Press.

Camagni, R. (1991) *Innovation Networks: Spatial Perspectives*, London: Belhaven Press.

Capriello, A. and Rotherham, I.D. (2008) Farm attractions, networks, and destination development: A case study of Sussex, *Tourism Review*, **63**(2), 59-71.

Cooper, A.C., Folta, T.B., and Woo, C. (1995) Entrepreneurial information search, *Journal of Business Venturing*, **10**(2), 107-120.

Das, T.K., Teng, B. (1998) Between trust and control: developing confidence in partner cooperation in alliances, *Academy Management Review*, **23** (3), 491-512.

Deeds, D.L., Mang, P.Y. and Frandsen, M. (1997), The quest for legitimacy: a study of biotechnology IPOs, in P.D. Reynolds et al. (Eds.), *Frontiers of Entrepreneurship Research*, pp. 533-543.

Freeman, J. (1999) Venture capital as an economy of time, in R.Th.A.J. Leenders and S.M. Gabbay, (Eds.), *Corporate Social Capital and Liability*, Boston: Kluwer Academic Publishing, pp. 460-482.

11

Gabbay, S.M. and Leenders, R. Th.A.J. (1999) CSC: The structure of advantage and disadvantage, in R. Th.A.J. Leenders and S.M. Gabbay, (eds.), *Corporate Social Capital and Liability*, Boston: Kluwer Academic Press, pp. 1-14.

Granovetter, M. (1973) The strength of weak ties, *American Journal of Sociology*, **78**(6), 1360-1380.

Granovetter, M. (1985) Economic action and social structure: A theory of embeddedness, *American Journal of Sociology*, **91**(3), 481-510.

Granovetter, M. (1992) Problems of explanation in economic sociology, in N. Nohria and R.G. Eccles (Eds.), *Networks and Organizations: Structure, Form, and Action*, Boston: Harvard Business School Press, pp. 25-56.

Hansen, E.L. (1995) Entrepreneurial network and new organization growth, *Entrepreneurship: Theory & Practice*, **19**(4), 7-19.

Hara, G. and Kanai, T. (1994) Entrepreneurial networks across oceans to promote international strategic alliances for small businesses, *Journal of Business Venturing*, **9**(6), 489-507.

Harrison, B. (1992) Industrial districts: old wine in new bottles?, *Regional Studies*, **26**(5), 469-483.

Haythornthwaite, C. (1996) Social network analysis: An approach and technique for the study of information exchange, *Library and Information Science Research*, **18**(4), 323-342.

Hopkins, H.W. (2001) Regional tourism micro-market development: strategic alliances or clusters for competitive advantage, in A. Haahti (Ed.) *Proceedings, entrepreneurship in tourism and the contexts of experience economy conference* ETCEE 1.

Ingram, P. and Roberts, P.W. (2000) Friendships among competitors in the Sydney hotel industry, *American Journal of Sociology*, **106**(2), 387-423.

Inkpen A.C. and Tsang E.W.K. (2005) Social capital, networks, and knowledge transfer, *Academy Management Review* , **30**(1):146-165.

Jarillo, C.J. (1988) On strategic networks, *Strategic Management Journal*, **9**(1), 31-41.

Jenssen, J.I. and Greve, A. (2002) Does the degree of redundancy in social networks influence the success of business start-ups?, *International Journal of Entrepreneurial Behavior and Research* **8** (5), 254-267.

Johannisson, B. (1988) Business formation: a network approach, *Scandinavian Journal of Management*, **4**(3-4), 83-99.

Johannisson, B., Alexanderson, O., Nowicki, K. and Senneseth, K. (1994) Beyond anarchy and organization: entrepreneurs in contextual networks, *Entrepreneurship Regional Development*, **6**(4), 329-356.

Jones, C., Hesterly, W.S. and Borgatti, S.P. (1997) A general theory of network governance: exchange conditions and social mechanisms, *Academy Management Review*, **22** (4), 911-945.

Kogut, B. (2000) The network as knowledge: generative rules and emergence of structure, *Strategic Management Journal*, **21**(3), 405-425.

Krackhardt, D. (1990) Assessing the political landscape: structure, cognition, and power in networks, *Administration Science Quarterly*, **35**(2), 342-369.

Kumar, K. and van Dissel, H.G. (1996) Sustainable collaboration: managing conflict and cooperation in interorganizational systems, *MIS Quarterly*, **20**(3), 279-300.

Lane, B. (1994) Sustainable rural tourism strategies: a tool for development and conservation, in B. Bramwell and B. Lane (Eds.), *Rural Tourism and Sustainable Rural Development*, Clevedon: Channel Views: pp. 102-111.

Larson, A. (1991) Partner networks: Leveraging external ties to improve entrepreneurial performance, *Journal of Business Venturing*, **6**(3), 173-188.

Larson, A. and Starr, J.A. (1993) A network model of organization formation, *Entrepreneurship: Theory and Practice*, **17**(2), 5-15.

Lazonick, W. (1992) *Industry clusters versus global webs*, New York: Department of Economics, Columbia University.

Lin, N. (1999) Building a network theory of social capital, *Connections*, **22**(1), 28-51.

Lipparini, A., Lorenzoni, G. (1993) Organizational architecture, inter-firm relationships and entrepreneurial profile: findings from a set of SMEs, in Churchill, N.S., et al. (Eds.), *Frontiers of Entrepreneurship Research*, pp. 370-384.

Long, P. (1996) Inter-organisational collaboration in the development of tourism and the arts 1996, in M. Robinson, N. Evans, and P. Callaghan, *Culture as the Tourist Product*, Sunderland: Business Education Publishers, pp. 255-278.

Lorenzoni, G. and Lipparini, A. (1999) The leveraging of inter-firm relationships as a distinctive organizational capability: a longitudinal study, *Strategic Management Journal*, **20** (4), 317-338.

MacDonald, R. and Jollife, L. (2003) Cultural rural tourism: evidence from Canada, *Annals of Tourism Research*, **29**(3), 720-742.

Marshall, A. (1964) *Principles of Economics*, London: Macmillan.

McEvily, B. and Zaheer, A. (1999) Bridging ties: A source of firm heterogeneity in competitive capabilities, *Strategic Management Journal*, **20**(12): 1133-1156.

Nelson, R. (1988) Institutions supporting technical change in the United States, in G. Dosi, C. Freeman, R. Nelson, G. Silverberg and L. Soete (eds.), *Technical change and economic theory*, London: Pinter Publishers, pp 312-329.

Novelli, M., Schmitz, B. and Spencer, T. (2006) Networks, clusters and innovation in tourism: a UK Experience, *Tourism Management*, **27**(6), 1141-1152.

Paché, G. (1990) The role of small business in the development of network organization: The case of France, *International Small Business Journal*, **8**(4), 71-76.

11

Palmer, A. (2002) Cooperative marketing associations: an effective investigation into the causes of effectiveness, *Journal of Strategic Marketing*, **10**(2), 135-156.

Pavlovich, K. (2003) The evolution and transformation of a tourism destination network: the Waitomo Caves, New Zealand, *Tourism Management*, **24**(2), 203-216.

Piore, M. and Sabel, C. (1984) *The Second Industrial Divide*, New York: Basic Books.

Porter, M.E. (1990) *The Competitive Advantage of Nations*, London: Macmillan.

Portes, A. (1999) Social capital: its origins and the application in modern sociology, *Annual Review of Sociology*, **32**(2), 1-24.

Powell, W.W. (1990) Neither market nor hierarchy: network forms of organization, in L.L. Cummings and B.M. Staw (eds.), *Research in Organizational Behavior*, vol.12, Greenwich CT: JAI, pp. 295-336.

Pruitt, D.G. (1981) *Negotiation Behavior*, New York, NY: Academic Press.

Pyke, F., Becattini, G. and Sengenberger, W. (1990) Introduction, in F. Pyke, G. Becattini and W. Sengenberger (Eds.), *Industrial districts and inter-firm cooperation in Italy*, Geneva: International Institute for Labour Studies, pp. 1-9.

Reynolds, P.D. (1991) Sociology and entrepreneurship: Concepts and contributions. *Entrepreneurship: Theory & Practice*, **16**(2), 47-70.

Roberts, N.C. and Bradley, R.T. (1991) Stakeholder collaboration and innovation: a study of public policy initiation at the state level, *Journal of Applied Behavioral Science*, **27**(2), 209-227.

Roome, N. (2001) Conceptualizing and studying the contribution of networks in environmental management and sustainable development, *Business Strategy and the Environment*, **10**(2), 69-76.

Rosenblatt, P.C., de Mik, L., Anderson, R.M. and Johnson, P.A. (1985) *The Family in Business*, San Francisco: Jossey-Bass.

Rowley, T.J. (1997) Moving beyond dyadic ties: a network theory of stakeholder influences, *Academy of Management Review*, **22**(4): 887-910.

Saxena, G. (2005) Relationships, networks and the learning regions: case evidence from the Peak District National Park. *Tourism Management*, **26**(2), 277-289.

Saxenian, A. (1991) The origins and dynamics of production networks in Silicon Valley, *Research Policy*, **20** (5), 423-437.

Scott, A. (1988) *Metropolis: From the division of labor to urban form*. Berkeley/London: University of California Press/Ashgate. pp. 67-86.

Scott, A.J. and Storper, M. (1989) The geographical foundations and social regulation of flexible production systems, in J. Wolch and M. Dear (eds.) *The Power of Geography: How Territory Shapes Social Life*, Boston: Unwin Hyman, pp. 21-40.

Scott, N., Baggio, R. and Cooper, C. (2008) *Network Analysis and Tourism. From Theory to Practice*. Clevedon: Channel View Publications.

Selin, S. (1999) Developing a typology of sustainable tourism partnership, *Journal of Sustainable Tourism*, **7**(3/4), 260-273.

Smeltzer, L.R., Van Hook, B.L. and Hutt, R.W. (1991) Analysis and use of advisors as information sources in venture startups, *Journal of Small Business Management*, **29** (3), 10-20.

Starr, J. and MacMillan, I.C. (1990) Resource cooptation via social contracting: Resource acquisition strategies for new ventures, *Strategic Management Journal*, **11**, 79-92.

Stuart, T.E., Hoang, H. and Hybels, R. (1999) Interorganizational endorsements and the performance of entrepreneurial ventures, *Administration Science Quarterly*, **44** (2), 315-349.

Szarka, J. (1990) Networking and small firms, *International Small Business Journal*, **8** (2), 10-22.

Teece, D.J. (1987) Profiting from technological innovation: Implications for integration, collaboration, licensing, and public policy, in D.J. Teece (ed.), *The Competitive Challenge*: Cambridge, MA: Ballinger Publishing, pp. 185-219.

Thorelli, H.B. (1986) Networks: between markets and hierarchies, *Strategic Management Journal*, **7**(1), 37-51.

Tremblay, P. (2000) An evolutionary interpretation of the role of collaborative partnerships in sustainable tourism, in B. Bramwell and B. Lane (Eds), *Tourism Collaboration and Partnerships: Politics, Practice and Sustainability*, Clevedon: Channel View Publications, pp. 314-332.

Uzzi, B. (1997) Social structure and competition in interfirm networks: the paradox of embeddedness, *Administrative Science Quarterly*, **42**(1), 35-67.

Van den Berg, L., Braun, E. and Van Winden, W. (2001) *Growth clusters in European metropolitan cities, a comparative analysis of cluster dynamics in the cities of Amsterdam, Eindhoven, Helsinki, Leipzig, Lyons, Manchester, Munich, Rotterdam and Vienna*. The Netherlands/England: European Institute for Comparative Urban research, Erasmus University Rotterdam/Ashgate Publishing Ltd

Williamson, O.E. (1985) *The Economic Institutions of Capitalism: Firms, Markets and History*, New York, Free Press.

Williamson, O.E. (1999) Public and private bureaucracies: a transaction cost economics perspective, *Journal of Law, Economics and Organization*, **15**(1), 306-342.

Zimmer, C. and Aldrich, H. (1987) Resource mobilization through ethnic networks: kinship and friendship ties of shopkeepers in England, *Sociological Perspective*, **30**(4), 422-445.

11

12 Responding to Disasters: Strategies for Tourism and Hospitality Entrepreneurs

Gabrielle Walters, University of Queensland, Australia

Introduction

The hospitality and tourism industry is highly vulnerable to interruption by natural disasters owing to its heavy reliance on positive perceptions of safety, functioning infrastructure and visitor mobility (Laws and Prideaux, 2005; Ritchie, 2009). The increasing occurrence of natural disasters across the world has demonstrated the catastrophic impact such events can have on the tourism industry. Small businesses in particular are often those hit hardest when disaster strikes and it is therefore necessary for small businesses to understand the potential implications of a natural disaster and the role they can play in the recovery process to minimise extensive loss of trade.

The purpose of this chapter is to develop your understanding of the impacts of a natural disaster on tourism and small hospitality businesses and, more importantly, how small business entrepreneurs can expedite the recovery process for both the destination and their own enterprises. In particular, by the end of this chapter you should be able to:

- Discuss the impacts of disastrous events on destinations and hospitality and tourism small businesses;
- Discuss how small businesses can prepare for disastrous events;
- Explain how small businesses in the hospitality and tourism sector can adequately respond to disastrous events.

This chapter begins with a discussion on the impacts a disastrous event can have on tourism destinations. A number of preparation strategies useful to small hospitality and tourism businesses in particular are then discussed. Following this, a number of practical response and recovery strategies are presented.

The impact of disastrous events on the tourism and hospitality industry

Disastrous events, whether they be natural (e.g. cyclones, wild fires, hurricanes, earthquakes, disease outbreaks) or man-made (economic downturn, terrorism events, political instability) will inevitably influence global travel patterns as tourists avoid unnecessary travel to destinations that are affected. There are winners and losers among the tourism sector following a disastrous event. Winners are those destinations that may not have been considered prior to a disaster taking place, e.g. an Australian tourist planning to travel to Thailand before the tsunami may choose to travel to Bali instead. There is often a spiked growth in domestic travel as tourists decide to stay closer to home in response to global media coverage of a significant event that instils fear and uncertainty among travellers. The focus of this chapter however is on destinations that miss out on the tourism income they would have received had the disaster not occurred

Over the past decade we have witnessed a significant increase in the quantity and intensity of natural disasters in particular. The 2004 Indian Ocean tsunami had a significant impact on major tourist destinations such as Thailand, Indonesia and the Maldives. In 2005, Hurricane Katrina devastated the popular tourist destination of New Orleans in the US state of Mississippi, resulting in the closure of nearly 1500 tourism and hospitality businesses (Pearlman and Melnik, 2008). In Australia, the 2009 Black Saturday fires in Victoria resulted in an estimated loss of $400 million in tourism revenue, while in New Zealand, the Christchurch Earthquake in 2011 resulted in a 35% downturn in visitor numbers in the twelve months following the event. Other significant events that have caused major disruptions to the global tourism and hospitality industry include; the 2011 Queensland Floods, which were closely followed by Cyclone Yasi; Tohoku Earthquake in Japan in 2011 and Typhoon Haiyan that hit the Philippines in 2013. The specific impacts such events are likely to have on an affected destination are discussed in detail below.

12

Downturn in visitor numbers

One of the first problems a destination will face in the wake of a disastrous event is cancellations from would-be visitors. Tourists, regardless of their existing travel plans, will generally stay away from a disaster-affected destination at the time of, or soon after, an event for a number of reasons. These include fear of interfering with recovery efforts, of being physically injured, or of being emotionally traumatised by witnessing the devastation and destruction; a wish to avoid negative or tragic circumstances; and the perceived financial and physiological risks associated with simply enduring a bad experience at the destination (Walters *et al.*, 2012).

In severe cases cancellations will occur because it is simply not possible to continue with travel plans owing to a loss of infrastructure. For example, the hotel they intended on staying in may have been destroyed or the destination simply rendered inaccessible. However, it is important to note that many small businesses will encounter cancellations as much as twelve months in advance simply because they are located in the same vicinity – whether this be the same region, state, or in some instances, even the same country (Walters and Clulow, 2010).

Loss of tourism generated income

A downturn in visitor numbers will inevitably lead to a substantial loss of tourism-generated income. In 2009, the Black Saturday Bushfires cost Victoria's tourism industry in excess of $400 million despite the fact that only one hundred tourism businesses were directly affected by the fires and fifty businesses were destroyed. In New Orleans, Hurricane Katrina resulted in an estimated loss of US$4.2 billion in tourism-related income. For those destinations, whose economies are heavily dependent on tourism expenditure, a disastrous event can cause long-term socio-economic problems that hinder the destination's recovery efforts. Consider the 2004 Indian Ocean Tsunami and the Thailand tourism industry, for example, where a large majority of entrepreneurs directly hit by the Tsunami did not have insurance to cover the loss of their small hotels and restaurants. Faced with a total loss of income and continuing bank loan repayments, these entrepreneurs often had to walk away from the industry (Karatani, 2008). Thirty percent of small business entrepreneurs had to return to their pre-tourism occupations (boating, fishing and farming) following the 2002 Bali bombings, while 16% had no alternative income source (Cushnahan, 2004).

Demise of destination image

Echtner and Ritchie (1993) propose that a destination's image has both an attribute-based component made up of measureable, observable characteristics (such as accommodation facilities and attractions) and a more abstract, holistic component, which includes intangibles (such as friendliness, safety, and atmosphere). Information relating to attribute-based components is relatively easy to source for the tourist, particularly if the destination is providing regular updates on the status of its facilities and attractions. The long-term difficulty for destination managers seeking to recover their image lies in the restoration of the destination's holistic reputation and this is harder to achieve. Holistic components of destination image, such as perceptions that the destination would not be safe, represent significant challenges to destination marketing authorities. They need to find a balance between marketing the destination in a 'business as usual' manner and acknowledging the perceptions of tourists that their destination is unsafe or unready to receive visitors (Avraham and Ketter, 2013). Consider those small businesses who do not incur any physical damage but, as a result of the disaster, experience a significant downturn in tourist numbers due to the negative image perceptions towards the destination itself. In 2009, the Black Saturday Bushfires resulted in a substantial decline in tourist numbers for the entire state of Victoria, despite the fact that only five percent of the state was physically affected (Destination Gippsland, 2009).

Decrease in tourism and hospitality work force

The loss or displacement of the labour force that occurs as a result of a disastrous event affects the destination at both an operational and a destination level. It is unrealistic for hospitality and tourism entrepreneurs to expect their staff to take unpaid leave while they are closed for business. Nor is it reasonable for employees to expect to be compensated by business owners who are not only missing out on regular income but are investing what funds they do have in the re-establishment of their business. This situation therefore leads to a significant decline in skilled tourism and hospitality workers as they seek employment in different tourism destinations or different industry sectors. When employees move elsewhere and the population declines, so too do the business opportunities. Further job losses result, causing further population loss, all inevitably becoming a problem for the entire destination (Regional Australia Institute, 2013). The loss of human capital is a significant issue, particularly for the hospitality and tourism industry that already experiences a labour shortage (Solnet *et al.,* 2010).

12

Lack of accessibility

When access in and out of destinations is temporarily lost, there are significant logistical implications for tourism entrepreneurs and the entire community. Destination managers need to be mindful of those tourists who are not part of the community but still require assistance should there be an emergency situation. Reduced accessibility can also present significant problems for businesses who rely solely on tourist-generated income. For example, the road closures that occurred around the time of the Queensland floods and Cyclone Yasi resulted in parts of North Queensland being out of reach for many tourists traveling via road. While these road closures were only temporary, they would have had implications for the current and future travel plans of tourists. Chang (2003) describes transportation disruption due to inaccessibility as one of the most common sources of economic and social loss. For hospitality and tourism entrepreneurs, when land (rail and road) transport is also compromised, this also has implications for the recovery process as access to supplies and services necessary for the continuing operation of their businesses becomes problematic.

Preparing for disastrous events

In many situations, small business entrepreneurs or their local tourism managers have some advanced warning that a disaster or crisis may occur. For example, in the event of fires, flooding, cyclones and severe storms, the region's emergency services networks will often notify the community of the potential hazard and its severity. With the help of technology, such as smart-phone applications and satellite meteorology systems, entrepreneurs themselves can track significant weather events and make their own assessments of the potential risks. Unfortunately, some disastrous events occur without any warning, for example earthquakes and tsunamis, terrorism incidents and flash flooding, leaving little time to prepare for their impact. It is essential that small business entrepreneurs be pro-active when it comes to preparing for the unexpected. Sullivan (2003) emphasises the importance of a long-lasting partnership between individuals, businesses and public institutions. In a tourism context, membership and active involvement with a region's local or state tourism association provides entrepreneurs with access to support ranging from preparation advice to recovery assistance.

The checklist featured in Text box 1 represents a real-world example of a Crisis Preparedness Checklist that provides operators with a self-assessment of their readiness. This checklist was compiled by Tourism Victoria, a destination management organisation (DMO) in Australia. Note the reference to other information that has been made accessible to hospitality and tourism entrepreneurs to assist them with their planning. For more details visit their website listed below.

Text box 1: Crisis essentials checklist

Have you:	Yes	No
1. Prepared an emergency management plan for your business - which includes your responsibilities to clients and staff?		
2. Secured adequate insurance coverage for your business to cover issues such as asset damage and loss and business interruption?		
3. Identified the emergency management arrangements for your area and made contact with local emergency services?		
4. Found out who to contact and how you will stay informed in the event of an emergency?		
5. Developed an appropriate policy and procedures to deal with cancellations, curtailment or forward bookings?		
6. Listed your business with the nearest accredited Visitor Information Centre and/or the database of your regional and local tourism associations?		
7. Identified the protocol for working with the media during an emergency especially the need for a sole regional spokesperson on tourism?		
8. Prepared a business continuity plan?		

If you answered yes to 7 or 8 questions - you are well on your way to deal effectively with a crisis. Spend time reviewing the Respond section to ensure you are ready to act in an emergency.

If you answered yes to 5 or 6 questions - your business is quite well-prepared but you need to undertake some tasks to increase your capacity to cope with an emergency. Spend time reviewing the Emergency planning section

If you answered yes to 4 or fewer questions - you do not currently have adequate processes in place to respond effectively to a crisis, and your preparation requires urgent attention. Review the Managing risk section and develop a risk management plan.

Source: Tourism Victoria Corporate Website: Crisis Management Guide
www.tourism.vic.gov.au/business-tools-support/crisis-management-guide/prepare.html

This checklist is just one example of the useful support resources offered by DMOs in their bids to assist small hospitality and tourism entrepreneurs to prepare for and respond to disastrous events (Ritchie, 2009). In the case of the Queensland Floods and Cyclone Yasi, the state and federal governments provided various means of recovery support including, but not limited to:

12

- Financial assistance;
- Free or subsidised marketing opportunities;
- Resilience building educational programmes;
- Trade advisory support.

Another advantage of being closely tied to a region's tourism industry association is the opportunity to be a part of or benefit from a response and recovery committee. The role and importance of response and recovery committees to disaster-prone tourism destinations is demonstrated in the text box below.

Text box 2: Destination Gippsland's response and recovery committee

Gippsland is a tourism region located in the south east corner of Australia. The region's natural assets include some of Australia's most pristine national parks and lakes districts. However, the prominence of these nature-based attractions combined with climate patterns of heavy rainfall in the winter and extremely dry summers leave the region particularly vulnerable to natural disasters such as floods and bushfires. Acknowledging the threat as a reality for this region and its tourism operators, Gippsland's DMO together with its local tourism associations formed a response and recovery committee. This committee comprises a number of stakeholders likely to be involved in the preparation, response and recovery phases of a disaster. These include emergency services, local entrepreneurs, destination managers and tourism officers, government officials and media representatives. The committee convenes at the beginning of the region's bushfire and flood seasons to assess the region's preparedness and put into place their response and recovery strategies. The committee offers numerous benefits to the Gippsland tourism industry as its primary goal is to minimise the impacts, both physical and reputational, of a potential disaster and expedite the recovery period. The committee achieves this by:

- ☐ The sharing of destination-specific information;

- ☐ Consistency across the industry in terms of policies, messages and media management;

- ☐ The preparation of cooperative marketing messages ready to roll out post- disaster;

- ☐ The provision of a platform on which relevant stakeholders (i.e. emergency services) can present important factual information relating to the disaster;

- ☐ The opportunity for entrepreneurs to evaluate/share past experiences and 'brainstorm' how to improve the preparedness and recovery processes;

- ☐ The implementation of an effective media management strategy.

Responding to disastrous events: recovery strategies for small businesses

When viewing the tourism industry from a systems perspective and acknowledging its interconnectedness, a destination's recovery success requires a united and cohesive approach from all stakeholders. The decisions and recovery of one entity will impact not only the decisions and recovery of others, but also the destination as a whole (Marshall and Schrank, 2014). While the literature in this area is yet to come to a consensus on what recovery looks like, researchers agree that the recovery process is seldom orderly and no two disaster recovery attempts are the same (Chang, 2010; Jordan and Javernick-Will, 2013; Marshall and Schrank, 2014). This diversity presents extreme challenges for destination managers seeking to learn from and replicate successful cases of disaster response and recovery at the destination level. However, from a small business perspective there are some well-founded examples of effective response strategies that may expedite the recovery process.

Managing cancellations and encouraging visitation

We have learnt that in the event of a disaster the tourists' initial response is to avoid the destination, regardless of whether they have existing travel plans or intentions to visit. While in the short term there may be difficulty convincing tourists that the entire destination is open for business, entrepreneurs can certainly do their share to discourage unnecessary cancellations, promote visitation and educate their target market in terms of the status of both their business and the destination. If the business is unable to open, then the entrepreneur should ensure they have a clear cancellation policy to sustain the goodwill of their current client base. Cancellation policies are legally-binding agreements between businesses and their customers. These policies should dictate what happens if the operator or the customer cancels a booking. In the event of a disaster, such policies will vary according to the extent of the damage incurred directly by the business or the destination. For example, while the business may not be directly affected, accessibility may be restricted or authorities may deem the area as not safe to enter. In this case, both parties are released from the contract. If the business and its immediate surrounds are not directly affected, then it could be that the cancellation policy stands in which case the customer will incur the set cancellation fee if they cancel their visit. Individual entrepreneurs do have some discretion in the enforcement of a cancellation policy and it is strongly advised that operators be fair and mindful of future customer relationships when making this decision.

12

Should the business and its surrounds be in an optimal position to continue offering a satisfying visitor experience despite the broader community being affected, it becomes the responsibility of the small business owner to promote their business directly to their customers (Walters *et al.*, 2014). Such promotional efforts need to cut through media hype surrounding the event and try to mitigate the negative perceptions that may exist in the tourism market as a result of sensationalist and misleading reporting (Walters and Mair, 2012). Examples of cost effective promotional activities include:

- Use of social media to post images and regular updates on the status of the destination and the small business;

- Direct marketing to the business's existing customer base (Walters and Mair, 2012) as repeat visitors are more likely to return to a disaster-affected destination than those who have not visited previously;

- Provision of factual information to help visitors make informed decisions.

Diversifying product and target markets

Market diversification is one solution for small business entrepreneurs wishing to sustain their business operations and overcome their dependency on the tourism trade in the aftermath of a disaster. Following the Black Saturday fires for example, regional townships in Victoria temporarily filled their accommodation facilities and restaurants with journalists and emergency services personnel who had travelled there to report on the event or assist in the recovery process. Following the 2011 Christchurch Earthquake, accommodation facilities had to cater for tradesmen and construction workers who had flown in from all over the world to assist with the city's redevelopment. With regard to product diversification, the Hong Kong tourism industry's response to the SARS outbreak presents a good example of how businesses, in particular accommodation providers, diversified their product offering to maintain some form of income. Over the period that Hong Kong was deemed inaccessible, the hotel trade hired their hotel rooms for video-conferencing and temporary office space. These temporary facilities were used by local business people who, in ordinary circumstances, may have met with their international colleagues face-to-face (Lo *et al.*, 2007). The local or domestic tourism market should also not be forgotten in times of crises. The perceptions held by the domestic or local tourism market are likely to be more consistent with the actual circumstances, given their familiarity with the actual as opposed to the often 'sensationalised' facts surrounding the event (Walters and Clulow, 2010) Further, research has suggested that domestic tourists are also more likely to feel a sense of empathy towards their local tourism industry and are therefore more willing to contribute to its rapid recovery (Walters *et al.*, 2014).

Mitigating negative destination image perceptions

Small business entrepreneurs play a crucial role on both a collaborative and an individual level when it comes to mitigating negative perceptions that may prevail as a result of the sensationalist and imbalanced media reporting of a disaster (Walters and Mair, 2012). Collaboratively, small hospitality and tourism entrepreneurs need to deliver a consistent message that supports the destination's post-disaster marketing strategy. It is also important for business owners to resist the temptation to speak to the media about the event to ensure that the destination manager has full control over the messages relayed to media regarding the status of the destination. The promotion of safety and security measures is also advised for the purpose of mitigating consequent risk perceptions held by potential tourists (Sharifpour *et al.*, 2014). Individually, entrepreneurs should advertise that they are open for business, providing concrete evidence (i.e. photos, testimonials, weather forecasts) that they are ready to receive visitors. According to a study by Walters and Clulow (2010), tourists may refrain from visiting a destination at the time of, or immediately following a disaster, as they fear the local community may perceive them as inhibiting recovery efforts. Marketing messages that promote community readiness are therefore recommended.

Retaining the tourism and hospitality work force

Given high levels of turnover and the consistent shortage of skilled workers faced by the hospitality and tourism sector, small business entrepreneurs should take all necessary measures to retain their current work force. While a decline in business may not allow small businesses to offer their staff full-time work, there are a number of options available to entrepreneurs. These options include:

- Reducing working hours of casual employees;
- Offering paid or subsidised training opportunities that will allow employees to increase their own skill set and on their return enhance the business services;
- Negotiating a temporary decrease in pay – not likely to be popular but loyal employees with limited options may accept this in the short term;
- Finding temporary positions for staff with other establishments not affected by the event or that may be experiencing an influx of visitor numbers as a result (e.g. media, emergency service crews, armed forces, construction workers);
- Asking staff to take any accumulated leave;
- Cross-training full-time staff in multiple tasks across different areas – for example, a full-time barista may learn to prepare simple breakfast menu items, or a chef to cover steward duties;
- If part of a franchise, temporarily placing employees with another franchisee.

12

These measures will not only sustain the staff retention rates of small businesses but may develop a sense of loyalty among their employees, making them less likely to relocate or seek employment with another organisation.

Conclusion

This chapter has discussed the implications a major disaster or crisis can have for the hospitality and tourism sector and in particular its small business owners. The decline in visitor numbers at the time of, or immediately following, a disaster will present challenges for small business owners such as a loss of income, loss of staff and damage to their current image. The main objective in preparing for and recovering from a disastrous event is therefore to minimise both physical and perceptual damage to the small tourism or hospitality business and its host destination. Effective disaster recovery requires a collaborative effort from a number of stakeholders, and small business entrepreneurs in the hospitality and tourism industry need to acknowledge their role in the recovery process and ensure they are aware of the support available to them from the public and private sector.

Questions

1 Identify the different types of impact of natural disasters on small hospitality and tourism businesses.

2 Explain how hospitality and tourism businesses can prepare for natural disasters.

3 Identify possible courses of action that hospitality and tourism businesses could undertake to retain their workforce following a disaster.

4 Why is it important for destinations to mitigate negative image perceptions following a disaster?

5 Give examples of how a hospitality or tourism business could diversify its products or markets following a disaster.

References

Avraham, E. and Ketter, E. (2013) Marketing destinations with prolonged negative images: Towards a theoretical model' *Tourism Geographies: An International Journal of Tourism Space, Place and Environment,* **15**(1), 145-164.

Cushnahan, G. (2004) Crisis Management in small scale tourism. *Journal of Travel and Tourism Marketing* **15**(4), 332-338.

Chang, S.E. (2003) Transportation planning for disasters: an accessibility approach. *Environment and Planning A,* **35**. 1051-1072.

Destinationgippsland (2009) *Destination Gippsland - Inspired by Gippsland.* http://www. destinationgippsland.com.au (viewed 15 January 2015).

Echtner, C. M. and Ritchie, J. B. (1993) The measurement of destination image: An empirical assessment. *Journal of travel research,* **31**(4), 3-13.

Jordan. E., and Javernick-Will. A. (2013) Indicators of community recovery: content analysis and Delphi approach. *Natural Hazards Review* **14**, 21–28

Karatani, Y. (2008) Tourism industry losses and recovery process from the Indian Ocean Tsunami, *The 14th World Conference on Earthquake Engineering,* October 12-17, 2008, Beijing, China.

Laws, E. and Prideaux, B. (2005) Crisis management: A suggested typology. *Journal of Travel and Tourism Marketing,* **19**(2/3), 1-8.

Lo, A., Cheung, C., & Law, R. (2007) The survival of hotels during disaster: A case study of Hong Kong in 2003, *Asia Pacific Journal of Tourism Research,* **11**(1) 65-80.

Marshall, M.I., and Schrank, H.L. (2014) Small business disaster recovery: a research framework. *Natural Hazards* **72**, 597-616

Regional Australia Institute (2015) *From Disaster to Renewal: The Centrality of Business Recovery to Community Resilience,* viewed 12 January 2015, http://www. regionalaustralia.org.au/wp-content/uploads/2013/08/From-Disaster-to-Renewal.pdf

Ritchie, B.W. (2009) *Crisis and Disaster Management for Tourism.* UK: Channel View Publications.

Pearlman, D., and Melnik, O. (2008) Hurricane Katrina's effect on the perception of New Orleans leisure tourists, *Journal of Travel and Tourism Marketing,* **25**(1), 58 – 67.

Sharifpour, M., Walters, G.A and Ritchie, B.R (2014) Risk perception, prior knowledge and willingness to travel, *Journal of Vacation Marketing,* **20**(2), 111-123 .

Solnet, D.J., Paulsen.N., and Cooper, C. (2010) Decline and turnaround: a literature review and proposed research agenda for the hotel sector, *Current Issues in Tourism,***13**(2), 139-159

Sullivan M (2003) Integrated recovery management: a new way of looking at a delicate process. *Australian Journal of Emergency Management* **18**, 4–27.

12

Tourism Victoria 2014, *Crisis Management Guide*, viewed 18 December 2014, http://www.tourism.vic.gov.au/business-tools-support/crisis-management-guide/prepare.html

Walters, G.A., Mair, J., and Ritchie, B. R. (2014) Understanding the tourist's response to Natural Disasters: The case of the Queensland Floods, *Journal of Vacation Marketing*, Published online, May 2.

Walters, G. and Clulow, V. (2010) The tourism market's response to the 2009 Black Saturday Bushfires: The case of Gippsland, *Journal of Travel and Tourism Marketing*, **27**(8), 844-857.

Walters, G. and Mair, J. (2012) The Effectiveness of post-disaster recovery marketing messages – the case of the Australian 2009 bushfires. *Journal of Travel and Tourism Marketing*, **29**(1), 87-103.

Concluding Remarks

Levent Altinay and Maureen Brookes, Oxford School of Hospitality Management, Oxford Brookes University, UK

This textbook has been designed to develop your understanding of entrepreneurship within hospitality and tourism. We can draw several conclusions from the text. The text has provided several examples of pioneering hospitality and tourism entrepreneurs who were proactive in developing products and services to address market inefficiencies. However, the hospitality and tourism industries have lately been criticised as 'traditional' in initiating and implementing change (Okumus *et al.*, 2010) and only 'reactive' following innovation driven by other industries (Harrington *et al.*, 2014). Given the dynamic and customer-focussed nature of these industries, this argument gives cause for concern. Today's consumers have more global consumption experience and have better access to 'market knowledge' given the growing integration of technology into the marketing and delivery of services. They can compare product and service options by using various online and traditional distribution channels. More importantly, global economic conditions make hospitality and tourism consumers more 'risk averse' and extraordinarily cautious with their consumption choices.

Hospitality and tourism industries need to engage in more entrepreneurial activities and drive innovation more than ever in order to meet the constantly changing needs of consumers and enhance their consumption experience. Entrepreneurship and innovation require the development of an enabling infrastructure in order to stimulate creative ideas. Institutions and governments, therefore, at international, national and local levels need to develop the appropriate policies and support mechanisms. However, these initiatives could only succeed if these parties acknowledge the synergistic and supportive role of the hospitality and tourism industries in the development of other economic activities and enhancing the competitiveness of destinations.

The skills and traits of entrepreneurs are crucial in the development of creative and entrepreneurial ideas that bring both economic and social change to societies. While some of the entrepreneurs are born with some of these skills and traits, others are not. Nonetheless, these skills and traits can be nurtured and developed through education. Universities have a responsibility to develop entrepreneurship programmes with a particular focus on hospitality and tourism in order to help individuals with this development. These programmes can be developed in collaboration with local authorities, destination management organisations and small businesses. Visionary thinking, proactiveness, innovativeness and risk taking are essential for the development of the requisite entrepreneurial skills and traits and thus should underpin hospitality and tourism entrepreneurship higher education programmes.

The entrepreneurship process involves the combination of unique resources for the exploration and exploitation of opportunities leading to economic and social change. These resources, including natural resources, financial, human, social, political and cultural capital are scarce and therefore require the implementation of careful resource mobilisation strategies. Resource mobilisation strategies should include stakeholders; hospitality and tourism entrepreneurs, customers/tourists, government representatives, local communities and residents and educators involvement and collaboration in the identification and exploitation of critical resources. It should also involve relationship development and empowerment strategies. Relationship development with these stakeholders groups and empowerment strategies can be particularly influential both in the mobilisation of critical resources and the 'co-creation' of innovative ideas.

Hospitality and tourism enterprises and social entrepreneurs can contribute to socio-economic development of communities particularly in developing economies if they acknowledge and cultivate a shared understanding and common voice of a wider vision for the role of hospitality and tourism in the local stakeholders' ecosystem. If the concerned destinations and communities are to benefit from social entrepreneurship, hospitality associations and tourism destination managers have the responsibility to harness stakeholder collaboration in order to enhance economic and social development simultaneously. In this vein, hospitality and destination managers should see themselves as part of the social entrepreneurship ecosystem and actively engage in its dialogues and resource exchanges, aiming to create collective meaning and understanding of social problems and solutions.

Culture and entrepreneurship interface need to be analysed in order to better understand how shared values and the socio-cultural backgrounds of entrepreneurs can shape their creative thinking and lead to the development of innovative hospitality and tourism products. A country's and destination's level of innovation and competitiveness can be enhanced through a thorough cultural assessment and evaluation of how different elements of culture affect the process of opportunity identification, innovative idea generation and evaluation, idea implementation and opportunity exploitation.

References

Okumus, F., Altinay, L. and Chathoth, P. (2010) *Strategic Management for Hospitality and Tourism*, Oxford: Butterworth.

Harrington, R., Chathoth, P., Ottenbacher, M. and Altinay, L. (2014) 'Strategic management research in hospitality and tourism: past, present and future', *International Journal of Contemporary Hospitality Management*, **26** (5), 778-808.

Index